Purcha

Fur 5/14/21

W. E. B. DU BOIS

B & N

91 Old Country Rd

Carle Place, N.Y.

Black Lives series

Elvira Basevich, *W. E. B. Du Bois*

W. E. B. Du Bois

The Lost and the Found

Elvira Basevich

polity

First published in 2021 by Polity Press

Polity Press
65 Bridge Street
Cambridge CB2 1UR, UK

Polity Press
101 Station Landing
Suite 300
Medford, MA 02155, USA

ISBN-13: 978-1-5095-3573-6
ISBN-13: 978-1-5095-3574-3 (pb)

A catalogue record for this book is available from the British Library.

Library of Congress Cataloging-in-Publication Data

Names: Basevich, Elvira, author.
Title: W.E.B. Du Bois : the lost and the found / Elvira Basevich.
Description: Cambridge, UK ; Medford, MA : Polity, 2020. | Series: Black lives | Includes bibliographical references and index. | Summary: "A totally fresh account of Du Bois and why his life and legacy remain as vital as ever."-- Provided by publisher.
Identifiers: LCCN 2020008754 (print) | LCCN 2020008755 (ebook) | ISBN 9781509535736 (hardback) | ISBN 9781509535743 (paperback) | ISBN 9781509535750 (epub)

Subjects: LCSH: Du Bois, W. E. B. (William Edward Burghardt), 1868-1963. | Du Bois, W. E. B. (William Edward Burghardt), 1868-1963--Criticism and interpretation. | African Americans--Biography. | African American authors--Biography. | African American civil rights workers--Biography. | Civil rights workers--United States--Biography. | African Americans--Civil rights--History.
Classification: LCC E185.97.D73 B367 2020 (print) | LCC E185.97.D73 (ebook) | DDC 323.092 [B]--dc23
LC record available at https://lccn.loc.gov/2020008754
LC ebook record available at https://lccn.loc.gov/2020008755

Typeset in 10.75pt on 14pt Janson by
Servis Filmsetting Limited, Stockport, Cheshire
Printed and bound in Great Britain by TJ International Limited

For further information on Polity, visit our website: politybooks.com for my teachers

Contents

Acknowledgments

Sections of chapters 2 and 6 have appeared in "W. E. B. Du Bois's Critique of American Democracy in the Jim Crow Era: On the Limitations of Rawls and Honneth," *Journal of Political Philosophy* 27(3) (2019): 318–40.

Sections of chapter 5 have appeared in "W. E. B. Du Bois's Critique of Radical Reconstruction (1865–77): A Hegelian Approach to American Modernity," *Philosophy & Social Criticism* 45(2) (2018): 168–85.

My warmest thanks to the following individuals who, at one point or another, provided the inspiration, support, and encouragement critical to the successful completion of this project: Linda M. Alcoff, Lawrie Balfour, Nelli Basevich (1917–2017), Rosa Basevich, Eric Edmond Bayruns Garcia, Lawrence Blum, Julia Davies, Jorge L. A. Garcia, Sally Haslanger, Adam Hosein, Chike Jeffers, Serene Khader, Frank M. Kirkland, Pauline Kleingeld, José J. Mendoza, Charles W. Mills, Jennifer Morton, George Owers, Alice Pinheiro-Walla, Isaac A. Reed, Melvin L. Rogers, Maureen Ritchey, Tommie Shelby, Inés Valdez, Alex Zamalin, and the anonymous reviewers for the press, especially Review #3.

Sat
5/15/21

Introduction

Du Bois Among Us:
A Contemporary, A Voice from the Past

In a tape-recorded conversation with Margaret Mead in 1971, James Baldwin described the problem of racism in the United States: "So that's what makes it all so hysterical, so unwieldy and so completely irretrievable. Reason cannot reach it. It is as though some great, great, great wound is in the whole body, and no one dares to operate: to close it, to examine it, to stitch it."[1] Baldwin discerned racism as an open wound that spans "the whole body" of the republic. Poets, philosophers, and social scientists struggle to explain its stubborn bloodletting rituals; like a chant, it has no clear beginning or end, pervading the legal and social conventions of our past and reaching out to cloud our future. In *Between the World and Me*, a spellbinding reckoning with white Americans' complicity in white supremacy, Ta-Nehisi Coates remarks that racism has left him wounded, unable to console his young son in the face of perpetual loss.[2] "I can only say what I saw, what I felt," writes Coates. "There are people whom we do not fully know, and yet they live in a warm place within us, and when they are plundered, when they lose their bodies and the dark energy disperses, that place becomes a wound."[3] If one were to place a stone or a flower at every tree, church basement, stairwell, or dark stretch of road where a person of color has lost their body and left there a wound still painful to touch, a cemetery could overlie the entire geography of North America. Marx had once warned of the specter of communism haunting Europe, whereas actual ghosts haunt the United States.[4]

In his characterization of American racism, Baldwin invoked two notions that, at first blush, appear to stand in opposition. He observed that reason "cannot reach it" and yet the "wound" remains open because "no one dares to operate: to close it, to examine it, to stitch it." Reason is both powerless against racism and an indispensable tool to combat it. And so one is left wondering if it is possible to mend the wound using the power of reason in some broad sense, employing persuasion, imagination, and fact-based arguments. The long history of racial violence and terror might suggest that racism is too resilient to crumble under public scrutiny or government intervention, however well intentioned. And yet Baldwin maintained that one must nevertheless "dare" to "close [the wound], examine it, stitch it." He thus asked his reader to redress the evil of racism. In doing so, we realize that racism, like all evil, as Hannah Arendt had put it, is "banal"; that is, it is a social phenomenon that, like any social phenomenon, originates in the human will and is therefore capable of being rooted from the world, however monstrous its proportions and stranglehold on institutions. What people have willed into existence, including a force as recalcitrant as white supremacy, by the same token can be willed out of existence. Racism is not a random and unstoppable event in the natural world, like an earthquake or the death of a star. To be sure, the fight against it must stretch the boundaries of the moral imagination, drawing on cultural and spiritual resources that are often overlooked as inspirations for democratic agency. The process must also support the transformation of major social and political institutions. But the prospect of a just world, nevertheless, remains viable. The question is only how and when to build it.[5]

The driving question in W. E. B. Du Bois's writings as a whole – a question that also inspired Africana philosophers from Frederick Douglass to James Baldwin – was the following: Can reason close the wound of racism that spans the whole body of the republic; and if reason cannot reach it, how else might it be closed? Africana philosophers do not all share the same optimism about finding solutions to anti-black racism.[6] But Du Bois had faith in reason – a kind of moral attitude of sustained hope for a better world – that the wound of racism *can* close and heal, even if it will leave an irremovable scar on the US republic and the world.

Though we cannot imagine that we can go back to a world untouched by racism, we have a moral obligation to figure out how to repair the world we have inherited, to put the ghosts of the dead to rest. The conviction that our profoundly nonideal world is reparable, I believe, is the conviction that inspired W. E. B. Du Bois's life and work. In his career as an academic, writer, and activist, this conviction motivated him to experiment with a great variety of methods for stitching shut the wound that racism has left on the body of the US republic and on the world. From the scientific method to literature and the arts, Du Bois dedicated his life to theorizing new approaches to anti-racist critique. In my mind, his originality and willingness to adopt new methods sets him apart from most political theorists. His methodological experimentation is perhaps why his thought is both so exciting and so challenging to reconstruct using general philosophical principles.

With the aim of presenting some of the principal methods Du Bois developed to combat anti-black racism and to build a more just world, this book provides an account of the life, activism, and scholarship of W. E. B. Du Bois. In a storied and prolific life, Du Bois's accomplishments were considerable and wide-ranging. He is recognized in the United States and around the world as an influential civil rights leader of the twentieth century. He co-founded in 1910 the National Association for the Advancement of Colored People (NAACP) and was the editor of *The Crisis* (1910–34), the official magazine of the NAACP, widely circulated in the segregated black community during the Jim Crow era. What is more, as a social scientist, he pioneered empirical methods to study black neighborhoods, founding modern "scientific" sociology.[7] His spellbinding *The Souls of Black Folk*, published in 1903, is a foundational text of Africana philosophy and African-American arts and letters. During his lifetime, he adopted liberal, Marxian, pan-African, and black nationalist frameworks to fight anti-black racism; and he published poems, short stories, and novels, and was involved in the Harlem Renaissance to use the arts to enhance the moral literacy of the white-controlled republic about racial matters. The characters who people his creative writings move through an uncertain world, burdened with slavery and segregation, wondering if it is still reasonable to hope for a better world in the aftermath of so much suffering.

In this book, I take the view that Du Bois is a modern political philosopher for whom the idea of basic civil and political rights for all, as well as the ideal of racial inclusion in the political, social, and economic spheres, is an indispensable basis for combating anti-black racism and for achieving racial justice. My presentation of Du Bois's thought, in part, builds on and puts pressure on the noted philosopher Charles W. Mills's recent argument that Du Bois is a "black

radical liberal") who aimed to realize the public values of
freedom and equality for all in order to welcome black and
brown people, refugees, and immigrants into a reconstituted democratic polity.[8] Mills maintains that, for Du Bois,
the process of advancing true freedom and equality for all
requires a radical reorganization of modern American society from the point of view of historically excluded groups.
Mills thus offers a theoretical exposition of Du Bois's original claim that a color line draws a "veil" over communities
of color by withdrawing respect and esteem from black and
brown people.[9] The readiness or otherwise of the American
public to dismantle the color line reflects whether or not the
republic is truly "modern" – that is, free and equal for all
persons regardless of race. As Du Bois put it, "the advance
of all depends increasingly on the advance of each," such
that respecting and esteeming historically excluded groups is
instrumental for the development of American modernity.[10] I
flesh out Mills's interpretation of Du Bois by looking at the
breadth of Du Bois's writings and activism, and present Du
Bois's changing positions as broadly consistent with a "radical" political liberalism. The challenge, of course, would be
to show what Du Bois packed into liberalism to make it "radical" and which liberal ideals are valuable in the first place.
Christopher Lebron provides an elegant definition about
what it means to be a "radical," one that complements Mills's
view and on which this book elaborates: "Radicalism is the
imagination and will to think and act outside the bounds of
the normally acceptable."[11] Rethinking the bounds of the
normally acceptable in social, economic, and political life is
the heart of Du Bois's political project for reconstituting the
US polity.

In this book, I introduce three themes that inform Du Bois's
critique of American democracy. These themes characterize
his political liberalism and map some of its radical potential:

(1) inclusion, (2) self-assertion, and (3) despair. In the beginning of his professional life (late 1890s–1934), Du Bois advocated the civic enfranchisement of African Americans *as* American citizens, a principle that is the hallmark of his political liberalism. By the early 1930s, he continued to assert that African Americans must become equal participants in modern American life, but grew skeptical about the white public's readiness to respect and esteem people of color. As a consequence, to the shock of the NAACP, he began to defend voluntary black self-segregation in order to shore up black civil and economic standing during the Jim Crow era. With the rise of McCarthyism in the 1950s, Du Bois was prosecuted by the US Justice Department and this marked the beginning of a period of something like despair. It was not, however, a time of his intellectual decline and unproductivity. The US federal government accused him of acting as a foreign agent for the Soviet Union because of his activism for world peace. He later shared: "I have faced during my life many unpleasant experiences: the growl of a mob; the personal threat of murder; the scowling distaste of an audience. But nothing has so cowed me as that day, November 8, 1951, when I took my seat in a Washington courtroom as an indicted criminal."[12] Although he avoided jail time, he was blacklisted and slid into poverty. He had confronted – time and again – the color line and had dedicated his life to fighting against it, only to be attacked by the state and abandoned by lifelong friends and allies. Like Socrates, he was rejected by the polity for whose soul he had so passionately fought. His prosecution ultimately drove him into exile under the patronage of Ghanaian President Kwame Nkrumah (in office 1960–66). Du Bois died in Ghana in 1963, the night before the March on Washington for Jobs and Freedom, when Martin Luther King Jr gave his famous "I have a dream" speech.

The themes of inclusion, self-assertion, and despair that I explore here do not exhaust the range of plausible interpretations of Du Bois's thought. Rather, on my view, they provide a helpful lens for establishing his unique place in modern political philosophy and the contemporary significance of his critique of American democracy. For example, in focusing on the ideal of civic enfranchisement, we can ask whether the US federal government could be a vehicle for racial justice in spite of its sustained attack on those who criticize it and its history of white supremacy. Though Du Bois held on to the emancipatory potential of the ideal of a racially inclusive polity, some of the questions that his political liberalism raises for us today include: Does the Trump presidency spell the decisive end of appeals to the government for racial justice? Or, on the contrary, does the ascendancy of white power movements confirm the importance of interracial grassroots movements to seize local, state, and federal power? Additionally, what role might black solidarity and self-segregation continue to play in democratic politics? Felony disenfranchisement, gerrymandering, and the suppression of voter rights remain destructive vehicles for disenfranchising communities of color; and the escalating attacks on and the criminalization of migrants and asylum seekers from Central and South America and the Caribbean illustrate that racial whiteness is still taken to be a marker of Americanness. It appears as if with each step forward the republic takes two steps back. The urgency of the questions above shows why Du Bois remains relevant in the struggle for justice today. For his work showcases how and why race defines who is to be considered a legitimate member of the American social fabric and what rights and resources political membership should entail.

Some might object to a presentation of Du Bois as centrally focused on theorizing domestic justice in the United States.

By foregrounding the US domestic context for most of this book, I do not mean to suggest that his political thought is exhausted by the ideal of civic enfranchisement. Neither do I believe that a focus on domestic justice bars thinking with Du Bois about cosmopolitanism and global justice or grassroots social movements in other countries. The Du Bois scholars Chike Jeffers and Inés Valdez offer rich analyses that extend the promise of Du Bois's cosmopolitanism with respect to his philosophy of race and pan-Africanism, respectively.[13] Juliet Hooker examines the influence of Latinx political theory on Du Bois, challenging assumptions about the role of the global south in his intellectual development.[14] To be sure, there is much to say about the intersection between domestic and cosmopolitan justice, as well as about the influence of Latinx and indigenous liberation movements on his theorization of the African-American struggle for emancipation. That is to say, Du Bois's political thought raises many rich avenues that I will not be able to pursue here. However, I do not take his critique of American democracy to foreclose other important lines for thinking with him about justice and democracy. Instead, I assume that his political thought consists of an interlocking system of concepts and principles that fashion a comprehensive, broadly liberal framework for theorizing global and domestic justice. To illuminate a mere element of this system is not to banish the remaining conceptual architecture to the dark.

One might also object to presenting Du Bois in the context of modern political philosophy or to my emphasis on his political liberalism. In providing a philosophical reconstruction of Du Bois's critique of American democracy, I establish, among other notable accomplishments, his contributions to modern political philosophy. I build bridges between Du Bois and major figures in the history of philosophy, including Immanuel Kant and G. W. F. Hegel. My aim

DuBois Renewed As Left Wing Marxist In 1950s. I wonder why?

is neither to canonize Du Bois in order to prove that he is a formidable political philosopher nor to chastise and chuck central philosophical figures for neglecting the problem of race and racism in general and of Du Bois in particular. Yet where racial violence abounds, and a nation still struggles to be free, it is instructive to see why more mainstream philosophical schools struggle to make sense of phenomena like the color line and double consciousness; and I believe that it is worth the effort to show their limitations. What is more, even in his so-called "late" period when Du Bois read Marx more closely, his major published works confirm that he continued to share some basic ideals with modern political philosophy, such as a commitment to civil and political rights and representational democracy; to be sure, he also experimented with political strategies and developed a critique of empire, colonialism, and global racial capitalism.[15] Even if political liberalism does not exhaust the richness of the Duboisian framework, it is nevertheless indispensable to it.[16] However, unlike most modern political philosophers, Du Bois concentrated on theorizing and tackling white supremacy, which he considered to be a defining obstacle to the advance of modernity.

Finally, I would like to briefly comment on my decisions regarding the structure of the book, as well as my personal motivation for writing it. The book has a rough chronological structure, though some chapters treat individual themes, such as Du Bois and the Black Lives Matter movement and his feminist thought, which incorporate different parts of his career and life. The second chapter opens with the birth of Du Bois and the conclusion of the book ends with his death. Most chapters begin with a brief biographical statement about the particular stage of Du Bois's life where we find him, where he was living and working, and his vision of political struggle at that point in his career, drawing in particular on D. L. Lewis's and Manning Marable's exquisite biographies of Du Bois. As a man who described himself as "bone of the bone" and "flesh of the flesh" of the people living and striving behind the color line, Du Bois noted that the "veil" too fell over his own life and that of his family.[17] His life provides some insight into his political thought, as he often reflected on his personal experiences to chart new directions in his research and activism. I therefore surmised that it would be helpful to include biographical information in an overview of his life and work. The inclusion of biographical information also meets the objective of the Black Lives series to represent the singular lives of powerful and neglected black thinkers.

I take the subtitle of the book, *The Lost and the Found*, from the dedication that Du Bois wrote to his children in *The Souls of Black Folk*: "To Burghardt and Yolande, The Lost and the Found." Du Bois's firstborn son, Burghardt, died from diphtheria in Atlanta in 1899, "The Lost." "I saw his breath beat quicker and quicker, pause, and then his little soul leapt like a star that travels in the night and left a world of darkness in its train."[18] A daughter, Yolande, was born the following year, "The Found." The Du Bois family, however, never fully recovered from the loss of their firstborn. In chapter 11 of *Souls*, "On the Passing of the Firstborn," Du Bois invites his reader to mourn the loss of his toddler with him, to join his family in its grief. Mourning is a sign of respect that is often denied to black children; and the loss of black life hardly bereaves a white-controlled world. The subtitle of the book is also a comment on the reception of Du Bois in academia and the American public. To suggest that Du Bois *is* the lost and the found is not just to foreground his life, work, and experience of the twentieth century. It is a call for the formation of new habits of judgment that realize his vision of a racially pluralistic democracy. In that sense, to "find" Du Bois is to learn to respect and esteem historically excluded groups and to move through the world from their perspective.

I would like to conclude my introduction with a brief note about my interest in Du Bois. As a white woman, I am often asked by well-meaning people for an "origin story," so to speak, explaining my interest in a black philosopher. I doubt my research would inspire as many calls for an explanation if it were limited to the study of Kant, Hegel, and analytic political philosophy. I reject the suggestion that a scholarly interest in Du Bois deviates from established norms; if this remains the widespread perception, then every new book on Du Bois must make a claim to "finding" him anew. Absurdly, Du Bois's prodigious writings would remain perpetually "lost," in spite of a growing body of Du Bois scholarship.

Yet it would be naive to ignore the connection between identity and the development of intellectual interests, though, on my view, family background and racial identity ultimately explain little. My family arrived in the United States as asylum seekers from the former Soviet Union. I grew up in a diverse immigrant community in south Brooklyn and remember Clinton's welfare reform of the 1990s not as a newspaper headline but through the gradual disappearance of my favorite breakfast items on the kitchen table. Because my parents did not speak English well, I was often the intermediary between public schoolteachers, welfare administrators, and census workers, translating my parents' fears and insecurity into a moral claim before the federal government. I felt like David slinging stones at Goliath, inserting myself and my family before a state apparatus that at any moment could leave us adrift or quash us. I struggled to explain on what basis anyone had any responsibility towards us – in what way were we part of a greater whole? The question preoccupied me, especially given the radical contingency of our being here in the first place. Why was our desperate need reason enough for someone to help?

In my philosophical studies, I focused on how social identity – especially racial identity – amplifies or mitigates a community's vulnerability to the excess of state power or the withdrawal of state resources. Whether one even has public standing to make a formal claim for rights, resources, and legal protection is often a reflection of one's position in a racial hierarchy. In a philosophy canon dominated by whites, I was fortunate to have teachers who turned my attention to Du Bois to help me theorize the influence of race on the organization of polities and inspired me to contribute to Du Bois scholarship.

On a more personal note, Du Bois's writing gave me a version of America that I can make my own inasmuch as it showed me a way of assuming responsibility for the white supremacist violence and racial trauma on which the republic was built. Even as my own family had experienced the vertigo of making formal claims before the federal government, so many communities of color and immigrant communities lack a formal platform to even assert their rights and to protect their needs and have existed – and continue to exist – outside the formal domains of political power. Their humanity remains invisible or, as Du Bois puts it, "veiled." With so much at stake in adopting the United States as my newfound homeland and making myself at home as a white person in a white-supremacist polity, Du Bois's vision of the future of American democracy gave me an opportunity to make sense of my own potential role in the country: I strive to make the future that Du Bois dreamt for America real. Only in a still-to-be-born America might I be at home. In a sense, I have accepted that to be fully committed to justice I must remain a refugee. Yet I am grateful to have been welcomed by a community of Du Bois scholars from whom

I have learned so much and will continue to learn. I am especially indebted to Du Bois scholars of color and the public alike who have placed a modicum of trust in my voice. I can only hope that my work can carry the moral faith to achieve what seems impossible in the light of the history of the irrevocable failures of white humanity: to rebuild an interracial political community in the aftermath of the sorrows of the past and the still burgeoning structural inequalities of the present.

My turn to Du Bois as a philosophy student coincided with the popular resurgence of white nationalist movements in the United States in the 2010s. With the aid of Du Bois, I aim to restore a vision of American democracy that dethrones white supremacy as the "true" meaning of our republican heritage and whiteness as the condition for being a "true" American. In turning to Du Bois, then, I would like to contribute, however little, to repairing the moral spirit of American democracy, telling a different story about how the parts relate to the whole that we are always building and rebuilding. With Du Bois, I refuse to believe that white fear and insecurity asserts complete sovereignty over the human spirit, though it will likely take uncharted moral imagination to properly mourn the black lives lost to bombs, nooses, and knives. I am grateful to the life and work of W. E. B. Du Bois and to the community of scholars and teachers who have taught me to feel the warmth and power of a new world being born and that what it means to be an American is an inversion of the inscription Dante read over the gates of the inferno: "Never abandon hope, all ye who enter here."

[Handwritten notes:]

† AFF • Why Do People of Color Stay In America?

• ↓ ↓   ↓ ↓ ↓ Continue To Come?

• Why Be Part of A Racist Capitalistic Country That Will Never Be Anti-Racist?

• Historically, Has Equality Ever Existed Anywhere?

Part I

Inclusion

1

Du Bois and the Black Lives Matter Movement: Thinking with Du Bois about Anti-Racist Struggle Today

During the March on Washington for Jobs and Freedom, on August 28, 1963, the prominent civil rights leader, Roy Wilkins, announced that Du Bois had died the night before: "If you want to read something that applies to 1963, go back and get a volume of *The Souls of Black Folk* by Du Bois published in 1903."[1] There are as many reasons why it is helpful to look to Du Bois today as there were in 1963 and in the early twentieth century. A voice from the past meditating on slavery, the Civil War, Reconstruction, and Jim Crow, Du Bois wrote about a world that appears bygone and foreign – a world that is not our own. One might wonder what his political critique can add to our understanding of the world today. His writings often conjure up images of dusty country roads, shaded by poplars, carrion-eating birds, and a fragment of dusk that approaches like a threat of violence. The takeaway from Du Bois's writings is that today – as in the past – any meaningful political analysis must underscore our racial realities. In the United States, racial matters constitute the *central obstacle* to the flourishing of the republic and the *central contradiction* between empirical reality and democratic ideals. This is why Du Bois asserted that the problem of the twentieth century was the problem of the color line.[2] The problem of race and racism implicates the entire nation and stretches across historical time. To motivate sustained public scrutiny of the significance of race remains a hurdle and explains, at least in part, why Du Bois's writings continue to spell both trouble and an opportunity to reflect on our world. In response to the Holocaust in Europe, Hannah Arendt warned that "once a specific crime has appeared for the first time, its reappearance is more likely than its initial emergence could ever have been."[3] In his foresight, Du Bois intimated that the problem of the color line will reemerge as the problem of our century.

For those new to Du Bois, one might wonder why he focused on race and racism. Perhaps to a white reader unaccustomed to viewing the world from the perspective of race – or viewing oneself as "raced" at all – the analytic lens of race might appear to be forced or overstated. After all, we embody multiple identities and it is not clear why race should center our sense of self and approach to democratic politics. Though he had much to say about class, gender, and nationality, Du Bois reaffirmed that the institutional and social practices that signify the withdrawal of respect and esteem from people of color generally and African Americans specifically mediate the overall structure of American society, wherein racial whiteness functions as a license to assert unconstrained power. He thus posited that the fate of roughly 12 percent of the population has and will continue to determine the fate of the republic. This strong connection between the part and the whole may be true for other social groups, but he aimed to show why it is true with respect to the African-American community.

Du Bois's abiding relevance for anti-racist struggle today offers insight into how the color line works today and how grassroots organizing might counteract it. The color line functions both to cause racial realities and to obscure their existence in a white-controlled polity. For Du Bois, to value black life across the color line is the central task of the republic, and successful grassroots movements illuminate disrespectful and derogating practices. In spite of the gains of the civil rights movement and the election of the first black president, the disrespect and derogation of the African-American community continues to undermine the legitimacy of the republic and test the commitment to democratic ideals for both vulnerable and privileged racial groups. A little more than a century after Du Bois published *The Souls of Black Folk*, the Black Lives Matter movement emerged to condemn the killing with impunity of African Americans by officers and vigilantes. Because structural inequalities bolster police violence, as the movement grew, it expanded its focus to show the intersection of police violence with mass incarceration, poverty, de facto segregation, the devaluation of labor, and the loss of housing and education opportunities in black and brown communities. The call to disrupt police and vigilante violence against African Americans is the heart of the Black Lives Matter movement; yet the call also serves to bring greater awareness of black vulnerability in social, economic, and political life.

The Black Lives Matter (BLM) movement was sparked by the acquittal of George Zimmerman in 2012. Zimmerman fatally shot a black 17-year-old high-school student Trayvon Martin in a gated community in central Florida. After a police dispatcher had instructed him to step down, Zimmerman pursued Martin, claiming, "This guy looks like he's up to no good, or he's on drugs or something." He continued, "These ***holes always get away."[4] Martin was unarmed and wearing a gray hooded sweatshirt; he had stepped out to buy snacks and it cost him his life. Zimmerman would later capitalize on his notoriety by selling online the gun he used to shoot Martin for US$139,000 and his amateur paintings of the Confederate and the American flags for as much as US$100,000.[5]

After Zimmerman's acquittal, the co-founders of the BLM movement, Alicia Garza, Patrisse Cullors, and Opal Tometi, demanded accountability for anti-black violence. In bringing the rash of legal lynchings into the national spotlight, the movement challenged public perceptions about the value of black life. For Du Bois, to counteract the phenomenon of the color line, the American public must be compelled to witness the black experience of America and to recognize that it stands in stark contradiction to democratic ideals. Not only do democratic institutions continue to fail to protect the most vulnerable members of the polity. The American public casts *doubt* about whether black lives are really in harm's way. Many *resent* the call to even pay attention to the possible racial dimension of policing practices; the color line thus *obscures* racial realities. As a consequence, the basic right to life – to have one's fair shot at being-in-the-world – is denied to African Americans; and it is extremely difficult to build more nuanced claims to justice when one's basic right to exist is insecure. Hence the radical power of the assertion that *black lives matter*.

In chapter 13 of *Souls*, Du Bois depicted the fictional tale of a young black man, John Jones, who has returned to his hometown of Altamaha, Georgia after receiving a college degree in the North. A white mob lynches Jones for defending his sister against a white rapist. Du Bois narrated Jones's last thoughts:

Amid the trees in the dim morning twilight he watched their shadows dancing and heard their horses thundering towards him, until at last they came sweeping like a storm, and he saw in front [a] haggard white-haired man, whose eyes flashed red with fury. Oh, how he pitied him, – pitied him, – and wondered if he had the coiling twisted rope. Then, as the storm burst round him, he rose slowly to his feet and turned his closed eyes towards the Sea.

And the world whistled in his ears.[6]

Though fictional, Du Bois's account of the last moments of Jones's life represents a moral truth about what it means to be a victim of racist violence. Jones was "swept like a storm" by the mob and, even as they asserted their gross claim to his physical body, he "pitied" his executioners; Jones saw their souls distorted by fury and fear in a way that they could not see themselves. In pitying his executioners, Jones asserted his spiritual sovereignty over them – that a vital portion of his self will not bend to their will. Of course, spiritual sovereignty can seem wanting against the destruction of the physical body. Du Bois's insight here, I submit, illuminates black insight into white souls disfigured by bigotry and asserts the right to black hope for liberation. "But not even this was able to crush all manhood and chastity and aspiration from black folk."[7] In his stark rendering of the white soul, for Du Bois, their "pitiful" deeds cannot be the final judgment about, and summation of, what it means to be a human being; instead, he cemented the victims of lynch mobs as the rightful judges of America, as those whose souls must live on in our collective consciousness. So too the Black Lives Matter movement upholds the value of the black lives lost and elevates their experience of violence as the true reflection of American racial realities. "We must exalt," implored Du Bois, "the Lynched above the Lyncher, and the Worker above the Owner, and the Crucified above Imperial Rome."[8]

After Reconstruction, lynching mobs exploded across the United States. Between 1882 and 1968, historians estimate 3,500 African Americans were killed. The destruction of the black body was a public festival, complete with the sale of photographs and souvenirs of the cut-up bits of the victims' bodies. In *Dusk of Dawn*, Du Bois recounted that when he found Sam Hose's knuckles on display in a shop window in Atlanta in 1899, a recent victim of a lynch mob, his faith in science as a tool for racial justice reform wavered.[9] Fact-based arguments alone could not stop anti-black violence or the family picnics around the burnt and mutilated remains of black people. He began to search for a more expansive way to combat the celebration of and complicity in racial terror. This history of violence has left a psychological imprint on the collective consciousness of the republic and today motivates, if not the celebration, then indifference and resentment against a movement to end police brutality. White nationalist groups have turned into an increasingly well-organized social force that seeks to reclaim the republic as a de jure racial caste system, reaffirming it as a white ethno-state. Today, as in the past, the claim that black lives matter is, in Baldwin's words, a spiritual "cross" that the republic bears: the recognition, or the lack thereof, of black lives continues to define its character and shapes the history of its future.[10] According to Du Bois, whenever the republic comes to value black life just a little more, it ushers in the radical reconstruction of modern American society.

The black lives lost

Recall that the color line withdraws respect and esteem from people of color in general and from African Americans in

particular. Though it cultivates a broad focus on racial realities, the Black Lives Matter movement highlights the racist
violence perpetuated and condoned by the state. To be sure,
the federal government had enabled the scourge of lynching
of the Jim Crow era, passing an anti-lynching bill in 2018,
a century after the bill was first introduced in the Senate.
Legal inaction fueled white mobs. This meant that local law
enforcement assured impunity for murderers, and police officials often played a role in lynchings, handing over victims to
mobs, standing idle, or lighting the match themselves. The
passage of the anti-lynching bill is a symbol of the ongoing
fight for accountability for racist police violence as much as
it is a symbol of the complicity of the state and law enforcement, then as now.

Du Bois believed that bearing witness to anti-black violence and the resultant trauma shapes the historical legacy
of black liberation struggles against white supremacy. In
his fictional and journalistic portrayals of the black lives
lost to racial violence, Du Bois wanted to stir in his reader
a sense of compassion and shared grief with the segregated
black community. He endeavored to portray the singular
and irreplaceable lives lost; and sometimes leaned on poetic
depictions of a person's subjective consciousness that is
snuffed out in death. Given the sheer number of deaths and
the lack of quality investigative journalism, with the exception of the efforts of Ida B. Wells and black-owned presses,
it is difficult to track all the victims of anti-black violence
over the centuries and to tell the story of their lives. Even
today, the few names reported by the press represent a frac-
tion of the many lives lost; and headlines often exclude black
women and members of the trans community whose lives are
notably at risk. For Du Bois, the task of political critique is to
defend the humanity of the vulnerable, while also capturing
the vast scale of anti-black violence and disenfranchisement

without reifying the lost lives into a statistic or an abstract status of "victimhood." His intuition was that empathizing with the individual behind the statistic would help the public resist the passive acceptance of white supremacist ideology and violence as a customary feature of modern American life.

The Black Lives Matter movement captures the black lives lost in routine policing practices across the country. By bringing attention to each individual victim with his or her diverse family background, gender, and class, the movement showcases how racial blackness mediates the public's perception of threat and exposes black lives to police violence.

Consider the brief life of Tamir Rice. In 2014, 12-year-old Rice was playing with a toy gun in a Cleveland park and a white man waiting for a bus called 911 to report him as an armed belligerent. Within seconds of arriving on the scene, a white officer fatally shot Tamir in the chest. On the day he died, his mother, Samaria, had packed him a turkey sandwich for lunch and had given him a few dollars to buy chips and juice from the corner store. Tamir still enjoyed playing with Lego and a *Teenage Mutant Ninja Turtle* video game; he was inseparable from his 14-year-old sister, Tajai. The Rice family had moved to the neighborhood in part to be close to the park in which Tamir was eventually killed. His older sister was the first to rush to her dying brother before the officer who had shot him tackled and arrested her as Tamir lay dying.

Consider, too, the brief life of Freddie Carlos Gray, Jr. He was 25 years old when he was "nickel dimed" by the Baltimore Police Department after being randomly targeted in his neighborhood. As he had done before, Gray ran at the approaching police vehicles and was then arrested. To "nickel dime" detainees is to bind their hands and feet without fastening their seatbelts, leaving them unable to protect their heads. Officers proceed to make sudden stops and sharp turns to fling their detainee inside the metal cage of the police van. Within an hour of his arrest, Gray's spinal cord was nearly 80 percent severed; essentially, he had suffered internal decapitation. A lifelong Baltimore resident, friends and neighbors called Gray "Pepper." He had a twin sister Fredericka; they grew up in crushing poverty, just a few blocks from where he was arrested. He had dropped out of high school in the ninth grade. Before being killed, he had suffered food insecurity and childhood lead poisoning so severe that a local attorney had filed a lawsuit on behalf of the Gray children; medical reports confirmed that they had permanent brain damage.

Although the deaths of black men and boys often dominate headlines, black women are extremely vulnerable to police violence. In Fort Worth, Texas, Atatiana Jefferson was killed during a wellness check in 2019; a neighbor had reported that her front door was ajar and was worried about the Jefferson household. Fearing an intruder, Jefferson approached her window to inspect the commotion outside. As she appeared in the window, an officer shot her *through* it. He had not announced who he was or why he was there. Atatiana had been playing video games with her eight-year-old nephew, Zion. A recent college graduate, she worked in the pharmaceutical industry and was planning to attend medical school. An only child, she was the primary caregiver to her parents, both of whom passed away soon after her murder.

In each of these cases, to this date, none of the officers have been held criminally responsible. Jefferson's killer was recently indicted, though convictions are rare. The above is just a snapshot of the many black lives lost. Each life tells a different story about the intersection of gender, class, and age in the devaluation of black lives. Like Atatiana Jefferson, African-American women are often killed by police in their own homes, including Korryn Gaines, Kathryn Johnston,

Yvette Smith, Aiyana Stanley-Jones, and Tarika Wilson, whereas black men are often targeted by racial profiling. In building a racial justice movement, Du Bois compelled white folk to conceive the world from the perspective of African Americans, i.e., to hear as they would hear the footfall of police boots at the front door, to feel their fear at an approaching police vehicle. Such an empathetic attitude is an essential tool for preventing future violence. And yet, when vulnerable voices share their distinct perspective on police practices (or the polity-at-large), they are often *distrusted* and *discredited*.

Trust: do you see what I see?

Du Bois argued that the color line cloaked racial realities. In part, it did this by cultivating distrust of black voices across the color line. Whites often reject the testimonies of black and brown communities, as if they do not bear witness to a shared reality with them. Conversely, after enduring long-standing scrutiny and indifference, understandably, victims of racial injustice come to distrust the white-controlled polity; and they doubt its willingness to listen to them or police departments' capacity to serve their communities, in which the police often function like an occupying military force. Mutual distrust strengthens the color line: whites refuse to acknowledge racial realities and, in turn, an interracial justice effort to dismantle the color line becomes impracticable. And yet there are moments when, as Du Bois puts it, the "veil" lifts and the black experience of the color line emerges, and is recognized, in public consciousness. The success of the Black Lives Matter movement is to have conveyed to the public the reality of anti-black violence at the hands of police and vigilantes that has long beleaguered African Americans.

Mutual trust is necessary to sustain the bounds of civic

fellowship and a shared sense of political fate. Trust often mediates what one takes to be true and is ready to accept as a feature of a shared reality that binds a stranger's destiny to one's own. In granting credibility to an interlocutor, one takes their experiences of the world to be a true representation of the world. Yet in an age of the rapid dissemination of information through the internet and social media, the refusal to trust black voices persists. Distrust and suspicion are the cause of racial violence – a fact exemplified in the killing of Eric Garner. The moments leading up to Garner's death were caught on cellphone video and watched by millions. A Staten Island resident, Garner was killed in 2014 in an illegal chokehold by ex-officer Daniel Pantaleo.[11] Yet there remains little consensus about what the footage means. Prior to his death, Garner repeated eleven times "I can't breathe," a phrase that is now a rally cry of the BLM movement. Pantaleo did not believe Garner that he really couldn't breathe; or else, he simply didn't care. Likewise, many members of the public still do not believe that Garner's death was avoidable, or else they simply don't care one way or another. In effect, they just don't trust that he really couldn't breathe.

In an interview, Garner's youngest daughter, Emerald Garner, responded to the news that four years after Pantaleo had killed her father he was finally fired: "We're grateful that someone sees what we see."[12] In contrast, the NYC police union leader, Patrick Lynch, denounced Pantaleo's firing. Lynch asserted that the firing encourages assaults on police officers. Of course, police officers' distorted perception of their own vulnerability to attack by African Americans rationalizes their use of deadly force in the first place. Moreover, officers often fabricate police reports to suggest a victim posed a threat, knowing that they enjoy the public's trust that their black and brown victims lack. The public's inclination to trust police officers and distrust their victims persists, in spite of video footage of fatal police encounters. In response to Lynch, Emerald Garner said:

> So, he's saying that de Blasio [mayor of NYC] left the police officers out on the street alone. Eric Garner was left on the street to die. And that's on video. So, if they're saying that the mayor abandoned them and they're so angry that a police officer broke the rules and got penalized for it, that's really what the problem is. The problem is they never thought in a million years that this cop would be fired because of a black man. And I think that's honestly what they thought. And the fact that he is fired, it makes them upset, because it's like, "We've been getting away with it for so long, so who are you to tell us to stop doing what we're doing?" And that's just how I take the whole situation, because a wrong was done. Like, at some point you have to stop and say Eric Garner was killed for no reason. He could have been saved. They neglected to save him.[13]

As Emerald Garner points out, Lynch never imagined – and resents – the idea that officers could face repercussions for their actions, even as most assailants like Pantaleo avoid criminal prosecution. The so-called "Blue Lives Matter" movement, which appeared in response to the Black Lives Matter movement, mobilizes the law enforcement community against police "vilification." In a press release, the "Blue Lives Matter" movement states that black rights activists "spread the absurd message that people were being shot by law enforcement simply because of the color of their skin. Even our political leaders pandered to these criminals and helped to spread this false narrative."[14] The distrust of black voices is so intense that the Black Lives Matter movement is dismissed as a cover for black criminality and as outright irrational. Equating black rights activists with "criminals," the countermovement invokes a timeworn racist theme that holding white-controlled institutions accountable for anti-black violence means somehow harming whites. Not only does it deny black vulnerability to police violence, it treats the call for police accountability as a *threat*.

Just as the white-controlled polity had once rationalized slavery – and wrote it into the Constitution – as if it were consistent with, rather than a contradiction, of liberal ideals, in our white-controlled polity today, public habits of moral judgment are often shaped by the denial of the moral and epistemic value of black voices. Du Bois believed that an effect of the color line is that the white public fails to register moral injuries against African Americans as a contradiction of democratic ideals. The white public struggles to "see" beyond the color line the people who live and strive there as making a legitimate claim on their will. And this failure to "see" black humanity can be so strong that even video footage of the destruction of the black body does not shake it.

The same year that the federal government enacted the first anti-lynching bill, Congress passed the "Blue Lives Matter" bill by a vote of 382 to 35. The Protect and Serve Act of 2018 makes it a federal crime to assault a police officer and categorizes attacks on law enforcement as a "hate crime."[15] The Senate is expected to pass the bill in 2020, at which point it will be ready for Trump to sign into federal law. A version of the bill has been proposed or passed in more than 30 states. The notion that the police constitute a maligned social group captures how much the federal government continues to distrust African-American claims that they are especially vulnerable to police violence. Though the days when Sam Hose's knuckles appeared in a shop window are thankfully gone, racial fault lines remain that influence public habits of moral reasoning about who to believe and who is really in harm's way.

Lifting the veil: de-colonizing the white moral imagination

The way the color line promotes distrust might suggest that each racial group is locked into its own version of reality. In a sectarian public sphere, social groups each have their own version of the world, bolstered by their preferred set of "alternative facts." Du Bois believed it was possible to repair the bonds of mutual trust torn apart by the color line. Cultivating a shared sense of political fate – the mutual recognition that the advance of each is a condition for the advance of all – is necessary to ensure that democratic politics does not become a mere public contest for grabbing power and asserting self-interest. But this is difficult to do if non-white racial groups inspire fear and resentment in the white moral imagination. Du Bois maintained that white Americans must carry the *onus* of reparative justice by developing their moral perception and demonstrating their trustworthiness to black and brown communities. In order for the polity to be reconstituted as a racially pluralistic whole, each member of the polity must feel as though their fate is an object of genuine concern for others. In cultivating a sense of interracial civic fellowship, Du Bois took pains to show the manner and depth to which white Americans have contributed to the problem of race and racism, i.e., the problem of the color line. He does this not to dismiss whites' capacity for advancing racial justice reform. Indeed, he always believed that white supremacy is eliminable from the polity. Rather, in offering a sober account of whites' role and complicity in white supremacy, he aimed to outline the forms of affective and cognitive labor that are necessary to restore their trustworthiness in communities of color. De-colonizing the white moral imaginations requires welcoming non-whites as civic fellows and showing that one is prepared, in turn, to undertake efforts and even sacrifices on their behalf. Consistent action to advance the standing of the worst off ultimately necessitates giving up an illicit claim to power. In return, one might repair the recognition of oneself as a genuine civic fellow, which is intrinsically valuable insofar as the pursuit of justice is an end in itself and is manifest when all persons believe that their life is an object of genuine concern for others.

In *Souls*, Du Bois's critique of modern American society begins with a discussion of the so-called "Negro Problem."[16] His formulation of this "problem" poses a question to the oppressed: "How does it feel to be a problem?"[17] With this rhetorical move, Du Bois at once represents the experiential quality of the first-person black experience of Jim Crow – that black people are made to feel like something is wrong with them, that *they* are the problem – and points forward to a new way of talking about race. Rather than presenting anti-black racism as a problem for black people, he makes it a problem for *white people.* To be sure, the kind of problem that race is for whites excludes subjection to racist disrespect and violence. Rather, Du Bois points out that the color line is nourished by white habits of judgment *about* non-whites. Whites render dark skin a "problem" by stigmatizing it and are often the wellsprings of racist hatred and ill will, as well as blank indifference or ignorance about racial realities.

For Du Bois, being morally illiterate about race is more than just not carrying ill will and hatred towards people of color. Being morally illiterate about race showcases habits of judgment that rationalize white fear, indifference, and ignorance, undercutting a sense of shared political fate with communities of color. To be sure, white moral illiteracy about race also *entraps* African Americans in a system of social values that can undermine the development of black positive

self-perception and establish the white-controlled world as
the arbiter of truth and value. For whites to de-colonize
their moral imagination takes more than just scanning the
brain and the heart for racist thoughts or ill will. It requires
a more nuanced account of the nature of white complicity in
white supremacy and the myriad informal ways that communities of color are rejected as civic fellows. To de-colonize
the white moral imagination, then, for Du Bois, entails illu-
minating a complex social architecture of domination and
subordination that preforms interracial social interactions.

In *Souls*, Du Bois introduces the idea of double consciousness, describing it as a "peculiar sensation."[18] One
begins to see oneself "through the revelations of the other
world."[19] Seeing oneself from the perspective of another is
an important way that humans develop self-consciousness.
From childhood to adulthood, when others see us in a positive light, their recognition enables us to form a strong and
well-defined sense of self. One's subjective consciousness of
being an honest, lovable, or smart person is confirmed in
the recognition of others. Once the "subjective" self fuses
with the "objective" self, which is reflected in the external
world, one develops an integrated sense of self. The difficulty for Du Bois is that in a white-controlled world, white
Americans "look on in amused contempt and pity" at African
Americans, and a "conflictual two-ness" results for those
standing behind the color line.[20] Du Bois noted, "One ever
feels one's two-ness, – an American and a Negro; two warring
ideals in one dark body."[21] One feels like one has to choose
between identifying as an American or as a person of color.
For the white perspective insinuates that a "true" American
is not a person of color – they are white. African Americans
can, then, feel compelled to "distance" themselves from
their own blackness in order to "win" whites' respect and
esteem. And so, when the white-controlled world attempts

to establish itself as the "measure" of the black "soul," black consciousness "doubles": the subjective self-consciousness of one's unconditional moral worth *as* black conflicts with the derogated image of blackness that the world imposes on subjective consciousness.

Paul C. Taylor explains that the "peculiar sensation" of double consciousness represents that African Americans are *in* the white-controlled world, but not *of* it.[22] The mere fact that one is there – a subject within a legal jurisdiction – does not mean that one has the formal capacity to assert democratic control over the terms of one's physical, social, economic, or political existence. "Imagine spending your life looking for insults or for hiding places from them – shrinking [. . .] from blows that are not always but ever; not each day, but each week, each month, each year [. . .] forcing your way among cheap and tawdry idiots."[23] Poor treatment, violence, and marginalization profoundly constrain one's scope of action. The fewer opportunities one has to exercise agency, the more one feels stuck "in" the white-controlled world as its dominated plaything rather than a free agent "of" a democratic republic. Fittingly, Du Bois employed the metaphor of a "prison-house" to illustrate black entrapment. For people of color are "imprisoned" in a world that does not welcome them and whose institutions they can hardly influence. And like a brutal warden, the white-controlled world is deaf to their outcry: "Why did God make me an outcast and a stranger in mine own house?"[24]

A white-controlled world shapes interracial social interaction to enable the black experience of double consciousness. To watch over one's shoulder as a police cruiser scopes out the neighborhood. To notice a security guard shadowing one's movement in a shopping mall. So too, Du Bois warned, whites have a psychological and material incentive to preserve the color line. Racial division stokes discord among the working poor, impairing the formation of a strong inter-racial labor alliance, which in turn bolsters the ascendancy of the superrich. Poor whites withhold solidarity with black and brown labor and undercut their own economic interests, which can only be advanced through an interracial alliance of organized labor. In compensation, poor whites receive "the wages of whiteness," a notion Du Bois formulated to illustrate the psychological feeling of superiority that incentivizes poor whites to reproduce white supremacist society that still leaves them poor and marginalized.[25]

Ironically, Du Bois imagined that the black experience of double consciousness could function as a window into building a utopian future inasmuch as double consciousness "gifts" African Americans with "second sight" about how to reconstruct the polity.[26] The challenge would be for a white-controlled world to cultivate the will to dismantle structural inequalities under black guidance, participating in anti-racist and interracial struggles as genuine allies of communities of color. Empathizing with the black experience of double consciousness can foment a shared sense of political and economic fate that substantiates the ties of interracial civic fellowship. With Du Bois, we can imagine the aftermath of white supremacy, when white Americans assume responsibility for racial realities, sacrificing their undue claims to power for the sake of a future without racial caste, state-sanctioned violence, and poverty. The success of the Black Lives Matter movement is that it has made the nation take responsibility for the racial realities it has created. Yet in forcing the white world to take responsibility for racial realities, the movement never makes black dignity contingent on white affirmation, as whites and white-controlled institutions slowly learn to achieve moral clarity about race.

Albeit Du Bois did not consider the limitation of the black/white paradigm at length, the color line in policing practices transcends the black/white paradigm. For white supremacy draws a continuum in which whites' social location tracks their power vis-à-vis non-whites; and the experience of racial marginalization targets multiple racial identities at once and in different ways. Hence, the #BrownLivesMatter and #MuslimLivesMatter have emerged to represent a more comprehensive experience of the color line in policing practices in order to refine the scope of public concern and intervention.[27]

Mourning and moral faith

In *Souls*, Du Bois shared his personal experience of the loss of his firstborn. The reader plunges with his young family into grief, from which his partner, Nina, never fully recovered, "never forgiv[ing] God for the unhealable wound."[28] But the white world, Du Bois wrote, saw no one worth mourning and closed in around them like a devouring mouth: "The busy city dinned about us; they did not say much, those pale-faced hurrying men and women; they did not say much – they only glanced and said, 'N******s!' "[29] To mourn is to feel the value of a life lost; public rituals of mourning show respect and a willingness to forge fellowship. Sharing in grief can even open a path to rebuilding shattered trust.

Of course, it is naive to assume that state-sanctioned rituals of mourning could spontaneously reconstitute a political community, especially if few measures are taken to redress structural inequalities. The philosopher Linda Alcoff cautions that even well-meaning whites are often ill prepared to do the difficult cognitive and emotional labor of interracial struggle. They would rather be portrayed as the saviors of the dark world, rather than an ally or a friend.[30] And yet a republic that once celebrated lynchings with a family picnic

– and sneered and continues to sneer at the death of black children – cannot forgo learning to mourn the lives lost to racial violence. In 1963, Baldwin reflected: "Morally, I think this nation should be, for the foreseeable future, in mourning."[31] After another unarmed black teenager, Mike Brown, was killed by a white police officer in Ferguson, Missouri, black residents built a makeshift memorial of flowers and teddy bears for Brown. The memorial was repeatedly run over by police vehicles; on one occasion, a police officer let his dog urinate on it.[32] "Later that night," Keeanga-Yamahtta Taylor writes, "the uprising began."[33] The destruction of Brown's memorial precipitated days of intense protests by black Ferguson residents, on whom the police fired tear gas and rubber bullets.

In his elegant defense of moral faith in the light of loss, Melvin Rogers notes: "The quest to transform the political landscape indicates that the legitimacy of democracy demands faith that sacrifice will be redeemed. Here the word 'redeem' indicates the possibility of mending wounds at the heart of the community, the end result of which is to include those who have otherwise been excluded from political life."[34] Likewise, Du Bois defined the power and limit of his faith in democracy: the moral redemption of the republic demands ongoing engagement with the history of black, Latinx, and indigenous losses. Though he had faith that it is possible to heal the wound racism has left on the republic, he knew white Americans would need to cross an uncharted "spiritual" territory to learn to atone for centuries of violence, a political gesture that has never been offered. The polity has not yet learned to mourn the dead. It has not even learned to be troubled by its direct role in the killings.

In the Jewish tradition, after a burial one observes seven days of mourning. The practice is called "sitting *shiva*." Mourners cover all the mirrors in their house and sit on low stools to show their humility before the dead. Unlike sitting *shiva*, there is no clear procedure in a constitutional republic of how to mourn or when to begin. Though the republic will never finish mourning the lives lost to racial violence, it is *necessary* and *possible* to begin the process of mourning. We must begin, as ever, with the conviction that *black lives matter*.

Every year on Martin Luther King Day, militia groups descend on Richmond, Virginia to protest gun-control legislation. That event organizers choose to hold their gun rights rally on a federal holiday that honors King suggests two things. First, the power of the Black Lives Matter movement remains its forceful assertion of the right of blacks to exist. Second, the forceful assertion of the right of blacks to exist is taken as a threat not just to the law enforcement community but to a fragile whiteness invested in the preservation of the color line. Their fear and insecurity betray them. The overwhelmingly white (and mostly male) militiamen nurse an elemental dread of black being-in-the-world. In the judgment of Du Bois's John Jones, the men who hold the noose remain "pitiful." And yet the losses they continue to inflict are incalculable, rendering precarious the day-to-day existence of communities of color. Born to former slaves, the poet Paul Dunbar reflects on what it is like to live a life to which one is made to feel unentitled. He notes that it feels like paying a debt: "This is the debt I pay just for one riotous day, / years of regret and grief, sorrow without relief / [. . .] / Slight was the thing I bought, small was the debt I thought, / poor was the loan at best – God! but the interest!"[35]

2

Student Days, 1885–1895:
Between Nashville, Cambridge, and Berlin

In thinking about Du Bois's significance today, it is helpful to visit his formative years as he developed his impressions of the postbellum United States. In this chapter, I provide a brief overview of his childhood and student days, tracking the development of his early political thought as it relates to Kantian political philosophy, a line of interpretation suggested by Charles W. Mills. In the chapter's first section, I discuss Du Bois's family background, from his birth in rural western Massachusetts to the completion of his doctoral degree in history at Harvard University. For the remainder of the chapter, I analyze Du Bois's conception of the ideal of black civic enfranchisement. Pursuing Mills's interpretation of Du Bois, I explain why Du Bois's ideal of civic enfranchisement is richer than the Kantian legalistic model of political inclusion.

Du Bois's childhood, formative experiences, and student days

Though perhaps best known as a political theorist of the Jim Crow era, Du Bois was born in the North in the town of Great Barrington, Massachusetts, not far from where the banks of the Housatonic River pickaxe a valley into the Berkshire Mountains. He was born in 1868, just three years after the end of the Civil War and five years after the Emancipation Proclamation. A textile and a paper mill were the two largest employers in the area, whose distinction was otherwise limited to possessing the largest barn in America and two poorly constructed iron bridges from which horses often accidentally fell.[1] As a child, he attended integrated public schools. In a poignant episode in *The Souls of Black Folk* (1903), he captured the moment in his school days when "it dawned on me with a certain suddenness that I was different from the others; or like mayhap, in heart and longing but shut out from their world by a vast veil."[2] Though he would pioneer the key concepts of the veil and double consciousness to theorize segregation in the South, he draws on his formative experience in his hometown.

Du Bois framed his life story within the historical narrative of a "New World" stained by the blood of enslaved Africans, the colonial genocide, and expropriation of indigenous lands. In American modernity, the significance of racial belonging originated in violent and oppressive white-controlled institutions that used the idea of race to justify political power. The antebellum political economy was forged in an uneasy alliance between a feudal slavocracy and industrial capitalism, which a de jure racial caste system helped stabilize. Du Bois's autobiographies begin with the bondage of his own ancestors. He constructed a personal mythology showing in the singular example of his life the passage of historical time through the historical consciousness of African Americans. His maternal great-great-grandfather, Tom, was captured on the coast of West Africa and purchased by a wealthy Dutchman, Coenraet Burghardt, who brought Tom to New England in the early 1730s. On his father's side, French Huguenots owned plantations in the Bahamas and Haiti. With an enslaved woman, Dr James Du Bois fathered his paternal grandfather, Alexander Du Bois, whom Du Bois would later meet as a teenager.[3] In *Darkwater*, Du Bois recounts, with subtle dramatic flourish, his light-skinned father marrying his "brown" mother.[4] By then, his father's older sister had already "passed over into the white world and her children's children are now white, with no knowledge of their Negro blood."[5] Unlike his cousins, the man who was fated to become the African-American man of letters *par excellence* was spared from being torn from his black roots. "The pronunciation of my name is *Due Boyss*, with the accent on the last syllable," he wrote, stressing the Americanized – not the French – pronunciation of his last name.[6] He even preserved his West African ancestry through a fragment of a Wolof song from Senegambia passed down on his mother's side of the family, a song "about confinement or captivity: 'gene me, gene me [*gene ma, gene ma*]!' – 'get me out, get me out!' "[7]

Du Bois was the only child of a domestic worker, Mary Salvina Burghardt, who raised him alone and championed his education. His Haitian-born father, Alfred Du Bois, was absent from his life, and the young Du Bois believed he was dead, when, in fact, his father worked as a barber and a preacher in Connecticut. Du Bois had insisted that he had a happy childhood, although his noted biographer, David Levering Lewis, speculated that a "reflexive bravura" likely papered over a "milieu circumscribed by immiseration."[8] On several occasions, Du Bois recalled idyllic scenes: in the backyard of his "clapboard" childhood home grew "unbelievably delicious strawberries."[9] Behind a railroad station, he disappeared with the children in the neighborhood into the Berkshire woods that grew as if out of a storybook. Yet his actual circumstances could not have been the stuff of idylls. There were few African-American families in Great Barrington and Du Bois was the only black student in his graduating high-school class. Partially paralyzed by a stroke years earlier, his mother died when he was 16 years old. "I can now see," Du Bois would later reflect, "that my mother must have struggled pretty desperately on very narrow resources and that the problem of shoes and clothing for me must have been at times staggering."[10] In his last autobiography, the 90-year-old Du Bois acknowledged that it was his mother's death that had prompted him to dedicate himself to his work. In spite of being "more alone than I had ever dreamed," he shared, "now especially I must succeed as my mother so desperately wanted me to."[11]

In *Darkwater*, Du Bois described his student days as "The Age of Miracles." And miraculous it was. Whatever he willed seemed to come to pass, as if the world were designed for his happiness – more a testament to his tenacity and support system than to Jim Crow America's recognition of the ambition and genius of black children. "Who was *I* to fight a world of color prejudice? I raise my hat to myself when I remember that [. . .] I did not hesitate or waver; but just went doggedly to work, and therein lay whatever salvation I achieved."[12] He aspired to attend Harvard University, where he would eventually enroll, becoming the first African American to receive a doctoral degree from the university in 1896, studying history. However, money was a problem. In an interracial effort, the local townspeople of Great Barrington raised funds through regional church networks to send him to college. He left Great Barrington at seventeen on a scholarship to Fisk University in Nashville, Tennessee, a historically black college, where he delighted in vibrant black cultural life:

> Disappointed though I was at not being able to go to Harvard, I merely regarded this as a temporary change of plan; I would of course go to Harvard in the end. But here and immediately was adventure. I was going into the South; the South of slavery, rebellion and black folk; and above all I was going to meet colored people of my own age and education, of my own ambitions. [. . .] I became aware, once a chance to go to a group of such people was opened up for me, of the spiritual isolation in which I was living. [. . .] I was thrilled to be for the first time among so many people of my own color or rather of such extraordinary colors, which I had only glimpsed before, but who it seemed were bound to me by new and exciting and eternal ties.[13]

In the South, he witnessed firsthand the racial realities of Jim Crow. He spent two summers working as a schoolteacher in rural Wilson County, teaching the children of black sharecroppers how to read. In *Souls*, he described establishing a one-room schoolhouse in a log cabin that had stored the corn of a white landowner. In the aftermath of slavery (1865) and Reconstruction (1865–77), the US federal government had done little to enfranchise former slaves and their children. Witnessing firsthand the limited opportunities and resources available in the postbellum black community, Du Bois began to discern the shadow that slavery cast on modern American society. The "afterlife" of slavery was manifest in the lives of children who lacked adequate access to basic amenities, including books and clothing. Denied land, viable employment opportunities, housing, and education, Du Bois's experience of black rural poverty prompted him to consider what kind of social and political programs could successfully incorporate the postbellum black community into the polity as free and equal persons.

Du Bois's early political thought

After graduating from Fisk in 1888, Du Bois transferred to Harvard University and studied philosophy with George Santayana, George Herbert Palmer, and Josiah Royce. During his student days, Harvard's philosophy department was a stronghold for German Idealism, spearheading the American reception of G. W. F. Hegel. Du Bois developed a close friendship with the philosopher William James. James is known as the founder of American Pragmatism. James often invited Du Bois to dinner in his Cambridge home.[14] Unlike other prominent intellectuals at the time, James offered mocking refutations of Social Darwinism, which was then popular.[15] After receiving his second BA from Harvard (he had to enroll as a junior after graduating from Fisk) as a doctoral student, he shifted from philosophy to the empirical study of social problems. Harvard had not then recognized sociology as a discipline. If it had, Du Bois would have likely studied sociology instead of history. After two years of graduate study at Harvard, he studied at the University of Berlin (now Humboldt University) under Gustav von Schmoller and Max Weber. At the turn of the twentieth century, the University of Berlin was the preeminent university of the Anglo-European world. In a series of letters written to the former president of the United States, Rutherford B. Hayes, Du Bois secured funding from the Slater Foundation to finance his trip abroad. Though the foundation refused to fund his doctorate at the University of Berlin – a major blow to Du Bois at the time – his experience in Germany profoundly affected him, professionally and personally.

In Germany, he began to see the United States in light
of its racial provincialism, a provincialism the entire world
did not share. He freely socialized with white students. He
danced at balls and wandered Berlin's Unter den Linden,
tipsy and unselfconscious. By the end of his stay in Berlin, one
of those dance partners came to hope that they might marry;
she would have followed him to America *gleich* – at once –
if he had invited her. White people's capacity for humanity
was a revelation to the young Du Bois. As it turns out, white
people were really just people. He also apprehended the
European racial caste system. Newspaper headlines about
Jewish pogroms, ghettoes, and the spread of interethnic conflicts across continental Europe heralded the coming world
wars. Traveling through German villages, cabdrivers sometimes deposited him at Jewish inns. He did not correct their
mistaken assumptions. He related a particularly horrifying
incident in Lübeck, a city north of Hamburg, where a gaggle
of townspeople "pursued" him until he fled by train.[16] In
Berlin, on the eve of his 25th birthday, he pledged that upon
returning to the United States he would dedicate his life
to fighting anti-black racism, declaring "Heaven nor Hell,
God nor Devil shall turn me from my purpose till I die."[17]
To achieve this, however, he had to first "drop" back into
"N*****-hating America." He returned to the United States
to submit his dissertation, *The Suppression of the African Slave-
Trade to the United States of America, 1638–1870*, under the
supervision of Albert Bushnell Hart; it became the first monograph (1896) published in the Harvard Historical Studies
book series on American history.

The normative basis of anti-racist political critique

Though Du Bois studied philosophy and social theory at
Harvard University and at the University of Berlin, short of

recounting the curriculum, he never explained its impact on his thought. His silence on the matter occasions an ongoing dispute about the best method for mapping the influence of German philosophy, particularly in his early years. A popular method for situating Du Bois's political thought in German philosophy (and American pragmatism) is philology. Philology is the study of language that traces the historical origin and usage of words. By reviewing the historical appearance of a word in popular discourse and print, a philological approach to "double consciousness" compares discussions of it in various texts across time. It is a popular method in literary criticism and historical linguistics. Such an inquiry can invite comparisons of Du Bois's notion of double consciousness to Ralph Waldo Emerson, Johann Wolfgang von Goethe, and Edmund Husserl, who each use the term "double consciousness" or a variant of it in their discussions of subjectivity and alienation. Early psychiatric diagnostic manuals even list "double consciousness" as a symptom of schizophrenia. Although philology presents an interesting survey of a concept, it neglects to provide a rational reconstruction of the meaning of a concept within the philosophical system in which it appears. Instead, philology outlines its function and relevant linguistic associations within a particular sociohistorical milieu.

My own method for reconstructing the normative foundation of Du Bois's political thought is built on my training as a philosopher, but I believe that it is also the most charitable, coherent, and comprehensive way of presenting his political thought as an integrated system. Save for the Afro-modern political tradition – and modern political philosophy more broadly – I do not believe it is worthwhile to argue that Du Bois "belongs" to any philosophical school or political program. I am not interested in proving that Du Bois is, in essence, a Germanist, nor do I shy away from thinking with Du Bois about the promise and limits of modern European philosophy. My method encourages productive engagement across disciplines and philosophical traditions to outline and advance the normative foundation of his anti-racist political critique.[18]

The is/ought distinction

To unpack the normative foundation of Du Bois's political thought, we must first understand the is/ought distinction.[19] The distinction is crucial in nineteenth- and twentieth-century American and German philosophy, enjoying prominence in the writing of Kant, Hegel, James, and Rawls among others. Even though he does not lay out a political treatise, we cannot begin to appreciate Du Bois's political thought without first understanding what normativity *is*. To be sure, for Du Bois, as an activist, journalist, social scientist, and historian, facts about the world – an accurate description of it – are crucial. He rejected what he called "car-window sociology" and established modern sociology by refining empirical methods for studying social problems, shirking overreliance on social theory. Even so, he did not just aim to give accurate descriptions of the world or to document people's bad experiences. Rather, he hoped to make it a fairer place for everybody. His commitment to social reform is paramount, showcasing his commitment to normative political critique. Even as a social scientist and historian, his political and philosophical commitments informed his empirical research, which was guided by a vision of social reform.

The is/ought distinction models two forms of judgment. First, we can represent the world as an empirical object that we find given in our experiences. Our mind *conforms* to the world by acquiring empirically verifiable facts about it. For example, Professor Basevich is 5 ft 7 in. tall, or most birds fly by flapping their wings in the air. These facts are reported by the senses and tools for measurement and observation. Facts are the essence of scientific thought that increase our knowledge *about* the world by describing it accurately. Hence scientific disciplines such as biology and chemistry are *descriptive*.

For Du Bois, the human mind is not a calculator or a thermometer that spits out facts about the world in response to sensory stimuli. The human mind also interprets the world. Indeed, the "ought" captures a form of judgment that is unique to the human animal. It provides a criterion or standard to which we expect the world to conform. Our capacity to make prescriptive judgments is part of the fundamental feature of human experience and an ineliminable condition of free purposive agency since prescriptive standards instruct us on what to *do* in the world. We can act in a way that *creates* the world that we think, ideally, ought to exist. With the "ought," the world conforms to the mind, rather than the mind to the world. It is a kind of judgment that makes a prescriptive demand by stipulating a standard for rightful conduct, such as a *principle* or a *norm* to guide what the world *should* become. Calls for change made by grassroots social movements and normative political theory are future-oriented, catalyzing reforms that aim to make the world better; and, ideally, such prescriptive demands force individuals and institutions to become aware of their shortcomings at living up to the principles or norms that would make the world a better place.

Consider the statements "The judge ruled in the case unfairly" or "The guards must treat prisoners with humanity and never beat them." The concepts of "fairness" and "humanity" function as criteria for rightful conduct that *should* be followed without exception, although they often are not followed in reality because so many judges are biased and so many prison guards are sadists. There are many reports about the world that confirm the *empirical fact* that it is unfair. However, reports about people acting badly and doing evil things to each other do not undermine the validity of the moral imperative that people really *ought* not to behave this way: that it is *wrong* for them to do so. Social movements aim to correct bad behavior and eliminate unfair social and institutional practices. The best and most challenging political thought is therefore *normative* inasmuch as it understands the world as it is, and yet it prescribes a moral or political ideal of what the world *ought* to become. Such a standard provides principles or norms by virtue of which anyone can evaluate the world's deviations from the requirements of morality and justice. Normative political theory can sketch a democratic political procedure for people to come together and construct standards of conduct together, or it can offer some combination of both principle-based and procedure-based approaches.[20] Du Bois thus declares that "the 'ought' is the greatest thing in human life."[21]

There remains the question, however, of which norms or principles drive the "ought" in Du Bois's political thought. Assuming that Du Bois was, in fact, committed to a program of social reform, this implies that he endorsed a conception of an ideally just world, which social reform should realize. There have been few *systematic* investigations of the normative foundation of Du Bois's political thought, though many have labeled him a "social democrat" or "liberal" turned "Marxist." I do not mean to suggest that these labels are inaccurate so much as they neglect to clarify the underlying normative basis of his critique.

A Kantian normative scheme in Du Bois's political thought

As noted in the introduction, the philosopher Mills argues that Du Bois is a "black radical liberal" committed to the liberal ideals of moral and political universalism.[22] He positions Du Bois in the tradition of Afro-modern political thought, an interpretation first advanced by the noted Du Bois scholar Robert Gooding-Williams.[23] A "genre-defining" feature of the Afro-modern thought is normative theorizing in the light of the black experience of modernity. The rise of modern states and of human rights discourse appeared with racial terror and subjugation in the West. In Du Bois's writings, the political and social organization of white supremacy is a critical reference point.[24] In the spirit of Afro-modern tradition, Du Bois employed a conceptual apparatus that he hoped would be useful for theorizing and combating anti-black racism in a white-supremacist society. His appropriation of the liberal ideals of moral and political universalism attests to his moral faith that racism is eliminable from the polity. However, he rethinks the ideal of civic enfranchisement to deal with the racial realities of post-bellum black disenfranchisement in the social, economic, and political spheres.

Mills builds on Gooding-Williams's position by offering a rational reconstruction of Du Bois's "Afro-modern" critique of American democracy. Drawing on his larger project of developing an immanent critique of political liberalism that uses universal liberal ideals to criticize liberalism, Mills argues that, for Du Bois, racism is a defining, rather than an anomalous, feature of modern liberal societies. Yet he maintains that Du Bois enlisted liberal ideals to dismantle racial caste and to "undertake a deracializing reconstruction of liberalism."[25] Du Bois's treatment of liberalism, Mills posits, focused on nonideal circumstances to rework liberal ideals in the service of black emancipation. Mills asserts that Du Bois is a "black radical liberal [. . .] centrally focused on *nonideal theory* – that is, the world of sociopolitical oppression and the challenge, in the United States in particular, of how

to overcome illiberal white supremacy in what was supposedly a liberal democratic state."[26] On his view, a deracializing
reconstruction of liberalism guides the radical transformation of a white-supremacist society; and Mills submits that
Du Bois's political thought offers precisely such a guide
to rethinking American modernity and modeling a racially
inclusive utopia.

In interpreting Du Bois as a nonideal liberal, Mills claims
that the United States treats people of color as "subpersons":

> People of color will originally have been conceptualized in
> [a] racist optic not as "persons" but as subpersons. This does
> not, of course, literally *make* them subpersons – I endorse
> the morally objectivist position that moral status is socio-
> independent. But it does mean that, assuming the capacity
> of white power to bring into existence a racially hierarchical
> society, the failure to attain "socially recognized" person-
> hood will have a profound effect on the psyches not merely
> of nonwhites but also of whites.[27]

There is much in Du Bois's writings to support Mills's interpretation. The contention that people of color occupy a
subordinate social and political status in spite of the polity's
nominal commitment to moral and political universalism is a
central concern for Du Bois.

Consider that Du Bois uses the idea of "the veil" in *Souls*
as a metaphor to signify the systematic racist misrecognition
of the moral equality of persons. For Du Bois, to be "veiled"
is to be rendered "invisible" to white people and white-controlled institutions as a person entitled to legal recognition,
moral respect, and social esteem. A person of color thus
stands "behind the veil" in the sense that whites refuse to
recognize their experience of exclusion and social derogation
as forms of moral injury. One can infer then, with Du Bois,

that whites fail to "see" black people *as* moral equals. The veil thus "unveils" African Americans *as* possessing a subordinate sociopolitical standing vis-à-vis whites. Or as Mills frames it, African Americans possess the subordinate status of "subpersons." To be clear, this does not mean that people of color actually *are* subpersons; equal moral status is a socio-independent – or transcendental – feature of persons. But it does mean that the equal moral status of blacks does not have social and political uptake in the polity at large. Black personhood is not, in Mills's words, "socially recognized." Consequently, black suffering seldom elicits compassion, public outcry, or state intervention.[28] As Du Bois observed in *Souls*, African Americans become "strangers" in their own "house," as the world seems more like a "prison-house" than a stage for the free pursuit of their interests.[29] The arbitrary violence directed at communities of color over the centuries is a powerful illustration of the racist misrecognition of their personhood. The veil represents a kind of spiritual homelessness that exiles Afro-descendant peoples from the Americas as their homeland, as they are denied a political community where they can feel safe, connected, and secure. Recall that Du Bois asked, standing with those behind the veil, "Why did God make me an outcast and a stranger in mine own house?"[30]

Given the racist misrecognition behind the veil, one might ask which principles can counteract the disrespect and derogation of people of color and advance their recognition as equal moral persons. Mills draws on the idea of moral personhood from Kant's moral and political philosophy to counteract black subpersonhood and to uphold a standard for universal political judgment in a nonideal polity.[31] If the veil misrecognizes black personhood, then the liberal ideal of equal moral personhood must anchor an anti-racist political critique that can tear through the veil. Although Kant held virulently racist views, Mills argues that Kant's practical philosophy provides an indispensable normative basis for building an anti-racist political critique. Unquestionably, the moral equality of people of color is a key principle in Du Bois's political thought. Mills advises, however, that the Kantian idea of equal moral personhood must be "revised" to better address the nonideal circumstances of illiberal white supremacy and that Du Bois gives us some insight into how to carry out the necessary revisions. To wit, Kant's "ideal-theory" formulation of moral personhood is an ideological abstraction ineffective for redressing the nonideal racial realities. Enter Du Bois: Mills interprets Du Bois as a "nonideal" political theorist who directly responded to the racial realities, about which Kant either did not care or on which he was not primarily focused, in order to advance black equal moral standing.

Legal versus civic equality

Unfortunately, in my view, there are at least two shortcomings in Mills's analysis of the Kantian conception of moral personhood (and subpersonhood) in relation to Du Bois's political thought. First, for Kant, the recognition of moral personhood, at best, protects via the state the negative liberty of non-interference and free choice. Even a "radical" revision of Kant must stretch beyond plausibility Kant's conception of legitimate state power. It is beyond the scope and purpose of this book to detail the limitations of Kant's philosophy of the modern state. Suffice to say that for Kant the modern state can only use coercive force to secure people's equal legal standing as rights-bearers. In other words, for Kant, to "recognize" or "see" another as a moral equal in the public sphere is to provide them with basic civil and political rights. The state, however, cannot force citizens to treat *each other* as moral equals. Individuals must be *free* to establish and pursue associations, even if they violate universal moral principles or fail to grant social esteem to civic fellows for no reason. So long as civil associations do not outright attack the body or property of others, the state cannot intervene to make citizens respect and esteem each other. For Kant, morality and virtue are *non-political* matters over which the state lacks legitimate domain in that it cannot influence the exercise of free choice, which characterizes persons' moral autonomy in the private sphere. Put another way, Christopher Lebron eloquently explains that "socially embedded power" preserves racial inequality without relying on explicit de jure racism: "socially embedded power is the ability for extant racial asymmetries to affect our sense of self and others such that those better positioned tend to hold beliefs and attitudes that motivate a lack of normative concern for the systemically disadvantaged, while those worse positioned are burdened in developing a full sense of being an equal democratic self."[32]

To be sure, I believe that Mills offers a powerful way to reframe the normative dimension of Du Bois's political thought inasmuch as Du Bois was emphatically concerned with the subordinate status of people of color in social, economic, and political life – a status Mills characterizes with the global label of "subpersonhood." However, in drawing on the Kantian ideal of moral personhood as a normative standard to counteract the phenomenon of subpersonhood, Mills does not appear to appreciate the distinction between the moral and the political in the Kantian framework. Kant was clear that the distinction must not be collapsed; if it does collapse, then the state runs the risk of obstructing the exercise of citizens' moral autonomy, which would make it an illiberal state in Kant's view. One must, then, acknowledge that in a Kantian political project, the recognition of moral personhood – and political resistance to the phenomenon of subpersonhood – is best conceptualized in terms of securing persons' equal legal standing as rights-bearers. Now the question emerges: is legal equality enough to secure racial justice for Du Bois?

Of course, Du Bois believed that securing basic rights and political liberties would be an enormous political win that has evaded the African-American community. Given anti-black police violence, black and brown mass incarceration rates, and the recent voter ID law controversies today, the universal recognition of basic rights and liberties for all is a goal that the United States is far from achieving. Yet I submit that Du Bois had a far richer conception of the recognition of black moral personhood than the Kantian legalistic (or moral) framework allows. Du Bois advanced the ideal of black civic enfranchisement to promote the political *and* social recognition of the moral equality of persons. Civic enfranchisement is therefore *not* reducible to legal enfranchisement. Ergo, legal equality is necessary but insufficient to secure racial justice.

To begin with, Du Bois did not consider the inculcation of the moral attitudes of respect and esteem for others, especially for historically marginalized racial groups, to be an illegitimate use of political power. To secure black *civic* equality, rather than just their legal equality, he advocated building interracial social relations outside of the state that fostered a substantive shared conception of the common good, which included cultural and economic considerations that are often neglected on the Kantian model of the state. The ideal of free and equal citizenship for all, then, in Du Bois's political thought *incorporates* and *transcends* the narrow legalistic framework of protecting basic rights and liberties in the modern state. To be clear, Mills agrees that a viable racial justice model must transcend a narrow legalistic reading and that Du Bois can help us rethink the ideal of black

enfranchisement; with Du Bois, my only contention is that
the Kantian model, however revised with the aid of Du Bois,
would struggle to incorporate the social virtues Du Bois
believed were necessary to advance the reciprocal relations
of nondomination, moral respect, and social esteem among
citizens.

Du Bois's difference from Kant about what it takes to recognize the moral personhood of vulnerable groups is not just
an interesting philosophical tidbit. It illuminates an important point about building successful social justice movements
in profoundly nonideal polities that were touched upon in
the previous chapter. Du Bois maintained that cultivating an
attitude of moral regard and social esteem for civic fellows
is *essential* for the advance of racial justice, especially when
the state is saturated by white supremacist ideology and con-
dones de jure and de facto racist disrespect and derogation.
The only way that the color line can be destroyed is if the
white strangers living beyond it – and the black and brown
souls striving behind it – take the initiative to learn about
and advocate for black and brown lives. And it is surpris-
ing how much liberal political theorists and philosophers
neglect to theorize the critical engine of the social virtues
of civic fellowship in grassroots political activity, which Du
Bois believed was necessary for the radical transformation of
modern American society. A sense of interracial fellowship
constructs the collective awareness of a shared political destiny that a people can only control if they risk working on
each other's behalf. Civic-minded moral attitudes, i.e., social
virtues, such as responsiveness to others, a sincere interest
in political advocacy, and mutual understanding, are difficult
to defend on the Kantian model of politics (or, really, most
mainstream liberal accounts of citizenship and the state).
The enactment of these social virtues corresponds to what
Christopher Lebron calls "moral realignment – the call for

Americans to act consistently from the values and principles of democratic freedom."[33]

What is more, Du Bois stressed that legal victories do not always translate into substantive gains for African Americans without an accompanying transformation of the general will and democratic habits of the people. (More on this point in chapter 5.) The legal abolition of slavery and the passage of the first Civil Rights Act and the Reconstruction Amendments did not secure black civic equality, even if it nominally secured legal equality. "Without effective voice in government," claimed Du Bois, African Americans were left "naked to the worst elements of the community."[34] Not only did the lack of goodwill among white Americans result in flagrant violations of and lack of enforcement of newfound black rights, but black social and economic spheres were left unprotected against white interference. In the aftermath of the civil rights movement, legal protection of black and brown Americans rings hollow as the US federal government does little to curb economic inequalities and growing de facto racial segregation; instead, the state finds legal pretexts to strip citizens of color of their rights by disproportionately criminalizing and incarcerating African Americans, which results in the loss of the franchise and viable employment opportunities in communities that have long suffered from economic destabilization. In addition, customary habits of citizenship have shored up recent anti-immigrant sentiment to bolster a policy of mass deportation of immigrants from Central and South America; in fact, the Trump administration's claim to legitimacy is anchored in the public's willingness to reject members of the black and Latinx communities as legitimate members of the US polity.

Du Bois did not *only* appeal to the state to promote black civic enfranchisement. Consider the social virtue of mutual understanding that he thought necessary for the advance of black civic enfranchisement. He used the social sciences to represent the truth about racial realities, and literature and the arts to cultivate the public's moral concern about racial exclusion. In his early years, he treated "objective" scientific scholarship as a tool for social reform and aimed to educate the public about black living conditions. For the young Du Bois, scientific truth could "heal" the wound racism had left on the republic; science should be a public value in a democracy. In his scientific research, he strove to provide an impartial description of black neighborhoods.[35] An accurate empirical representation of racial realities might lead whites to condemn segregation; he assumed that an increased theoretical understanding might improve moral literacy about racial matters. His noted biographer Manning Marable observed that, for the early Du Bois, the "ultimate evil was stupidity" and the "cure for it was knowledge based on scientific investigation."[36] In his later works, Du Bois continued to underscore whites' extraordinary "fear of the Truth."[37] So many white Americans today remain ignorant about the lives and histories of their non-white civic fellows, with whom they are unwilling to stand in interracial solidarity, even if they are otherwise inclined to support social justice reforms. For if we don't think there are any issues in our racial reality, what's there to support? If one does not understand racial realities, then racial justice movements will seem gratuitous and unnecessary. In fact, numerous reports confirm that, ironically, today more whites accept in principle the idea of racial equality but reject actually supporting racial justice reforms.[38] Social scientific facts about structural racism can guide the formation of political judgment by pointing out the ways in which racial exclusion and structural inequality still manifest themselves. Unsurprisingly, a major effort of BLM chapters is pamphleteering and running workshops to educate the public about racial realities that provide an accessible language for how to talk about white supremacist disenfranchisement and the history of anti-black and -brown violence.[39] I submit that Du Bois would view the effort to fight ignorance to be indispensable for achieving black civic equality today.

Additionally, unlike Kant, Du Bois strove to build a sense of political community and moral responsibility using music, literature, and the arts. Once Du Bois grew disillusioned with the idea that science alone can destroy the color line, he defended art as a form of "propaganda" that imparted the black experience of an anti-black world.[40] The development of aesthetic sensibility became an important tool for him to build a more just society and to fortify black cultural integrity against absorption into white America. For in his later years, he began to suspect that scientific research and political advocacy would do little to protect black interests if the white-controlled world did not recognize or respond to black evaluative judgments in the first place. Black voices lacked *credibility* as free agents, with thoughts and feelings and a rich subjective interiority. He surmised that the arts might awaken a nascent white moral imagination by inspiring civic fellow feeling and affective identification with the oppressed. Du Bois's conception of the political and moral function of art led him to participate in the Harlem Renaissance and to mentor young black artists throughout his life.[41] He also affirmed that the arts could sustain black resilience and a positive normative self-understanding in a white-controlled world that systematically devalued black life.[42]

Lastly, the feature of Du Bois's rich ideal of civic enfranchisement on which this book primarily focuses underscores the fluid interpenetration of the private and public spheres. Specifically, social values and practices outside of the state (in black-led civil associations such as churches and schools, for example) led to the reconstitution of political norms that, over time, restructured the modern American state. For example, according to Du Bois, black self-organization in the antebellum period and in segregated black communities during Jim Crow was the wellspring that provided the impetus and moral imagination for the radical reconstruction of the republic. As I explain in later chapters, Du Bois held that who and what gets to count as a right and privilege of US citizenship is an expanding bundle of goods that often showcased blacks' "second sight" about what should become a relevant political consideration at all.[43]

Ideal versus nonideal theory

An additional shortcoming of Mills's interpretation of Du Bois, in my view, is that Du Bois should be considered an *ideal* theorist rather than a nonideal theorist, as Mills claims. Mills observes that ideal-theory liberalism does not sufficiently address – in the formulation of the terms of its normative theorizing – the centrality of racial domination in modern life and the polity's failures to comply with the requirements of justice. For Mills, ideal-theory liberalism implicitly assumes, instead, that failures to honor the requirements of justice are mere exceptions, rather than a defining empirical fact of racialized modernity. By conducting normative theorizing in the light of Jim Crow segregation (and the historical legacy of black chattel slavery), Du Bois's liberalism responds to empirical reality by highlighting the impact that racial caste has on citizens' engagement with public institutions and each other. Though I concede that Du Bois was primarily focused on the social and political organization of illiberal white supremacy, I maintain that his original contributions to rethinking civic enfranchisement and political modernity position him as an ideal theorist whose focus on racial realities refined the "ideal" normative basis of his political critique without dissolving it into nonideal theory.[44]

On my approach, the liberal ideal of civic enfranchisement is a context-sensitive basis for grounding persons' transcendental claims for rights and resources. Even as an "ideal" theorist, Du Bois offered a sober account of the obstacles that racial caste poses for all citizens to develop a robust sense of justice, showcasing ordinary white citizens' longstanding and unreasonable complicity in the reproduction of racial caste. Yet he also highlighted that partial compliance with the "ideal" requirements of justice does not entail its complete absence from the polity. He thus endorsed what the influential political philosopher John Rawls called "the moral rights of citizenship," which are the moral duties of civility and public concern that assert the liberal principle of legitimacy: to advance, consider, and accept the reasonable claims of others in a democratic attitude of deliberative openness and to reject unreasonable claims and institutional arrangements that undermine universal equal moral standing. The ideal of civic enfranchisement thus grounds his critique of American democracy and models progressive social reform on an ongoing basis.

Du Bois argued that the exercise of the moral rights of citizenship directs black democratic agency under the conditions of systematic exclusion – what he described as the figurative "color line" that racial segregation draws to sanction unequal treatment in social and political life. His empirical investigations confirmed that the exercise of the moral rights of citizenship was a pronounced feature in the segregated black communities' struggle for justice. Fairmindedness, the willingness to listen to others, and the desire for its own sake for a world in which people are free, equal, and socially cooperative are striking features of black political culture. By underscoring the problem of partial compliance with the requirements of justice in the polity-at-large, Du Bois simultaneously defended a vibrant black political culture that flourished "behind" the color line that racial segregation drew and thereby showed the often overlooked work of African Americans to preserve and expand democratic ideals in the darkest of times.

Given Du Bois's warranted preoccupation with the United States, I emphasize his conception of the ideal of civic enfranchisement as a vehicle for achieving domestic justice in the United States. To be sure, for Du Bois, a people's sense of community must be porous enough to welcome newcomers; and so the normative standing of civic fellows does not strictly correspond to the legal status of those who currently hold American citizenship. Civic fellowship necessarily transcends the legal status of persons as citizens of a particular state; rather, it strengthens a collective moral obligation to welcome and address the needs of those outside the sovereign national territory of the United States. Moreover, for Du Bois, the ideal of civic enfranchisement is a method for rethinking the bonds of civic fellowship on an ongoing basis; any established legal precedents or rights are necessarily subject to scrutiny and transformation. Figuring out what it means to become a full-fledged "member" of a political community and what such membership must entail in terms of the universal expansion of rights, freedoms, social goods, and opportunities is an unending process. The idea of civic enfranchisement is a helpful way to model reform that sorts out the substantive meaning of political membership.

Additionally, the ideal of civic enfranchisement does not stipulate a fixed set of social goods, but it does assume that public institutions are primarily responsible to protect the needs and interests of the people and must recognize each person as a civic equal. The ideal aims to advance rights and privileges that are the *outcome* of the historical struggle for inclusion; and what counts as a right and a privilege of citizenship changes in response to grassroots pressures. For Du Bois, historical struggles for inclusion should foreground in the polity-at-large the normative self-conception and needs of historically excluded groups.[45]

I now turn to the ideal of civic enfranchisement and defend it as a principle that grounds the normative basis of Du Bois's critique of American democracy. Du Bois's commitment to the ideal of civic enfranchisement captures his expansive model of the social and political inclusion of persons as free and equal civic fellows. As we've seen, it calls for more than a narrow legalistic interpretation of persons as legal citizens with rights. Instead, Du Bois aimed to tap the "moral power" of excluded agents who in a nonideal public sphere assert their democratic rights and privileges. The ideal of civic enfranchisement motivated his activism at the NAACP and his scholarship – empirical, theoretical, and literary – especially in the early stages of his career. I explore in detail the promise of black civic enfranchisement in postbellum America in chapter 5 but introduce it here as a defining principle of his liberalism.

A different kind of ideal theory? Du Bois's ideal of civic enfranchisement and the inclusion/ domination paradigm

In recent years, scholars and activists have used the inclusion and domination paradigm to theorize racial justice. In evaluating the inclusion paradigm, the prominent political theorist Danielle Allen assesses the effort to desegregate Central High School in Little Rock, Arkansas. On the first day of school in 1957, an angry white mob, in concert with the Arkansas National Guard, barred entry to nine black students, later known as the Little Rock Nine. In an iconic photograph, a black 15-year-old student, Elizabeth Eckford, regal and solemn, wearing sunglasses and a black and white gingham dress, is flanked by a white mob, from which Hazel Bryan emerges like a meat-eating bird, her mouth distorted by cursing and scowling at Eckford.

Allen favors the domination paradigm over the inclusion paradigm to convey the social relation between Eckford and Bryan that the photograph captured. In that moment, Bryan dominates Eckford, which Allen identifies as a habit of citizenship among white Americans towards people of color. In her critique of the inclusion paradigm, Allen targets Hannah Arendt's claim in the essay "Reflections on Little Rock," published in *Dissent* in 1957, that whites who perpetrate injustice against others nevertheless preserve among themselves sound and healthy democratic habits. Arendt believed that even in a political sphere that supports Jim Crow segregation, modern American society was "essentially healthy."[46] On Arendt's inclusion paradigm, modern American society is "healthy in the sense," elaborates Gooding-Williams, "that the habits and practices of citizenship prevailing among white citizens were 'presumed to be reasonably decent.' "[47] Allen and Gooding-Williams instead claim that there is nothing "essentially healthy" about Bryan's disposition towards Eckford.

The inclusion paradigm assumes that white supremacy is an "extrinsic," rather than an "intrinsic," feature of the United States. On this paradigm, the struggle for racial justice requires that blacks fight against discrimination, as well as "assimilate" to the customs of democratic life: "An inclusive democratic citizenship involves two projects [. . .]: first, an effort to make political institutions fully inclusive; and second, an attempt to educate minorities to convert their fraternity within the group into the stuff of a broader citizenship developed by those within the political realm."[48]

To overcome their exclusion, marginalized racial groups are expected to master democratic skills and increase their practical knowledge of social and democratic life in order to become full members of society. Allen objects that inclusion in a toxic public sphere that supports habits of domination towards people of color is an undesirable political ideal for black liberation struggles. The inclusion paradigm assumes that public institutions do not require major structural transformation. Instead, African Americans should prioritize fitting into a world that doesn't want them.

Allen contrasts Arendt's inclusion paradigm with the domination paradigm proposed by Ralph Ellison and later developed by Robert Gooding-Williams and Charles Mills. The domination paradigm, Allen argues, calls out the customary habits of citizenship that encourage white domination and black acquiescence in a white-supremacist polity. In Little Rock, Bryan enacted a habit of citizenship based on an "etiquette of dominance," whereas Eckford performed an "etiquette of acquiescence," as she was forced to turn away from the doors of the high school and to wade through a mob ready to lynch her.[49] It was not just that Eckford was excluded and left alone to her own devices, but the white mob *arbitrarily intervened* in the pursuit of her life goals and demanded that she perform a public ritual of submission before them. Eckford thus suffered a traumatic loss because white power *dominated* her the moment she entered the public sphere, forcing her to sacrifice her right to learn to the mob.

Echoing Allen's critique of the inclusion paradigm, Gooding-Williams contends that Du Bois's ideal of inclusion incorporates an "anomaly" theory of white supremacy that views prevailing democratic norms to be "essentially healthy," even in a white-supremacist society. On Gooding-Williams's interpretation, Du Bois failed to recognize that white modes of domination over black people are an *intrinsic* feature of modern American life.[50] He argues that, like Arendt, Du Bois held that white supremacy is an *extrinsic* feature of US polity inasmuch as he believed that behavior like Bryan's was an "anomalous" deviation from the democratic habits of public life, rather than an intrinsic feature of the polity. The underlying democratic ideals of the polity were, in essence, still morally valid and should motivate the black struggle for inclusion. Furthermore, Gooding-Williams surmised that for Du Bois modern American society did not require substantive transformation to expunge anti-black racism. According to Gooding-Williams, Du Bois's use of the inclusion paradigm assumed that the United States has an essentially healthy public sphere; racial exclusion results from anti-black discrimination and black ignorance about the practice of democratic politics. To achieve full membership in the polity, African Americans should assert themselves against exclusionary laws and public policies, and assimilate to the norms of modern American society; and the failure to assimilate to American "folkways" exacerbates racial exclusion.[51]

Against the inclusion paradigm that he attributes to Du Bois, Gooding-Williams champions the *"revolutionary refounding* of the American polity, and hence a transformation of the norms of citizenship. Bearing witness to the degeneration and corruption of American citizenship, [one must] aim to unsettle its prevailing practices and beliefs, hoping thus to prompt its reconstitution."[52] And so Gooding-Williams agrees with Allen that the domination paradigm necessitates the *reconstitution* of essentially unhealthy habits of citizenship that exact black submission and sacrifice in the face of white-supremacist power:

Thus a movement beyond 1957 requires not merely the inclusion of the excluded within political institutions but

also, more fundamentally, a transformation of the citizenship of dominance and acquiescence into a single more truly
democratic citizenship shared by all, through which we
would aspire to make the citizenry [a] whole, *mutually trust-
ing and therefore healthy.*[53]

Similarly, Mills prefers the domination paradigm for theorizing racial justice. With Allen and Gooding-Williams, he
endorses the intrinsic theory of white supremacy and considers white habits of domination to be an essential feature of
modern American society. Modern states, Mills argues, have
created a social contract based on reciprocal relations among
whites and, at the same time, a racial contract that legitimized
and institutionalized the secondary status of non-whites as
subpersons. The racial contract is a domination contract that
has eliminated the black voices from public procedures of
democratic will formation. Black citizens were consequently
subject to arbitrary interference and naked white power,
which neither major institutions nor their white civic fellows
bothered to prevent. To sum up, Mills identifies the following features of the domination contract: it (1) focuses on the
nonideal circumstances of illiberal white supremacy; (2) is
"necessarily historical" in that it "talk[s] about the human
creation of sociopolitical institutions as the result of previous sociohistorical processes, not *ex nihilo* from the state of
nature"; (3) makes groups "the key players" in its social ontol-
ogy; (4) assumes the groups in power have a vested interest
in keeping their power and that inequality is the de facto
social norm; and (5) considers social identities such as race,
class, and gender to be social constructions, rather than the
fixed "natural" features of persons.[54] Traditionally, the social
contract tradition imagines that prior to establishing a state,
people exist in the state of nature and agree to join a civil
condition; on the racial contract model, African Americans

join the modern state, but their membership within the state facilitates a white etiquette of dominance over their lives along the five axes outlined above.

Given the descriptions of domination by Allen, Gooding-Williams, and Mills, I grant that the domination paradigm is an extremely powerful way of talking about racial injustice and the potential limitation of the liberal ideal of inclusion. The domination paradigm cautions against people of color joining a white-controlled polity that does not truly welcome them or only offers them a de facto secondary "subperson" status as a condition of their political membership. As Martin Luther King, Jr poignantly put it to his friend and civil rights organizer Harry Belafonte: "I've come upon something that disturbs me deeply[.] We have fought hard and long for integration, as I believe we should have, and I know that we will win. But I've come to believe that we're integrating into a burning house."[55] The domination paradigm shares a skepticism about the possibility of building a pluralistic political community from the starting point of our present racial realities. Allen, Gooding-Williams, and Mills caution against black acquiescence and submission to white power. Yet it strikes me that Du Bois's conception of civic enfranchisement shares their concerns about the danger of white habits of domination. In other words, Du Bois's conception of civic enfranchisement is not reducible to the liberal ideal of the inclusion paradigm.

Du Bois agreed that it was necessary to transform dominant norms and habits of citizenship in the nonideal public sphere. However, a revolutionary refounding would not abolish the polity or mitigate the democratic ideal of building genuine interracial civic fellowship; it would just, well, "refound" the polity on principles all can accept as fair. Allen, Gooding-Williams, and Mills each appear to endorse some version of the project of the democratic restructuring of a constitutional democracy, where all persons finally stand free and equal within the circle of civic fellowship. Gooding-Williams claims that he aims to transform *"the norms of citizenship,"* suggesting that some version of political membership would be ideal for overcoming domination. So, too, Allen defends the virtue of political friendship in a nonideal public sphere to repair democratic relations among citizens. For a people to refound the state in a way that is no longer white supremacist, presumably, the people must commit to the idea of forming a political community in the first place, one that is circumscribed by a major public institution, with a set of procedural norms grounded in the public values of freedom and equality for all. At the very least, even as a people transforms the norms of citizenship, they implicitly affirm constitutional democracy as a viable and meaningful object of democratic self-determination. It is hard to imagine what the transformation of democratic norms would otherwise amount to as a normative basis for political critique. In light of his defense of racial inclusion in his early political thought, Du Bois has been accused of being an elitist and an assimilationist who prizes the norms of Anglo-European modernity and, in turn, blames African Americans for their cultural "backwardness" and lack of preparation for modern American life. My presentation of his defense of the ideal of civic enfranchisement stresses, instead, the importance of the democratic reconstitution of a racially pluralistic polity. The process of democratic reconstitution entails a public procedure for deliberation that foregrounds the shared experiences of racial exclusion, as those experiences are conveyed and interpreted by the most vulnerable members of society.

Ultimately, on my view, the distinction between the exclusion and domination paradigms breaks down once we define which norms and principles must actually guide emancipatory ideals. To wit, both the inclusion and domination paradigms posit racism *is* eliminable in a white supremacist society. It seems that even for critics of an inclusion model, public institutions must serve to actualize the democratic self-determination of the people. If one cannot partake in the democratic adjudication of the terms of political membership, then one's existence within a particular polity would be subject to arbitrary interference in social, economic, and political life. Exclusion, then, *constitutes* and *exacerbates* domination.

Du Bois had hoped that a just polity would emerge from the ashes of the Civil War to form a more rational social order. It is true that for Du Bois white supremacy is *not* intrinsic to the United States. He held that America does not "belong" to white people. "Your country?" he asks, "How came it to be yours?"[56] A future must arise that makes it possible for one to be both black and an American and to reconcile "two unreconciled strivings, two warring ideals, [. . .] merg[ing] his double self into a better and truer self [. . .] without being cursed and spit on by his fellows, and the doors of opportunity closed roughly in his face."[57] So, too, Baldwin asserted: "The terms of the revolution are precisely these: that we will learn to live together here or all of us will abruptly stop living. And I mean that. This is not, and never has been, a white nation. [. . .] I am an American."[58] The claim "I am an American" strikes like a thunderbolt, a startling assertion of the self as black and as American. The notion that America is for white people is the myth that white nationalists tell to rationalize the historical exclusion of people of color.

That said, Du Bois would not accept white domination as a condition of racial inclusion. Consider his discussion of the history of slavery and the function of a democratic politics. In his first book, *On the Suppression of the African Slave-Trade*, he articulated the relation of the institution of slavery to the lax policies of the federal government:

One cannot, to be sure, demand of whole nations exceptional moral foresight and heroism; but a certain hard
common sense in facing the complicated phenomena of
political life must be expected in every progressive people.
[. . .] It behooves the United States, therefore, in the interest
both of scientific truth and of future social reform, carefully
to study the chapters of her history as that of the suppression of the slave-trade. The most obvious question which
this study suggests is: How far in a state can a recognized
moral wrong be safely compromised? And although this
chapter of history can give us no definite answer suited to
the ever-varying aspects of political life, yet it would seem
to warn any nation from allowing, through carelessness and
moral cowardice, any social evil to grow.[59]

Du Bois's historical study of the trans-Atlantic slave trade
examined "how far" a state can "allow [. . .] social evil to
grow." He acknowledged that it is often difficult for a
nonideal public sphere to recognize the "moral wrong"
it perpetrates; and yet, he contended that the difficulty of
forming sound political judgments does not let the polity
off the hook. Sound judgment requires neither "moral foresight" nor "heroism." In other words, it is always possible for
a people to avoid complicity in "evil." That is, complicity in
white supremacy is not "baked" into modern society nor the
public sphere, however nonideal they might be. Instead, Du
Bois invoked the ideal of civic enfranchisement for former
slaves and their descendants to criticize white supremacist
habits of democratic citizenship.

In contrast, Kevin Bruyneel objects that Du Bois's postbellum vision of the black democratic transformation of,
and inclusion in, the federal government relied on a "settler memory" that condoned the expropriation of indigenous
lands in favor of a policy of land redistribution for recently

emancipated slaves.[60] Endorsing a version of the domination contract paradigm, Bruyneel observes that black freedmen's participation in the state dovetailed with the state's violent suppression of indigenous communities' territorial sovereignty.[61] "There is a constitutive presence and absence of Indigeneity and settler colonialism in [Du Bois's] *Black Reconstruction* that we need to attend to [. . .] Indigenous people and also settler colonial practices that produced [land] dispossession remain, at best, barely visible to it."[62] The influential theorist of indigeneity Dale Turner analyzes the nature of the dispute over claims to land in the Canadian context: "Herein lies a fundamental disagreement between Aboriginal peoples and Canadian sovereigntists: many Aboriginal peoples believe to this day that they own their lands, yet the Canadian state continues to assert and enforce its unilateral claims to sovereignty over Aboriginal lands."[63] Dale argues that there has been a failure "to reconcile these two seemingly incommensurable positions" and that the main reason for this failure "is that the 'form' of reconciliation, if it is to occur at all, must evolve out of a very special kind of dialogue – one grounded in a renewed and more respectful legal and political relationship."[64]

To be sure, Du Bois did not address with consistency and care the historical plight of indigenous peoples in North America or around the globe. Yet I believe that his conception of the ideal of civic enfranchisement has something meaningful to add to the discussion about indigenous resistance to state expropriation and genocide. Recall that the normative status of civic fellowship overlaps with but does not strictly correspond to legal citizenship, which renders a person subject to the coercive power of the Kantian state. The circle of civic fellowship will always be wider than that of legal citizenship for two reasons: (1) the former is the basis for the ongoing reconstitution of the latter and it unfolds on a higher moral terrain, one that appeals to the universal scope of an imagined shared moral community that guides the democratic will formation of "the people."[65] In articulating their ideal vision of human togetherness, civic fellows invest the state with legitimacy; (2) the sense of civic fellowship – and the attitudes of moral regard it elicits – is attached to our equal moral status as human beings and so surpasses legal standing and national boundaries. The upshot is that you can stand in a relation of civic fellowship with a person without forcing her to join your state or to accept your legal and political framework in her understanding of herself as a free democratic agent. And so Du Bois's expansive conception of the ideal of civic enfranchisement allows not only for the assertion of the right to self-determination of indigenous peoples as sovereign nations, including opening a public discussion about the redistribution of land and honoring perpetually violated treaties. It also sketches a form of democratic engagement to bolster legal responsibilities of a state *towards* the social groups it oppresses. The ideal of civic enfranchisement provides a shared normative basis for entering a dialogue that *recognizes* indigenous peoples' claims to rights and resources. Within the circle of civic fellowship, the normative self-understanding of historically excluded and vulnerable social groups must set the ground rules for social interaction.[66] For one fails to treat a person as a civic fellow if you rob them, enslave them, or steal from them.

For Du Bois, the recognition of the civic equality of persons does not entail that the state must give the same bundle of rights, privileges, and goods to everyone, whether they like it or not. Nor does it assume that the state has legitimacy outside of the democratic will formation of the people, that is, the ongoing process of civic fellows reimagining the pull and significance of their civic bounds. Civic enfranchisement is not, therefore, akin to joining a state, though it might solicit legal responsibilities from states towards civic fellows outside their territorial boundaries, including enabling indigenous communities to assert sovereignty over their ancestral land.

The ideal of civic enfranchisement thus functions in different ways in its domestic, continental, or global orientation. It is an attitude of moral regard that one holds towards strangers and neighbors alike, and it is a shared perspective that simultaneously transcends and develops one's legal standing as a rights-bearer. In fact, for Du Bois, the ideal of civic enfranchisement is the normative basis through which an existent schedule of rights is reimagined and redistributed by the people redefining their collective self-understanding of what it means to be a people. In his ideal of the modern American state, Du Bois adds that historically powerless groups have a special authority – or "insight" – to reimagine who should belong and how that should impact the existent power structure, interpolating rights claims to mitigate a shared vulnerability.

Clearly, whether an entity as historically unjust as the US federal government can ever truly be the object of the universal democratic self-determination of all – and legitimated by *all* historically excluded racial groups, including black and indigenous communities – is a contentious matter. In fact, with the rise of explicit white supremacy and anti-immigrant sentiment, many have come to doubt that the republic is even rhetorically committed to racial equality. Be that as it may, Du Bois had faith in democratic politics and the ideal of civic enfranchisement, even in profoundly nonideal polities. He favored a procedure for public deliberation that focuses on the relation between the shared experience of exclusion and the actualization of democratic ideals in nonideal circumstances.

Any polity could come to actualize the ideal of civic enfranchisement on the basis of a shared sense of civic fellowship. However, the color line remains the most significant obstacle to the creation of a just state. White supremacy is still a central organizational principle in the United States. But it is just that: an organizational principle that the people can delegitimize and dethrone. The ideal of civic enfranchisement is thus a *normative* ideal. It retains its validity in spite of the history of slavery, exclusion, and denigration in black, Latinx, and indigenous communities. Du Bois's ideal theory thus takes the world as it is and yet provides an ideal of what the world *ought* to become. The organization of institutions is informed by the past without being *fixed* by it: "No matter how crude or imperfect the past may be, with all its defects, it is the foundation upon which generations to come must build."[67] His point is precisely to imagine the polity, bolstered by a sense of interracial civic fellowship, that makes it possible for the federal government, and all major public institutions, to be the condition rather than the obstacle to the innate right to freedom *for all*.

In response to Belafonte's question of what to do about integrating into the burning house of America, Martin Luther King replied, "I guess we will have to become firemen."[68]

3

The Emergence of a Black Public Intellectual: Du Bois's Philosophy of Social Science and Race (1894–1910)

In the fall of 1906, crowds poured into the Bronx Zoo in New York City to see an exciting new addition to the monkey and orangutan exhibit. Ota Benga, a Congolese man, stood among the animals. A sign on the cage, giving his age, height, and weight, read "Exhibited each afternoon during September."[1] Benga had survived the slaughter of his people in the Belgium invasion of what was then the Congo Free State. His wife and children were among the dead. Sold into slavery, he eventually came into the possession of the anthropologist Samuel Phillips Verner. Verner shipped Benga to the St Louis World's Fair to live in an attraction recreating Native Americans, Inuit, and Filipinos in their "natural" environments. Upon first arriving in New York City, what remained of Benga's belongings and the man himself were housed in the American Museum of Natural History. Benga wandered the halls of the museum after hours before he was moved uptown to the zoo. He shot himself in the chest ten years after his debut in the zoo, homesick, penniless, and alone.[2]

To say the least, racial science has had a fraught history. Pseudoscientific anthropology was instrumental in the emergence and justification of the modern race concept.[3] Phenotypical differences in skin color, hair, and facial features among human beings bolstered the myth of fundamental biological differences that the early "science" of race used to defend a natural racial hierarchy. In tandem with the rise of the modern state, race science rationalized political campaigns of enslavement, genocide, colonialism, and the sterilization of non-white racial groups. Against this flood of ignorance, as a young journalist and social scientist, Du Bois set to work to find a meaningful way to talk about racial differences that was both scientifically objective and that empowered vulnerable racial groups. Du Bois's goal was nothing less than to vindicate the dignity of African and Afro-descended peoples as equal human beings and to set the development of the social sciences on the right course. Yet the question of what makes race "real" or "scientifically" confirmable remains controversial.

Du Bois premised the scientific study of race on, first, the principle of universal moral equality and, second, the conviction that "scientific" knowledge is a potential basis for cultivating interracial civic fellowship. He defended quality scientific scholarship to mitigate anti-black racism, rejecting the racist pseudoscience of eugenics and Social Darwinism that championed classical racialism, the view that there is a biological hierarchy of races that reveals heritable differences in intelligence, temperament, and character. At this point in his career, he assumed the dual role of public intellectual and civil rights leader, organizing the Niagara Movement in 1905, a civil rights organization that prefigured the formation of the National Association for the Advancement of Colored People (NAACP), which he co-founded with Ida B. Wells-Barnett and others in 1909. He began his scientific inquiry, like his political activism, with the radical postulate that African and Afro-descendant people are ordinary human beings, with all the features of human personality possessed by anyone else. To wit, blacks are complete, self-standing practical agents. In sum, "Du Bois's sociological studies on Negro life stood virtually alone against a flood of nonscientific and virulently racist dogma."[4]

As we saw in the previous chapter, an advantage of Du Bois's robust conception of the ideal of civic enfranchisement is his defense of the social virtue of knowledge to mitigate anti-black racism and white ignorance about the effects of the color line. Du Bois had hoped that cultivating the virtue of knowledge in a nonideal public sphere would help whites resist rationalizing racially exclusionary social practices and laws. To be sure, he grew skeptical about the power of science in a nonideal public sphere that sometimes did not appear to be even nominally committed to universal moral equality. In 1906, the same year Benga was displayed in the Bronx Zoo, a pogrom destroyed black neighborhoods in Atlanta, where Du Bois was then living. He bought a Winchester double-barreled shotgun to protect himself and his family, later admitting, "If a mob had stepped on the campus where I lived, I would have without hesitation sprayed their guts over the grass. They did not come."[5] As he gripped his shotgun, he gave up his faith in science as a means of social reform and in whites' capacity to cultivate a real understanding of race and racism.

And yet in the public sphere today, voices reemerge that invent alternative facts to legitimize a growing white nationalist movement. Today, just as at the height of Jim Crow, prominent officials in the White House entertain notions of a natural racial hierarchy, aspiring to redeem the nation from nefarious non-white elements. In a barrage of racist statements that could rival a Jim Crow legislator, President Trump has claimed that Mexicans are rapists and dangerous

criminals and that Haitians "all have Aids."[6] Studies still seek
to find a genetic basis for the IQ test results of black children.[7] Just as the director of the Bronx Zoo and the *New York
Times* had lamented the closing of Benga's exhibit in 1906 as
a loss to science, some scientists today caution that a naive
belief in "biological egalitarianism" is a potential barrier to
scientific research.[8] Racist convictions still aspire to find justification in facts that don't exist. All the while, "color-blind"
legislators refuse to pass bills that redress racial discrimination in housing, education, and employment, dismissing
claims about structural inequality as illusory and social scientific analyses that highlight racial disparities in access to basic
social services as "racist" or "playing the race card."

In this chapter, I show why Du Bois maintained that his
philosophy of social science and race was a tool for social
reform. At the intersection of science and race, Du Bois
asserted that there could be a meaningful and respectful
way to talk about racial differences without invoking the
assumptions of classical racialism. Although he rejected the
biological essentialism of the latter doctrine, he defended a
controversial racialist view that posited that racial differences
are cultural and that African and Afro-descended peoples,
especially in the United States, share, or ought to share, a
unified race "ideal" that defines a shared sense of purpose.
His philosophy of race also upheld a cosmopolitan ideal of a
utopian future. Racial justice need not entail the elimination
of racial differences. Instead, the reciprocal recognition of
racial differences *ought to constitute* interracial civic fellowship.

The unhesitating sociologist (1894–1911)

After Du Bois returned to the United States from Germany,
he received an invitation to teach at Wilberforce in Ohio in

1894 at the age of 26. Although he had earned the most prestigious education possible, he struggled to secure a university appointment in the United States. He was so grateful for the opportunity that he turned down more lucrative offers that arrived weeks later, including one from the Tuskegee Institute, directed by a man who was fated to become a bitter rival, Booker T. Washington. The parochial university tried his patience and he soon grew unhappy in Ohio. Classes were periodically suspended for impromptu rivals.[9] "What business had I, anyhow, to teach Greek when I had studied men?"[10] A silver lining in his experience in Wilberforce is that there he met his future wife, an undergraduate student, Nina Gomer, and they soon started a family.

After just two years in Ohio, in 1896, Du Bois accepted a temporary appointment at a reduced salary at the University of Pennsylvania, which provided him with neither an office nor institutional support customary for a university-appointed researcher. With his indefatigable will, however, he undertook a seminal sociological study of the Seventh Ward in *The Philadelphia Negro*, published in 1899. Philadelphia had the largest black population in the North at the time, and he conducted thousands of interviews there.[11] In the end, "he had before him life histories of the entire black population of the Seventh Ward – nearly ten thousand men, women, and children."[12] Professionally, the risk paid off. The following year, in 1897, he secured a professorship in economics and history at Atlanta University, relocating with his young family to Atlanta, Georgia. His responsibilities at Atlanta University (1897–1910, 1934–44) included organizing an annual conference and publishing its proceedings, which, for roughly a decade, profiled original scholarship by black scholars on black America. He led what would become known as the Atlanta School of Sociology, predating the Chicago School that academics have thought founded modern sociology.[13]

Du Bois's philosophy of social sciences

In the essay "Sociology Hesitant" (1905), Du Bois outlined his philosophy of social science, drawing on the distinction between theoretical and practical reason.[14] Theoretical reason employs the empirical sciences to discover causal connections in the external world in relation to "outer culture," whereas practical reason outlines the principles that determine autonomous judgment and action in its aspect as "inner thought."[15] Du Bois defined the theoretical object of sociological study: "amid the bewildering complexities of human life ran great highways of common likeness and agreements in human thoughts and action."[16] As an exercise of theoretical reason, sociology must account for observable patterns that structure outer culture, i.e., ethical customs and social systems that govern behavior. In examining the nature of practical reason, Du Bois located the freedom of the will in self-conscious agents and characterized their capacity for agency as "the Kantian absolute."[17] The "Kantian absolute" is the unconditioned ground of free choice whereby a self-conscious agent gives herself the ground or reason to motivate her judgment and action. Du Bois did not posit that human beings mechanically respond to environmental pressures or natural law.[18] His social scientific and historical studies posit, in contrast, the free self-determination of social groups in history. For Du Bois, this meant that African and Afro-descendant peoples too act on the basis of shareable reasons – and always have.

This simple premise has radical implications for the development of the social sciences and democratic politics, according to Du Bois. Consider that the bondage and exploitation of Benga encapsulated the racial science of the twentieth century, which placed blacks closer to the natural world of monkeys and apes, than that of modern "civilization," fetishizing black skin and African and African-American cultures as akin to the living fossils of a subhuman race too underdeveloped to count as a full member of the human species. Though not as extreme in his remarks, the then democratic nominee for president Barack Obama gave a speech in 2008 criticizing African-American culture for producing broken families and generational poverty.[19] In 2007, then president of France Nicolas Sarkozy said that "the tragedy of Africa is that the African has not fully entered into history. [. . .] There is neither room for human endeavor nor the idea of progress."[20] Although nearly a century apart, these observations share the same racist trope that rendered Benga an object of public fascination and abhorrence: blacks have failed to reach a threshold of social development and are more determined by nature than by the self-given laws of a modern culture.

In refashioning G. W. F. Hegel's concept of spirit, Du Bois affirmed that African and Afro-descended peoples are fully self-determining agents who are deficient in neither physiology nor culture but are always already in the process of "shaping themselves" into a social whole under "universally binding directives."[21] Hegel noted that the historical development of spirit, or the self-consciousness of a people as free and self-determining:

> expresses in concrete ways all the aspects of consciousness and will, its entire reality: the shared stamp of its religion, its political system, its ethics, its system of law, its customs, as well as its science, art, and technology. These special characteristics are to be understood in the light of the *universal character* that is the particular principle of the people.[22]

At least for Du Bois, African and African-American culture, religion, and ethical customs have a "universal character" that occupies the same fundamental level of human development: the giving and sharing of reasons that motivate (or not) a shareable basis for judgment and action.[23] The recognition of the normative force of historical reason is the engine in the social development of a people; and it establishes African and Afro-descended peoples as always already *within* world history, not outside of it, entrapped in nature.

Du Bois continued, "I conceived of the idea of applying *philosophy* to an historical interpretation of race relations. In other words, I was trying to make my first steps toward sociology as the science of human action."[24] His ethnographic work describes the world – and African-American communities in particular – not just through the lens of statistics and quantifiable data. He applied "philosophy" to illuminate the "peculiar principle" or "race ideal" that furnished a common sense of purpose under the conditions of racial exclusion.[25] As a social scientist, he captured the normative structure of historical reason through which black agents understood themselves to be free in body or spirit. The power of his "philosophical" approach stood out against a historical context that perceived African and Afro-descended peoples to be animals, rather than thinking and feeling persons who *judge* and *transform* the world on the basis of universalizable reasons. Du Bois thus asserted that blacks' agential power was manifest in the historical exercise of practical reason, as expressed in the race ideal that has shaped black identity and culture and, ultimately, the democratic ideals of the republic, which African Americans have redefined in their struggle for emancipation.[26]

In essence, Du Bois's philosophy of social science highlighted at least three types of sociological research. First, a sociologist studies the "social conditions" that influence "human development." Social conditions are features of the external world that mediate subjectivity formation; to an untrained eye – ignorant of sociology and history – the behavior of individuals might appear to be random, but "Sociology is the study that seeks the limits of Chance in human conduct."[27] It is not just that social conditions determine social outcomes. Rather, social conditions should be improved upon to produce *better* social outcomes. Sociology must therefore endorse the philosophical idea of human perfectibility – that human beings are capable of improving social conditions according to a model of human flourishing. For Du Bois, sociological research is inevitably political, even as it seeks to be "objective." For it raises the critical question about what should count as an ideal model for organizing the labor market, civil society, and the constitutional state in order to facilitate universal social development. The better the organization of these institutions, the more likely they are to promote the social development of all. And so, for Du Bois, scholars must dedicate themselves to democratic politics to advance a conception of flourishing that might secure the well-being of all. Hence, Du Bois advocated for science as a means for social reform not only because it dispelled racist myths about human biology; a social scientist could also illustrate the deformation of vital social institutions in vulnerable communities in order to create, over time, a more rational social order.

Second, unlike other disciplines, sociology can reveal the implicit (and explicit) organizational principles that constitute the color line and chart the negative impact of racial exclusion on black well-being at a particular place and time. Sociologists can thus "gain intelligent insight into conditions and needs, and [provide] enlightened guidance" for the social development of segregated black communities.[28] Du Bois refused to attribute pervasive social ills in African-American communities to a cultural backwardness. Neither did he believe that social ills were somehow beyond explanation or public intervention, as if they were natural phenomena or the will of God. He underlined that the social conditions that produced gross racial inequalities and hurt social development had a societal origin, traceable to failures of local and federal government. He characterized the reluctance to acknowledge the societal origin of social ills by likening it to "[e]xactly the same attitude with which the man of a century or so ago fought disease: looked about for the witch or wondered at the chastening of the Lord; but withal continued to live in the swamps."[29] He added, "If you degrade a people the result is degradation and you have no right to be surprised by it."[30] The cultivation of the virtue of scientific knowledge could help a polity achieve democratic control to safeguard the social development of the African-American community.

Finally, Du Bois maintained that sociology, and historical sociology in particular, can build a "science of human action" that presents a systematic account of the norms that undergird customs and social systems but possess a "universal character." Such insight into the "inner thought" of a people constitutes social scientific knowledge. Du Bois used it as empirical "evidence" or "confirmation" of the agential power of black historical actors, charting the intragroup ties of black political solidarity during slavery, Reconstruction, and Jim Crow. Against popular received histories that either eliminated or denigrated the role of African Americans, Du Bois established their central role in American history.

Because the historical exercise of practical reason showcased shareable reasons for judgment and action, Du Bois's notion of a "science of human action" also opened a conceptual space for the philosophical reconstruction of the normative foundation of judgments about the beauty and fairness of the world from the African-American point of view. To wit, Du Bois illustrated that black political and cultural agency preserved blacks' sense of themselves as free, in spite of harrowing circumstances. What is more, their positive normative self-understanding was an impetus for the reconstruction of American democracy, which came to recognize the normative "force" of the exercise of historical reason in the African-American community. The exercise of historical reason in the African-American community was *interpenetrated* with the development of the political culture of the polity at large; not only is there an overlap of shareable reasons for action and judgment in the two spheres, but the black perspective on the republic developed and actualized its democratic ideals.

Thus, for Du Bois, African and African-American culture was not a living fossil of a primitive subhuman race. Rather, he affirmed that a universal capacity for self-determination rendered every racial group an equal on the world stage. To be sure, like Obama, his discussion of the black racial ideal sometimes led him to condemn the shortcomings of the African-American community, which he criticized for sexual impropriety, laziness, and political disorganization. In this respect, he too wavered in his conviction of the ethical integrity of black "inner thought."

Du Bois's philosophy of race: reconsidering racialism

In the politics of race and critical race theory today, the notion of a race "ideal" that supposedly defines a racial identity across history and intragroup differences should raise eyebrows. After all, what does African-American culture and African culture really have in common? Why impose a Latinx "race" on the myriad ethnicities and nationalities in Central and South America? It seems like these so-called races have nothing in common, far less share enough to constitute a unified racial ideal. What is more, if we give up the notion that race has a biological foundation, why should we hold on to the idea that races exist at all? Scholars and activists alike have rightly rebuked the contention that African and Afro-descendant peoples share some sort of hive mind that makes all black people think and act alike. To posit a race ideal, and to attach it to skin color, stinks of nineteenth-century racist pseudoscience that mapped racial essences in the service of a white ethno-nationalist discourse.

Although he rejected a biological foundation for race and racial hierarchy, Du Bois was a realist about race; he did not believe that it was racist to affirm and cultivate racial differences. According to his racialist doctrine, a race ideal tracks the inner thought that inspires the cultural or spiritual life of a people. Physical differences cannot explain spiritual differences, but those spiritual differences should be "conserved" to deliver a "particular message" to the world.[31] In Du Bois's Hegelian language, a racial ideal is the "peculiar principle" that shapes the spirit of a people and structures their shared historical sense of moral imagination and practical agency. Du Bois interpreted the modern concept of race as an "instrument of progress."[32] A racial ideal posits "a distinct sphere of action and an opportunity for race development."[33] Black self-organization displayed a collective self-consciousness of the prospect of real freedom; and the sustained drive to be free helps humanity achieve the cosmopolitan condition of global justice and interracial civic fellowship.

In a speech given to the American Negro Academy, "The Conservation of Races" (1897), Du Bois presented his original philosophy of race:

> Although the wonderful developments of human history teach that the grosser physical differences of color, hair and bone go but a short way toward explaining the different roles

which groups of men have played in Human Progress, yet there are differences – subtle, delicate and elusive, though they may be – which have silently but definitely separated men into groups. While these subtle forces have generally followed the natural cleavage of common blood, descent and physical peculiarities, they have at other times swept across and ignored these. At all times, however, they have divided human beings into races, which, while they perhaps transcend scientific definition, nevertheless, are clearly defined to the eye of the Historian and Sociologist.[34]

The "subtle forces" which followed the "natural cleavage of common blood [. . .] have divided human beings into races" and yet "transcend scientific definitions," even as they generate observable patterns to historians and sociologists. Du Bois continued, explaining the interrelation of descent and culture:

But while physical differences have followed mainly physical race lines, yet no mere physical distinctions would really define or explain the deeper differences – the cohesiveness and continuity of these groups. The deeper differences are spiritual, psychical, differences – undoubtedly based on the physical, but infinitely transcending them [. . .] [through] a common history, common laws and religion, similar habits of thought and a conscious striving together for certain ideals of life.[35]

Race thus "infinitely transcends" physical differences and is grounded, instead, in the ethical customs and "spiritual, psychical differences" that manifest in the "striving" of a racial group.

In an influential essay, Kwame Anthony Appiah argues that Du Bois inadvertently relied on the racial science of his day that linked culture to "common blood."[36] "The scientific notion [of race], which presupposes common features in virtue of a common biology derived from a common descent, is not fully transcended."[37] A race ideal, in the end, bunches together individuals on the specious basis of common descent, attaching the reality of race to physiology. On Appiah's anti-realist position, because race is not grounded in human biology, we must give up the idea of race altogether: "there are no races: there is nothing in the world that can do all we ask race to do for us."[38] Appiah's criticism of Du Bois's philosophy of race has inspired a flurry of discussion. Below I consider two ways of talking about the reality of race that are consistent with Du Bois's account.[39]

Political and cultural theories of race

Among critical race theorists, the political theory of race is perhaps the most popular philosophy of race today.[40] The political theory of race holds that race is a by-product of racial discrimination – it is "real" to the extent that racial discrimination exists. Although race has no biological basis, the material conditions of racial reality reveal a structural racism that profoundly impacts individuals' life chances, establishing unequal access to rights and resources along racial lines. Du Bois often spoke in this register. In *Dusk of Dawn*, he wrote that to be black is to ride Jim Crow in Georgia.[41] Or, as Paul Taylor elaborates, black racial identity "means being vulnerable to the everyday insult of being mistaken for a Pullman porter or to the assault of the lynch mob."[42] One might add that being vulnerable to police violence also delineates the material conditions of black racial reality. On this view, the political project of fighting for rights and resources eliminates race inasmuch as structural racism and a racialized vulnerability to violence and insult disappear.

In contrast, the prominent Du Bois scholar Chike Jeffers defends a cultural theory of race. "A cultural theory of race," notes Jeffers, "does not see the cultural characteristics of races [in terms of] either [a] straightforward biological inheritance or as the inessential by-product of the political situation that creates races in the first place."[43] On Jeffers's reading, Du Bois is a cultural pluralist about race who celebrates racial cultural diversity as an essential feature of the human condition:

> What it means to be a black person, for many of us, including myself, can never be exhausted through reference to problems of stigmatization, discrimination, marginalization, and disadvantage, as real and as large-looming as these factors are in the racial landscape as we know it. There is also *joy* in blackness, a joy shaped by culturally distinctive situations, expressions, and interactions, by stylizations of the distinctive features of the black body, by forms of linguistic and extralinguistic communication, by artistic traditions, by religious and secular rituals, and by any number of other modes of cultural existence. There is also pride in the way black people have helped to shape Western culture, not merely by means of the free labor and extraction of resources that economically supported this culture but also directly through cultural contributions, most prominently in music and dance. These contributions are racial in character – that is to say, they are cultural contributions whose significance can only be fully understood when they are placed in proper context as emerging from a racialized people.[44]

Black racial identity is not merely a stigma that marks the subordinate status of a person. There is a joy and beauty in blackness. Racism does not wholly determine what it means to possess a racial identity. In a racial utopia, Jeffers argues that racial cultural differences can – and indeed, must – harmoniously coexist. The ideal of interracial civic fellowship and racial equality presupposes the existence of racial differences and that those differences are meaningful. If the condition for fellowship and equality requires assimilation into white America, then neither genuine fellowship nor equality is achieved. Jeffers defends black equal rights without black absorption into white America. Racial identity can remain intact after the end of racism. Jeffers adds, "There is, in fact, reason to think that the historical memory of creating beauty in the midst of struggling to survive oppression can and should persist as a thing of value in black culture long after that oppression has truly and finally been relegated to the past."[45]

The political and cultural theories of race offer two compelling ways for thinking about the reality of race without relying on racial biology. Du Bois's call to "conserve" the "race ideals" would entail: (1) a future-oriented political function that dismantles the color line; and (2) a past-oriented continuation of cultural traditions and rituals whose intrinsic cultural value (independent of politics) attests to a people's ethical character in the face of harrowing circumstances. On both readings, race remains an instrument of progress in the broad sense that race "perfects" humanity's understanding of itself as a free, self-determining agent. Both readings illuminate shareable reasons for judgment about justice and beauty. A race ideal can also come to motivate the action and judgment of the members of the polity-at-large and thereby transcend racial lines.

Both lines for thinking about race are supported by Du Bois's writings. With respect to (1), Du Bois emphasized that vulnerable racial groups must mobilize along racial lines to fight discrimination. The cultivation of a race ideal is then tantamount to the cultivation of a democratic ideal that secures freedom and equality for all. The black "message" to the world is then a "gift" that delivers substantive freedom to a nominally free polity in (hopefully) the not-too-distant future. Racial conservation is an indispensable, future-oriented tool for achieving reciprocal relations of recognition. The race ideal that sustained the spiritual world of the segregated black community during slavery and Jim Crow reveals a moral interpretation – and condemnation – of an unjust world. Under certain nonideal circumstances, a race ideal can thus guide the development of the republic and capture how racial realities contradict the public values of freedom and equality.[46]

With respect to (2), Du Bois advocated conserving the ideal of race inasmuch as it outlines a distinct cultural world that structures a *historical* sense of practical agency. The race ideal is thus past oriented and can continue to impart a positive normative self-understanding to a group that strengthens their personal sense of resilience, joy, and beauty. The black "gifts" of song, "spirit," and literature, claimed Du Bois, reflect humanity's capacity for self-mastery in spite of harrowing circumstances, and have intrinsic aesthetic and normative value.[47] Victories against racial injustice should not be taken as "a new sign that the world ought to be rid of racial difference and thus also black cultural difference."[48] On this reading, by reflecting on the accomplishments of the past, race still functions as an instrument of progress that teaches "the world" what it means to "strive": to create in actuality the stuff of a people's dreams and hopes.

Revisiting Hegel's concept of spirit

The German Idealist philosopher G. W. F. Hegel might be an unlikely ally for fleshing out the "spiritual" reality of race on Du Bois's account. In his lectures in *Anthropology*, Hegel asserted that African and Afro-descended peoples are steeped in "natural spirit" and banished from the stage of world history. He mocked the prospect of their acting under the idea of freedom, that is, as self-determining agents. Hegel admitted in his 1830 lectures on history that the normative character of the United States is just emerging and – at least from his vantage point – is too inchoate to judge: "America is therefore the land of the future."[49] Ironically, when Hegel looked to "the land of the future," he hardly envisioned the politics of race as being instrumental in the development of American modernity. Du Bois asserted that "the race spirit, the race ideal [. . .] shall help to guide the world nearer and nearer the perfection of human life."[50] Whether Hegel likes it or not, then, I submit that the owl of Minerva has flown further and Du Bois saw in which direction it flew. In a Du Boisian vein, Frank Kirkland observes, "Although the principle of th[e] exercise [of the principle of free self-determination] has its origins in Europe, it is not distinctly European, because its validity cannot be measured by its point of origin."[51] Racial matters are the necessary departure point for political and cultural critique in the United States and for theorizing modernity for any republic founded on black chattel slavery, the expropriation of indigenous lands, and colonialism.

Save for Du Bois's philosophy of race, Hegel's concept of spirit is unique in having a simultaneously forward- and backward-looking conception of human perfectibility. Revisiting Hegel's concept of spirit (or culture) clarifies the forward- and backward-looking aspects of Du Bois's philosophy of race. My intention is not to demonstrate Du Bois's Hegelianism. Du Bois's primary concern is the substantive emancipation of his people, not getting Hegel "right." A Hegelian lens can nevertheless unpack Du Bois's claim that in moving forward, a people must "re-remember" the past.[52] In fact, the importance of preserving the historical memory of racial trauma and the triumph of the human spirit in the face of adversity is a persistent theme in modern Africana philosophy, art, and literature.[53]

In a Hegelian move, Du Bois maintained that historical memory can "guide future development" in providing (1) a people's *motivation* to continue the political struggle for freedom and (2) the distinctive *content* of a people's ethical character as self-conscious and self-determining agents.[54] Recall that for Du Bois an ideal is a shareable reason for judgment and action. We can now specify the *kinds* of reasons the race ideal refines through a reliance on historical memory. With respect to (1), historical memory can bolster a person's sense of self-worth, psychological fortitude, and grit. A history of political struggle often motivates one to participate in political action and strengthens one's moral faith in eventual triumph. After all, members of a vulnerable racial group tend to stand in the same relation to the past, on the same side of the color line, and often have similarly limited access to rights and resources. To be sure, anyone can choose to join the fight for racial justice, but a common historical memory is more likely to motivate one to do so. Historical memory sharpens the psychological feeling of personal power and provides insight into why it is important to carry on the struggle for justice. So, too, a vulnerable people can protect their positive sense of self-worth in the face of perpetual losses. For Du Bois, the "soul" and "striving" of his people reveals *unrealized* hopes and dreams for a better future in the aftermath of slavery, the failure of Reconstruction, and the emergence of Jim Crow.[55] The reality of race, then, positions racial groups in a different relationship to the past that enables one not only to delight in historical accomplishments but also motivates one to make real the unrealized hopes and dreams of one's forebears.

The recent controversies about the removal of Confederate

monuments in the United States underscore the power of historical memory to mobilize racial groups. Whites' sense of personal power and self-worth remains tied to the vindication of the history of the Confederacy, founded on the defense of slavery and white supremacy. This is why historical memory alone is *never* sufficient to mediate subjective will formation and must be articulated through a dialectical mediation of the ideal of civic enfranchisement, that is, a democratic ideal that advances the freedom and equality of all. Historical memory is powerful but it could also be abused when it is employed to motivate a people to *narrow* their sense of civic fellowship with others. What is more, a group's psychological sense of personal power and drive for belonging can never trump the norms of "Spirit," which entails the free self-actualization of all in a constitutional state.

With respect to (2), historical memory also forms the distinctive *content* of the normative self-understanding of a people. For example, Du Bois held that slavery and Jim Crow elicited patterns of cultural responses that represent a unique collective self-consciousness that is preserved in African-American cultural artifacts, such as song, literature, dance, and stylized comportment. Hegel argued that ethical customs and social systems' ruling behavior attest to a people's consciousness of themselves as free. Culture is the means through which we shape ourselves into fully self-determining agents through historical time. Culture educates us – shapes our subjective will – so that we can advance universalizable reasons to reconstitute our political community in perpetuity. Or, as Hegel puts it, culture or spirit is "the distinct particularity [that] actually constitutes the characteristic principle of a people."[56] To identify the *content* that structures the normative self-understanding of a people, one must look backward in time as one comes to understand the meaning and significance of the historical deeds of one's people and the impact that they have had – or have yet to have – on the world.

It is the essence of Spirit to *act*, to make itself explicitly into what it already is implicitly – to be its own deed, and its own work. Thus it becomes the object of its own attention, so that its own existence is there for it to be conscious of. That is the case with the Spirit of a people: it is a definite Spirit, one that builds itself up into an entire world, which subsists and persists, here and now, in its religion, its forms of worship, its customs, its forms of government and political laws, in the entire scope of its institutions, its deeds and events. This is its work – it is what a people *is*. A people is what its deeds are.[57]

By assuming a relation to the past, "The individual discovers the being of his people as a firm world, already there, into which he must incorporate himself."[58] Du Bois did not believe that in a racial caste society one is "free" to lose one's racial identity, as if through the sheer force of the will a person can rise above the effects of the color line. To locate racial difference in the historical exercise of practical agency does not mean that racial identity is determined by an unconstrained free will. Rather, Du Bois appreciated that racial identity is not a static object but a dynamic and unstable practical orientation that informs one's relation to the past, other people, and the world. Yet individuals can still freely reinterpret what their shared social location and common history means to them and experience anew the feeling of joy, personal power, and delight in the historical accomplishments of one's people.[59]

Du Bois claimed that a black race ideal, while defining a distinct racial identity, also makes a "peculiar contribution

[. . .] to the culture of their common country."[60] The distinct content that characterizes the ethical character of the black race ideal thus interpenetrates the development of the "ethical spirit" of the American republic:

> We are the people whose subtle sense of song has given America its only American music, its only American fairy-tales, its only touch of pathos and humor amid its mad money-getting plutocracy. As such, it is our duty to conserve our physical powers, our intellectual endowments, our spiritual ideals; as a race we must strive by race organization, by race solidarity, by race unity to the realization of that broader humanity which freely recognizes differences in men, but sternly deprecates inequality in their opportunities of development.[61]

And so, in Du Bois's racialism, the conservation of race functions as *both* a political instrument to dismantle the color line and as a vehicle to preserve intrinsically valuable "ideals of life." "What, then, is a race?," asked Du Bois, "It is a vast family of human beings, generally of common blood and language, always of common history, traditions and impulses, who are both voluntarily and involuntarily striving together for the accomplishment of certain more or less vividly conceived ideals of life."[62] The black race ideal galvanizes at once the growth of the modern American state, American popular culture, and the positive normative self-understanding of African Americans.

Interracial civic fellowship and the cosmopolitan condition

Lastly, as an instrument of progress, the race ideal employs culture and the arts to advance the ideal of interracial civic fellowship and a global cosmopolitan condition of the harmonious coexistence of peoples. A major feature dictating the relevance of the role of race in history is the unacknowledged *trauma* that has been inflicted on communities of color. For the promise of civic fellowship to make sense in the aftermath of so much suffering, that suffering must be acknowledged by those who have long ignored it. Our conception of what justice is must be expanded to incorporate public engagement with the historical memory of racial trauma. Specifically, public engagement with cultural artifacts that have preserved the historical memory of racial trauma can substantiate the ideal of interracial civic fellowship and show a genuine willingness to understand and atone for the history of white supremacy.

In the *Dusk of Dawn*, published in 1940 some forty years after Du Bois gave his first address to the American Negro Academy, he commented:

> But one thing is sure and that is the fact that since the fifteenth century these ancestors of mine and their other descendants have had a common history; have suffered a common disaster and have one long memory. [. . .]. But the physical bond is least and the badge of color relatively unimportant save as a badge; the real essence of this kinship is its social heritage of slavery; the discrimination and insult[.][63]

As we've seen, in order to recognize "difference" as civic fellows, a public must work through the spiritual and cultural fabric of diverse race ideals – to wit, the cultural artifacts that document a racial group's shared dreams, hopes, and self-expression; and the reciprocal recognition of differences constitutes interracial civic fellowship. But, more to the point for Du Bois, the public must learn to engage with the *pain* encapsulated in African-American music, literature, and art.

In particular, in the essay, he cautioned against "forgetting the slave trade and slavery, and the struggle for emancipation; [and] forgetting abolition[.]"[64]

Du Bois's discussion of the Sorrow Songs is an excellent example of a distinct black cultural response to the color line that highlights the pain of his people. He dedicated the final chapter of *Souls* to the sorrow songs, a bar of which opens each chapter of the book. The Sorrow Songs, he wrote, are "weird old songs in which the soul of the slave spoke to men. [I]t stands today not simply as the sole American music, but as the most beautiful expression of human experience born this side of the seas."[65] The sorrow songs convey the first-person experience of bondage; they impress upon the reader the historical reality of antebellum America. As cultural artifacts, they carry a distinct aesthetic value. As Du Bois says, they are "the most beautiful expression of human experience born this side of the seas." Yet, because they signify the historical memory of racial trauma and are created by enslaved Africans, for Du Bois their moral value in a democracy founded on black chattel slavery transcends aesthetic, cultural, or music theory. The songs should elicit an attitude of moral regard that symbolizes respect for enslaved Africans and their descendants and achieves some form of moral repair for the trans-Atlantic slave trade and the institution of slavery. Frank Kirkland adds, "Only through recollection can African-Americans of a future-oriented present virtually compensate for the violation of the principles of modernity [. . .] and achieve some kind of virtual compensation for the breach."[66]

The trauma of slavery has in a way cemented a racial fault line in habits of citizenship today. According to Du Bois, by understanding the "meaning of [the] music," the American public must learn to acknowledge the pain of bondage.[67] The sorrow songs, Du Bois explained, "are the music of an unhappy people, of the children of disappointment; they tell of death and suffering and unvoiced longing toward a truer world, of misty wanderings and hidden ways."[68] The public's reluctance to listen to the sorrow songs reflects the persistent reluctance to acknowledge black and brown traumatic experiences of the color line. The same public sentiment that once judged slavery to be consistent with constitutional norms today judges white vigilantes and police officers to be the *victims* of the Black Lives Matter movement.

Instead, Du Bois asked the public to join the African-American community in the condemnation of the history and persistence of anti-black violence and white supremacy. He hoped that the sorrow songs might provoke affect in white readers to discern their *sorrow*:

> In these songs, I have said, the slave spoke to the world. Such a message is naturally veiled and half articulate. Words and music have lost each other and new and cant phrases of a dimly understood theology have displaced the older sentiment. Once in a while we catch a strange word of an unknown tongue[.] Purely secular songs are few in number, partly because many of them were turned into hymns by a change of words, partly because the frolics were seldom heard by the stranger, and the music less often caught. Of nearly all the songs, however, the music is distinctly sorrowful.[69]

In rejecting a revisionist history, he refused to rationalize slavery as a beneficial institution that, in the long run, "schooled" enslaved Africans, promoting their welfare, technical expertise in industry and farming, or sociocultural literacy, as evidenced by the conversion to Christianity or the adoption of Anglo-European languages on slave plantations.[70] In short, in spite of popular black caricatures of

smiling mammies and jovial Toms, Du Bois asked his reader
to seriously consider that slaves were *unhappy*; that no puta-
tively beneficial consequences rationalize the institution or
its historical legacy; and, moreover, that it should have never
existed in the first place.[71] To discern the sorrow of the
sorrow songs is thus a crucial step in foregrounding enslaved
Africans' own interpretation of what had happened to them
and respecting their humanity as persons who had, all along,
an innate right to be free.

What is more, racial groups' relation to the past captures
another racial fault line in habits of citizenship. The African-
American community strives to honor the past, whereas the
white world strives to distance itself from it. The historical
memory of slavery remains alive in the African-American
community and it is passed down through an oral folk song
tradition. Du Bois hoped that, if properly understood, the
sorrow songs can make the republic face its past and thereby
educate the public spirit to reform long-standing habits
of judgment that exclude – and ignore – its most vulnerable members. He concluded that the duty to conserve race
remains at least until "the ideal of human brotherhood has
become a practical possibility."[72]

Du Bois envisioned a cosmopolitan condition where all
racial groups stand together on the world stage as equals
and "freely recognize[s] differences in men."[73] A unified race
ideal is necessary to fight discrimination and foster cultural
difference, which is an ineliminable feature of the human
condition. One cannot fully "instrumentalize" cultural heritage for the sake of democratic politics. Indeed, Du Bois
affirmed the intrinsic value of black cultural traditions in a
global society. "The modern theory of the world's races," he
wrote, "no longer looks upon them as antagonistic hatred-
cultivating groups[.] Races and Nations represent organized
Human effort, striving each in its own way, each in its own

time to realize for mankind the Good, the Beautiful, and the True [. . .] blending and harmonizing into vast striving of one humanity."[74] The challenge of mapping the color line today is finding the right language to talk about differences without essentializing difference or overgeneralizing its political significance. Du Bois entertained the possibility that racial identities as we know them may one day break down, though he advised against making "self-obliteration" a goal.[75] In any case, the concept of race still has a lot of work to do to improve the world. To speculate about a future where it has no pull – or a radically different kind of pull – is to imagine a world so far off that we've little guidance for our speculation. To be sure, today a color-blind politics *masks* the persistence of racially exclusionary practices by attacking the credibility and judgment of those who bring such practices to light. The claim that the civil rights movement and the election of Obama has "solved" the problem of racism in America rationalizes a lack of motivation to act for racial justice reforms or to meditate on the significance that race continues to have in our society.[76] Du Bois's philosophy of race encourages democratic reasoning that articulates a shared sense of political destiny and repairs the bonds of mutual trust and civic fellowship to foster a peaceful future.

A certain form of respectful cultural consumption among members of the public can provide a moral education for democratic citizenship, demonstrating how looking backward at the past helps a nation learn how to rebuild the republic of the future. Du Bois thus supposed that a vibrant popular culture should underlie democratic politics to strengthen relations of mutual recognition among citizenry.[77] In closing, I would like to offer a fragment of a poem by Du Bois which celebrates his racial identity and condemns the color line, "I am darkening with song/I am hearkening to wrong":

"The Song of the Smoke" (1907) (excerpt)[78]

I am the Smoke King,
I am black!
I am darkening with song,
I am hearkening to wrong!
I will be black as blackness can –
The blacker the mantle, the mightier the man!
For blackness was ancient ere whiteness began.
I am daubing God in night,
I am swabbing Hell in white:
I am the Smoke King
I am black.

Part II

Self-Assertion

4

Courting Controversy: Du Bois on Political Rule and Educated "Elites"

In 2017, Patrisse Cullors, a co-founder of the Black Lives Matter movement, shared in an interview with the *Los Angeles Times* where she saw the movement in four years: "One of the biggest places that I see us will be in local and national government. I think you'll see not just black people, but black folks and our allies really pushing to be a part of local government, city government and national government – to move to be mayor, county board of supervisors, to be on boards."[1]

Cullors envisioned the future BLM movement seizing local, state, and federal power. She concluded the interview speculating about whether she might run for public office one day. Cullors, who earned her baccalaureate degree at UCLA and was a Fulbright scholar, had dedicated herself to police reform after witnessing the brutalization of her brother in the Los Angeles jail system. In her memoir, she clarifies her view of the relationship between electoral politics and social justice, explaining her decision to continue organizing after Trump's election:

[T]here is so much work to do as we push to fight this presidency and stop its Jim Crow-era aggressions. We are working collaboratively to create sustainable rapid response networks to violence and ICE raids. But we are also deeply committed to building Black political power and supporting bold leadership like Chokwe Antar Lumumba's in Jackson, Mississippi, and Stacey Abram's in Georgia. We are committed to working closely with [. . .] Three Point Strategies, the Washington, DC-based consulting firm that works at the intersection of electoral politics and social justice. We can elect Black women to office who are committed to advancing human-centered agendas, leaders who understand and honor the truth that real leadership must be earned, not appointed. Or stolen. Or arrogant.[2]

Cullors proposes a *hybrid* model of radical black leadership, invigorated by community engagement and collaboration. She emphasizes that electoral politics should not be an arena of compromise, where the people choose the lesser of two evils; rather "real" leadership must redress "Jim Crow-era aggressions." Real leaders earn the respect of those they represent. Neither focusing on *nor* discounting electoral politics, she supports progressive campaigns around the country, particularly those of black women.

Typically, the question of optimal strategy reemerges with the fall of one generation and the rise of a new generation of organizers. Cullors's hybrid model of leadership encourages cooperation between organizers and leaders. It contrasts from, but also complements, a recent trend from the Occupy to the BLM movements that favors decentralized, youth-led, and de-institutionalized political mobilization.

Du Bois is widely associated with the old vanguard model of leadership, as encapsulated by his controversial essay "The Talented Tenth" (1903), which dates back to the early civil

rights era and affirms the college-educated visionaries as
the rightful leaders of the African-American community. A
tenth of the African-American population – the "talented
tenth" – were the "exceptional men" charged with "saving"
through social "uplift" the black working class.[3] Pushing
against this reading, in this chapter I show the value of
his defense of leadership in chapter 3 of *Souls* in which he
rejected Booker T. Washington's accommodationist politics.
Further, as early as 1904, he began to rework his model of
leadership in favor of a hybrid model resembling Cullors's
proposal, grounding effective leadership in direct community engagement and representation. I thus synthesize Du
Bois's comments on leadership to present a hybrid model of
leadership grounded in community engagement for thinking
about political mobilization today.

In the first section below, I recount Du Bois's debate with
Washington to sketch the value of Du Bois's early notion
of leadership. Next, I reexamine his defense of the "talented
tenth" to explain why the role he assigned to black leaders
was viable in the historical contexts of the ante- and postbellum United States and remains viable today inasmuch as
it endorses a hybrid model of leadership that is grounded
in direct and ongoing community engagement. In the final
section, in order to present the hybrid model of leadership
in action, I present recent community organizing efforts
to desegregate neighborhoods and schools on Long Island,
New York – one of the most segregated counties in America,
in spite of having a thriving suburban black middle class.
Access to quality public schools in black and Latinx neighborhoods in Long Island remains a crushing barrier to equal
opportunity, a symbol of re-segregation in counties across
the United States.

With this chapter, I introduce the second theme of the
book: black *self-assertion* against anti-black discrimination

and exclusion. To wit, Du Bois maintained that African Americans should become free and equal citizens, but advocated black self-assertion to bolster their right to *seize* power and resources from the state.[4] Through self-assertion, one *takes* what one is morally entitled to. The theme of self-assertion outlines one of two avenues for black self-organization that Du Bois proposed during the Jim Crow era: the turn *outward* to seize state power or the turn *inward* to self-segregate. In despair later in his life, as we'll see, he pursued the second option.

Washington–Du Bois debate

With the publication of *Souls*, Du Bois's rising political profile was set in opposition to Booker T. Washington. Their dispute brought to the national stage the reality of diversity and disagreement among black voices. In 1895, Washington delivered his now infamous "Atlanta Compromise Speech" to national acclaim. In the speech, Washington outlined his accommodationist stance to racial segregation: "In all things that are purely social we can be as separate as the fingers, yet one hand in all things essential to mutual progress."[5] He proposed that former slaves refrain from fighting for equal rights. Instead, he suggested focusing on economic self-determination. Black business owners should create job opportunities to uplift poor black laborers. He did not advocate for civil and political rights, interracial labor unions, or labor rights. Instead, he defended, particularly for the working poor, the virtues of self-reliance, insisting on thrift, hard work, and self-sacrifice of a nascent black capitalism, opining "The great human law that in the end recognizes and rewards merit is everlasting and universal."[6] In 1900, he established the National Negro Business League, a cooperative of black business owners designed to facilitate the growth of a black middle class.[7] Additionally, he supported the vocational training of black children for skilled and semi-skilled labor, rather than their access to a liberal arts education. Their concern should be earning an "honest wage," rather than securing civil and political rights.

Washington was born into slavery and yet seemed to find a silver lining in racial segregation in the hard work of the poor. His speech won the praise of the Jim Crow South and the industrial North, establishing him as a public authority on the so-called "Negro Problem." Even Du Bois initially supported Washington's emphasis on economic self-reliance to counter the destructive effects of the free market on black freedmen. Though it might be hard to imagine today, Washington had enormous influence at the dawn of the twentieth century. His reputation for being a "race leader" enjoyed the support of prominent black public figures. The poet Joseph Seamon Cotter even wrote poetry in honor of the National Negro Business League.[8]

Although Du Bois initially supported Washington – and congratulated him after his Atlanta Compromise Speech – in *Souls*, Du Bois comes out in opposition to Washington. Du Bois asserted that the voting franchise is inalienable and that the segregated African-American community must seize political power from the state. In particular, the voting franchise represents the dignity of black humanity and cannot be sacrificed for economic expedience. Rights belong to black persons simply because they are persons. One need not "prove" one's moral equality through hard work and self-sacrifice. Washington's emphasis on black self-reliance, as Du Bois put it, ultimately "shifts the burden of the Negro problem to Negro shoulders and [makes whites] stand aside as critical and rather pessimistic spectators; when in fact the burden belongs to the nation."[9] For a politics of self-reliance made the problem of race and racism a problem primarily for African Americans, not for white people, and thereby exculpated whites' role in the perpetuation of racial segregation, violence, and economic exploitation.

Washington's reluctance to condemn segregation ensured external funding for the Tuskegee Institute, the school of industrial training which he directed. As his program for industrial training grew, he opposed the newly founded NAACP, publicly denouncing it as "nonsense."[10] It has since surfaced that Washington anonymously financed desegregation campaigns and penned editorials attacking racial segregation in housing and schools. Yet his reluctance to *publicly* criticize Jim Crow segregation or to support the NAACP impeded the struggle against lynching, voter suppression, and economic exploitation.[11]

In contrast, Du Bois upheld the voting franchise in order to advance the fair equality of opportunity and the interests of black labor, including access to a quality higher education. He viewed the franchise to be essential for the advancement of black economic interests through equitable and effective representation in government. And so he favored a politics oriented around "rule," but a politics of rule, in his mind, was not "anti-democratic" but an essential means for black labor to engage a constitutional state in order to grab rights and resources.[12] In other words, as Cullors proposed in 2017, even if he had initially overstated it, Du Bois did not discount the importance of engaging electoral politics and the modern American state.

What is more, he rejected the suggestion that vocational training was preferable to the liberal arts model of higher education. He resented Washington's notion that it was inappropriate to teach black children "impractical" subjects such as literature and the French language.[13] He emphasized the innate moral value of the right to education. Throughout his life he maintained that all children who showed an interest and aptitude for learning should have the right to learn whatever they want, including pursuing a college degree. Furthermore, for Du Bois, Washington's proposal was ineffective for building black wealth. He doubted that industrial training alone, in the long run, led to economic advancement. Were a black household somehow to secure capital through luck and hard work, they would have little legal recourse against white mobs, abusive employers, and white neighbors. In what became known as "the red summer" of 1919, white mobs burned down entire black neighborhoods and commercial districts, targeting black laborers organizing for fair wages from Chicago, Illinois to Elaine, Arkansas.[14] Instead, Du Bois argued that the voter franchise would enable African Americans to pursue their economic interests in the free market inasmuch as it protected their legal standing as contract laborers and property owners. As he reconsidered voluntary black self-segregation in the mid-1930s, Du Bois would inch closer to Washington's original defense of independent black businesses and grow pessimistic about the willingness of the state to desegregate and expand fair equality of opportunity.

In rejecting Washington's accommodationist stance, Du Bois entered the political fray. A promising young scholar, he emerged as a black public intellectual prepared to confront anyone to weather public scrutiny. No one was above criticism. Yet his promulgation of the term "the talented tenth," coined by the philanthropist Henry Lyman Morehouse to solve the "Negro Problem," remains perhaps Du Bois's most controversial act. Although he rejected Washington's accommodationist stance in his early years, Du Bois's own proposal to secure equal opportunity for the segregated black community invited doubt. It seemed to favor affluent male professionals as the rightful rulers of the working poor, as Du Bois did not address the politics of sex and gender until the 1910s, as the women's suffrage movement was gaining traction. In *Race Men*, Hazel Carby points out that Du Bois "assumes and privileges a discourse of black masculinity."[15] Yet, even in *Souls*, one can appreciate his emphasis on a politics of rule in relation to the electoral participation of a systematically disenfranchised group.

The role of the "talented tenth"

Du Bois's idea of the "talented tenth" has greatly influenced the reception of his writings.[16] In the eponymous essay (1903), he explained that the "talented tenth" are college-educated professionals who constitute a small elite. They must assume responsibility for the "uplift" of the black working poor: "The Negro race, like all races, is going to be saved by its exceptional men."[17] Du Bois described at least two generations of the "talented tenth" who each had a political purpose that corresponded to their sociohistorical period. First, in the antebellum period, he stated that black leadership must abolish slavery.[18] Then, in the aftermath of the legal abolition of slavery, they must fight "half-serfdom" or "second slavery" through the expansion of a schedule of rights and liberties.[19] He encouraged the second generation of race leaders, of which he was a member, to "plead for black men's rights."[20]

> It is the fashion of today to sneer at them [the first generation of black leaders] and to say that with freedom Negro leadership should have begun at the plow and not in the Senate – a foolish and mischievous lie; two hundred and fifty years that black serf toiled at the plow and yet that toiling was in vain till the Senate passed the war amendments [i.e.,

the 13th, 14th, and 15th Amendments]; and two hundred and fifty years more the half-free serf of today may toil at his plow, but unless he have political rights and righteously guarded civic status, he will still remain the poverty-stricken and ignorant plaything of rascals.[21]

The second generation of leaders must fight for "political rights" and "civic status," which in turn enabled a person to rise from poverty and avoid economic exploitation.

Access to education emerged as a crucial "political right" for securing black civic equality in the late nineteenth and twentieth centuries; it represented black citizens' moral entitlement to equality of opportunity. His model of leadership asserted meaningful political representation that expanded access to education. Du Bois's presentation of the second generation of leaders, then, advocated for universal access to education, among other major concerns for black labor. Du Bois stressed "the peculiar value" of schools and colleges in a historical context when few endorsed public schools as a legitimate moral entitlement of American citizenship in the first place.[22] Today, a quality higher education remains a key vehicle of social mobility; the push of for-profit charter schools increasingly contests whether free and open public education should be a right of US citizenship at all.[23]

To be sure, Du Bois often used inflammatory language to describe black poverty and illiteracy. Notably, Joy James and Robert Gooding-Williams argue that the idea of the "talented tenth" betrays Du Bois's elitism, which elevated himself and other college-educated "race men" as the rightful leaders of the unwashed black masses, unlettered in modern American folklife.[24] "[E]ducators of the black masses should be *cultured aristocrats*," writes Gooding-Williams, "individuals who can expose their black brothers and sisters to the whole range of characteristically modern behavior and attitudinal norms."[25]

Gooding-Williams concludes that the idea of the "talented tenth" confirms Du Bois's politics of "expressive self-realization" through which black elites pushed "backward" black masses into modern cultural refinement.

In my view, it is uncharitable to infer that a focus on expunging black illiteracy and lack of access to education in the aftermath of slavery meant Du Bois viewed the masses as "backward." This line of interpretation mischaracterizes the postbellum political purpose of the "talented tenth," which was to advance the equality of opportunity through the universal expansion of access to education. Du Bois's remarks about the apparent lowliness of black serfdom were meant to highlight a rigid racial caste system that forced black freedmen into body-breaking, immiserating, and often uncompensated drudgery in the forms of sharecropping and industrial labor. One can condemn exploitative drudgery without condemning the people who do it or even the social value of such labor.

On the heels of his dispute with Washington, Du Bois waged a campaign against the Tuskegee machine that aimed to eclipse black professionalization with its vocational training. In the early twentieth century, so little public value was placed on educating black children that schools sometimes "used student labor for the erection of their buildings."[26] At the very least, Du Bois's proposal aimed to shore up resources for black schools and historically black colleges, so that they would grow to be powerful social institutions in the aftermath of the legal abolition of slavery. After all, college-educated teachers were needed to teach in segregated black schools, even if many children were to conclude their schooling with vocational training. Students would still have to learn to read and write and to learn about black history and culture. Du Bois asserted that African-American teachers were desperately needed in black classrooms. He was adamant on this point.[27] To decry it as elitist minimizes the impact of receiving a quality education on a person's sense of self-worth, civic status, and equality of opportunity in the job market.

One might object that a focus on education nonetheless presents a narrow vision of the flourishing of the oppressed. If an education is a necessary objective and qualification for leadership, then that condition restricts to an elite few those who can legitimately rule the unlettered many. Moreover, it leaves in place the capitalist structure of industry that exploits the majority of laborers. To answer this objection, it is helpful to consider who, concretely, comprised the "talented tenth" in Du Bois's view. In "The Development of a People" (1904), Du Bois explained: "I care not what their vocation may be – preacher, teacher, physician, or artisan, this person is going to solve the Negro problem."[28] The group consisted of black teachers in segregated black schools, black politicians in government, black preachers in churches, black investors in segregated neighborhoods, among others. They are formal and informal leaders who must be prepared to "fight an army of devils" for their people.[29] Some thirty years later, in *Dusk of Dawn*, Du Bois admitted the classist dimension of his early formulation of leadership and began to think about workers' democratic control of the workplace. He would grow skeptical that a small black middle class would remain in solidarity with the working poor once it achieved professional success and affluence.[30]

Du Bois, then, continued to develop a more expansive vision of political mobilization and hit on a *hybrid* model of leadership grounded in direct community engagement and collaboration that addressed the concrete needs of the many. To wit, a rule-based politics is not just about the importance of having black politicians and professionals. That is necessary but insufficient. For black leadership is ineffective in disrupting the color line if, like the white-controlled polity, it loses touch with the black working poor. Leaders derive their legitimacy from the communities they must represent and advocate for. Public scrutiny should heighten organizers' sense of responsibility towards the people and commit them to a protracted struggle for fair wages, rights, and resources. His conception of leadership thus evolved to espouse a hybrid model of rule that presupposed a diversity of voices and sustained grassroots organizing. It incorporated electoral politics without limiting the push for social justice to winning elections. Notably, he also refused to discount the importance of state and federal government on the life prospects of the oppressed.

In his later works, Du Bois stressed that the moral literacy requisite for advancing political struggle is not conferred with a college diploma, social status, or wealth, even though he continued to lobby for blacks' rights to earn a higher education and enter high-status professions, such as doctors, lawyers, and professors. Moral literacy is conferred through the ongoing participation in informal and formal social practices that recognize the equal moral value of all and evince compassionate recognition of the shared experiences of exclusion. For him, the distinct spiritual and cultural world of the segregated black community is the ultimate springboard for political mobilization; and habits of citizenship that prevail there should undergird the development of formal representational politics.

In an original interpretative move, the political theorist Arash Davari reinterprets Du Bois's model of leadership to redirect the organizational tactics of contemporary anti-racist struggle. Davari observes that a strong preference for leaderless and decentralized tactics in social movements dovetails with the neoliberal consolidation of power. These tactics facilitate the "dissolution" of the people "into a gathered mass of individuals" ineffective at resisting economic exploi-

tation that targets labor rights.[31] Davari does not call for a
return to traditional models of leadership by (male) professionals. Rather, he advances a hybrid model of leadership in
a "radical democracy" that champions "the constant movement of individuals and perspectives in and out of positions
of authority on the basis of differences in lived experience."[32]
Responding to the ebb and flow of the democratic redistribution of power, democracy should consist of a productive
exchange between the leaders and the led – this he takes to
be the non-elitist promise of Du Bois's model of leadership.[33]

Taylor elaborates on Davari's point in her assessment of
the strategies of the BLM. She notes that overemphasis on
leaderless and decentralized action can inadvertently function to sideline political newcomers and make a movement
less effective:

> #BLM has reinvigorated the Occupy method of protest,
> which believes decentralized and "leaderless" actions are
> more democratic, essentially allowing its followers to act
> on what they want to do without the restraint of others
> weighing in. But at a time when many people are trying
> to find an entry point into anti-police activism and desire
> to be involved, this particular method of organizing can
> be difficult to penetrate. In some ways, this decentralizing
> organizing strategy can actually narrow opportunities for
> democratic involvement of many in favor of the tightly knit
> workings of those already in the know.[34]

Neither a return to the old vanguard of rule nor total decen-
tralization is optimal. Rather, a hybrid model that learns
from the past and empowers the rising generation of organizers would ensure the most inclusive and effective grassroots
political mobilization.[35]

Many of the same issues that Du Bois had hoped black

leadership would solve in the postbellum era remain pressing problems today: universal access to education, voter and economic enfranchisement, and equitable representation in public office. The question of how to dismantle the color line in the fight against anti-black prejudice and institutional racism return us to the very same starting point with which Du Bois began his political career. In the final section, I turn to the issue of residential segregation and unequal access to education to show the hybrid model of leadership in action.

The politics of leadership and desegregation in Long Island, New York

For many residents of New York City, Long Island represents the American dream, a suburbia of large family homes and quiet, tree-lined streets, just a short drive from Manhattan. Dotted with wineries and beaches, it is a coveted destination for those families planning their escape from urban life. Long Island also includes some of the most segregated counties in the United States. According to a recent investigative study by *Newsday*, it "has 291 communities. Most of its black residents live in just eleven."[36] Real-estate agents continue to practice redlining, the illegal practice of steering prospective homebuyers of color into black or mixed neighborhoods, and white prospective homebuyers into predominantly white neighborhoods. As a consequence, in the last decade, Long Island has become both more diverse and more segregated.

Residential racial segregation cuts across class lines. Wealthier families of color are still funneled into integrated neighborhoods, even if they could afford homes in mostly white areas. To be sure, residential racial segregation on Long Island is not new. Some towns, such as Levittown, were founded on an explicit whites-only residential covenant for servicemen returning from World War II, becoming the nation's first sanctified modern American "suburb."[37] Levittown's covenant aligned with a national pattern of severe and systematic housing discrimination. Across the United States in the mid-twentieth century, the federal government and commercial banks refused to give low-interest, federally backed loans and mortgages to black and brown applicants, while approving whites for new home purchases.[38] Redlining is a major source of racial economic inequality that persists today. Home value passes down intergenerational family wealth; without access to this form of capital, a family's economic health suffers. Shortly after King's assassination, Lyndon B. Johnson had signed into law the landmark Fair Housing Act in 1968. The act prohibits "discrimination against any person in the [. . .] sale or rental of a dwelling [. . .] because of race, color, religion, sex, familial status, or national origin."[39] Even so, the federal government has consistently failed to intervene or redress discriminatory housing practices. Under the control of Ben Carson, appointed by Trump, the Department of Housing and Urban Development (HUD) has rolled back federal initiatives to enforce the Fair Housing Act. Carson indefinitely suspended the review of all pending cases of housing discrimination filed under the Obama administration. He then "instructed HUD officials to delete the words 'inclusive' and 'free from discrimination' from the agency's website."[40] He joins the rank of presidential appointees whose function is to raze the federal organizations they run to "streamline" big government.

The devastating consequences of racial segregation in housing are well documented. White flight undermines black and brown upward social mobility. The value of black-owned homes plummets in areas of residential racial segregation, intensifying the intergenerational wealth disparity between black and non-black households. The transgender activist and director, Yance Ford, has documented the racial tensions on Long Island that spill over into racial violence, as segregation shores up resentment and ill will among neighbors. Ford's own brother, a black teacher, was killed in Central Islip, Long Island by a white 19-year-old autobody mechanic over a dispute about a car repair.[41] The public school system is perhaps most affected by residential racial segregation, directly impacting the demographics of the student body and city funding.

In 1976, whites made up nearly 90 percent of the student body in Long Island public schools. By 2018, less than 50 percent of white students were still enrolled in public schools. With the influx of black and Latinx residents, white parents withdrew their children from public schools and placed them in charter and parochial schools. The result is the dramatic underfunding of the public school system, the channeling of public monies into for-profit charter schools, declining educational outcomes across the board, and the hyper de facto re-segregation of schools. With the passing of *Brown v. Board of Education* in 1954, it became illegal for public schools to use explicit racial guidelines for admission. The effort to resist the federal push towards integration sparked nationwide racial unrest. Yet the modest gains of the civil rights era are eroding, as the US public school system "has steadily re-segregated to levels last seen in the 1960s."[42] No longer is the major obstacle the legal protection of white-only spaces; now the failure to shore up the political will to integrate schools has accelerated the rise of de facto segregation, bolstered by an attack on public schools. In his State of the Union address on February 4, 2020, in a racist dog whistle, Trump referred to "rescuing children [. . .] trapped in failing government schools."[43] It does not take much to understand that his administration aims to "rescue" white children "trapped" in integrated "government" classrooms.

Black Long Island residents are steadfast in fighting for access to quality education and fair housing practices. To remedy the urgent situation on Long Island, several advocacy groups have developed a *hybrid* approach to radical black leadership, invigorated by community engagement and the leadership of local residents, often under the helm of black women. The public advocacy group ERASE Racism, an acronym short for Education Research Advocacy Support to Eliminate Racism, was founded by Elaine Gross in 2001. It focuses on curbing the re-segregation of housing and schools on Long Island. In a collaborative effort by teachers, lawyers, and volunteers, it spearheads public outreach programs that run educational workshops, anti-racist trainings, and visits to local public schools. ERASE Racism also "helps to draft legislation to address the problem and su[es] municipalities when their policies violate the federal Fair Housing Act."[44] As the advocacy group leans on college-educated black professionals, Gross prizes community participation to empower black residents on the island to take control of the development of their neighborhoods.

Though ERASE Racism does not concentrate on electoral politics, without question it acknowledges, as the historian Mark Naison states, that the cause of de facto re-segregation is "that most civil rights leaders have given up on integration" as a political project.[45] ERASE Racism *shores up* the political will to desegregate. Their approach markedly contrasts with a national trend to "improve" hyper-segregated schools by expanding school "choice" voucher programs – a tactic that *intensifies* de facto segregation. When black residents act against bigoted neighbors and lax federal laws, they are often the only defense left against the rollback of civil rights-era legislation. ERASE Racism thus incorporates an emphasis on rule-based politics and effective leadership that strives to restore and advance the gains of the civil rights era while strengthening grassroots advocacy in direct collaboration with Long Island residents.

To be sure, among organizers, the notion of a rule-centered politics oriented towards leadership (or the government) is not very popular after the civil rights era – and often for good reason. Self-appointed leaders sometimes assert their self-interest above the people, parachuting into local struggles without full knowledge of the situation on the ground or a vested interest in the people affected by injustices. There are numerous non-profits that court corporate donations and neglect the communities they are supposed to serve. But the hybrid model of leadership in action on Long Island suggests that Du Bois's views on leadership might offer a viable strategy for political mobilization today, one that combines the tactics of the civil rights movement with a newfound populist sensibility that is as inclusive and accessible as possible.

Undoubtedly, at the dawn of the twentieth century, Du Bois saw himself emerging as a race leader and the rightful heir of Frederick Douglass's legacy.[46] He often used prophetic imagery to suggest that he is the new self-appointed Moses to lead his people to the Promised Land. Yet his *justification* for a hybrid model of political leadership remains viable today. Following Du Bois, one can accept that organizing must transcend formal offices of political power, but it is still important not to lose sight of the fact that the state and economic markets aggregate real power along racial lines. My presentation of Du Bois's idea of leadership suggests that a representational politics – with a critical role for radical black leadership – still has a role left to play in the struggle for justice.

Finally, a lesson that is worth serious consideration today, Du Bois insisted that African Americans have to be the leaders of their own communities and spearhead their political mobilization.[47] It would be imprudent and inappropriate to rely on the goodwill of whites.[48] Those who are most likely to have sober and compassionate appreciation of the effects of the color line – and to communicate black interests to the American public – *are none other than black people*. In Du Bois's formulation, "Our one haven of refuge is ourselves."[49]

In the end, however, the most important thing for effective political leadership is to awaken the conscience of the republic – and that capacity for moral awareness transcends a person's race and social identity. Margaret Walker imagines a prophet, Amos, who, returning, "speaks to the captive hearts of America/He bares raw their conscience."[50]

5

A Broken Promise: On Hegel, Second Slavery, and the Ideal of Civic Enfranchisement (1910–1934)

[And the congressman from] Connecticut declared the [anti-slavery petition] "contained nothing but *a farrago of the French metaphysics of liberty and equality*;" and that "it was likely to produce some of the dreadful scenes of St Domingo [i.e., the Haitian revolution]."

W. E. B. Du Bois[1]

From 1910 to the mid-1930s, Du Bois established himself as a powerful advocate for racial justice and cemented his scholarly reputation as a sociologist, historian, and a civil rights leader in the NAACP. During this period in his academic scholarship, he turned to writing an alternative history of the nineteenth century, *Black Reconstruction* (1935).[2] The "farrago of the French metaphysics of liberty and equality" arrived on American shores in 1865 in the aftermath of the Civil War; and it shook the foundation of the republic in the Radical Reconstruction era (1865–77). In this "farrago," Du Bois saw a new story to tell about the intersection of race and democratic development. His turn to historiography charted the historical legacy of slavery in the twentieth century and identified key goals for future social justice movements grounded in the ideal of civic enfranchisement.[3]

Du Bois described Reconstruction as a time when "all the Southern land was awakening as from some wild dream to [. . .] social revolution."[4] The legal abolition of slavery signified the dawn of an unprecedented experiment of pluralistic democracy in the New World, which for the first time brought African Americans within the rarified circle of legal citizenship. In the postbellum era, African Americans assumed public standing with an innate right to freedom, a normative status that now posed an ostensible legal constraint on the free exercise of choice by whites. However, the public transition of black public standing from property to person was never fully completed despite the passage of the 13th, 14th, and 15th Amendments, which legally emancipated black labor. Du Bois warned that a "second slavery" would soon follow. Even as legal citizens, antebellum social practices and values continued to assail blacks' newfound status as free and equal civic fellows, eventually enabling the rise of a new racial caste system, Jim Crow.

The promise of freedom has yet to be delivered. Emancipation raised a troubling question that still haunts American democracy: how can we be confident that slavery has really ended if whites refuse – and even resent – constraining their actions with the idea of black dignity and equality? In other words, the dignity and equality of non-whites is still perceived to be an illegitimate constraint on the exercise of free choice and in the public adjudication of the terms of civic fellowship.[5] This racist vision circumscribes the limits of the public moral imagination: it is hard for the nation to imagine black labor that is not coerced for the extraction of productive value. And so "the idea of a meaningless emancipation looms large for Du Bois."[6] The lingering impact of second slavery today highlights the idea that black dignity and equality still fail to function as a constraint on the institutional conditions of the productive process. In the final section of this chapter, I reflect with Du Bois on what second slavery might mean today with respect to prison labor, Walmart, and Amazon workers.

Du Bois in Harlem

The early twentieth century brought the efflorescence of black cultural expression and widespread demographic changes, as the first Great Migration swept the country. Fleeing economic stagnation and Southern lynching bees, African Americans settled in the industrial cities of the North. Du Bois himself moved with his family to New York City to assume his editorial responsibilities at the Harlem office of the NAACP, though he remained affiliated with Atlanta University. By 1910, Du Bois had given up his tenured professorship to become the NAACP's director of publicity and research. He took up residence in Harlem, the vibrant black enclave in Manhattan that would soon serve as the backdrop of the artistic and literary movement of the Harlem Renaissance. In 1928, his daughter Yolande married the premier poet of the Harlem Renaissance, Countee Cullen. A lavish wedding party was thrown in Harlem.[7]

Living in New York City, Du Bois edited the NAACP's monthly magazine *The Crisis* from 1910 to 1934. His editorial position gave him considerable authority over the public image of the organization. Under his editorship, at its height, the magazine reached a circulation of nearly 100,000 in the years preceding the Great Depression.[8] On the heels of the Great Depression and the October Revolution in the Soviet

Union, a different kind of social phenomenon would sweep through the streets of Harlem, one that rattled Du Bois and became the object of his scorn in *The Crisis*: the Jamaican black nationalist Marcus Garvey. In the spirit of his debate with Washington a decade earlier, Du Bois did not shy away from a public confrontation with an influential figure.

Garvey gained a massive following in the 1920s. Hailed as a "black Moses" who would bring the black working poor to the Promised Land, he presided over celebratory parades in Harlem to mark a new epoch in black history. Converging with the aesthetic philosophy of the Harlem Renaissance, Garveyism hailed the emergence of a "New Negro" who was the master of his own economic fate. He advocated black racial unity and repatriation to continental Africa to escape Jim Crow America. Under the slogan of "Africa for the Africans," he financed a project to operate a line of steamships sailing from New York City to Liberia, returning African Americans to their ancestral homeland. The Black Star Line steamship company never launched a single ship and was plagued by problems of graft and fraud, for which Garvey would eventually serve three years in prison. Garvey also founded the Universal Negro Improvement Association (UNIA) in 1914, an organization that he hoped would establish black economic self-reliance and global pan-African hegemony.[9] Akin to Washington's National Negro Business League, the UNIA formed the Negro Factories Corporation to generate black wealth; it ran grocery stores, savings banks, laundries, and factories. Popular with the working poor, it employed and sold goods and services exclusively in segregated black neighborhoods.[10] Garvey's leadership captured the hope that black pride and economic self-reliance would free African Americans from racial terror and economic insecurity.

Many commentators, including Du Bois, observed that

Garvey's vision of a black utopia morphed into racial chauvinism that advanced a racial separatism that in the end would hurt, rather than aid, the black working poor. First, the failed steamship company lost investments from financially strapped backers and undermined the economic well-being of the most vulnerable members of the African-American community who had supported the project. Second, Garvey, like Washington before him, teetered towards accommodating white nationalism and attacked the NAACP for being liberal hacks. Garvey embraced the idea of "racial purity" that, paradoxically, aligned him with the Ku Klux Klan.[11] Du Bois denounced Garvey's meeting with Ku Klux Klan leaders in 1922.[12] With the KKK, Garvey supported anti-miscegenation and segregation laws. For both parties had *agreed* that people of color simply had *no future* in the United States. Hence the continents of North America and Europe are *for* white people, while Africa is *for* African and Afro-descendant people. For Du Bois, racial separatism – however prudent and necessary at times for black survival – when taken to the extreme inadvertently reconsolidates whites' monopoly on political power and suggests that racial justice is impossible. In effect, Garvey rendered the US government the "proper" object of control just for white people, a line Du Bois refused to endorse. Du Bois rejected the notion that whiteness was a prerequisite for membership in the American polity or American civic identity, however suppressed the ideal of black civic enfranchisement might appear in dark times.[13]

Second slavery and democratic theory

A legitimation crisis in the postbellum United States

Perhaps it is no surprise, then, that during this period Du Bois turned to undertake a revisionist historiography of the nineteenth century to retrieve the viability of the ideal of black civic enfranchisement and to outline key goals for future racial justice movements. Namely, genuine interracial civic fellowship could restructure American political and civil life, including the conditions of labor and love through interracial social cooperation. Indeed, the unprecedented gains of Reconstruction proved that such changes were still possible because they had happened before. History could help define the goals of a struggle for racial justice and show why even in the darkest of times hope is not lost in the uncertain and indefinite transition to freedom.

The abolition of slavery created a legitimation crisis in the postbellum United States that elicited the urgent call for the democratic reconstitution of major civil, economic, and political institutions. Institutions that were once taken to be legitimate – and beyond the realm of public intervention – betrayed their instrumental role in the domination of black persons and invited doubt about their normative authority in the public sphere:

> The true significance of slavery in the United States to the whole social development of America lay in the ultimate relation of slaves to democracy. What were to be the limits of democratic control in the United States? If all labor, black as well as white, became free – were given schools and the right to vote – what control could or should be set to the power and action of these laborers? Was the rule of the mass of Americans to be unlimited, and the right to rule extended to all men regardless of race and color, or if not, what power of dictatorship would rule; and how would property and privilege be protected? This was the great and primary question which was in the minds of the men who wrote the Constitution of the United States and continued in the minds of thinkers down through the slavery

controversy. It still remains with the world as the problem of democracy expands and touches all races and nations.[14]

Black participation in mainstream political channels threw modern American society into a new critical light which Du Bois referred to as "second sight." If ex-slaves were to join American society as equals, then major institutions would have to meet their emancipatory aspirations. For institutions lacked political legitimacy without the consent of the people, which now included ex-slaves. Antebellum America was founded and developed without reference to the critical autonomous judgment of black (and brown) folk. "Blacks formed no part of the 'imagined community' of Jefferson's republic."[15] In other words, were African Americans to enter the polity as free and equal legal citizens, not only must the federal government change its laws, but it must also reorganize civil society and industry, which had never before accommodated a free black labor force with state-backed political power.

Du Bois formulated the concept of second slavery to sketch a *normative standard* to judge the extent to which postbellum America welcomed ex-slaves into the polity under the moral auspices of free and equal citizenship; legal citizenship was a formal platform for recognizing their public normative authority to transform society as civic fellows.[16] Free black labor posed not just a technical problem about employment and housing. A feudal agrarian political economy, controlled by a slavocracy, had hitherto preserved the institutional conditions of black labor in the service of white power. The normative question of what kind of institutional transformations it would take to truly welcome ex-slaves into the polity is open ended and unresolved. The answer must lie in a democratic procedure that mitigates the circumstances of the worst off, responding to their claims of collective self-determination.[17] The concept of second slavery thus demonstrates that Du Bois considered emancipation both an unprecedented "social revolution" and an ongoing democratic process that has yet to be completed and guided to its fullest expression.[18]

Du Bois's philosophy of the modern American state

Du Bois advanced the concept of second slavery to reconceptualize modern freedom – or, "modernity in black" – through the principle of democratic self-determination.[19] Inasmuch as the system of slavery entailed an enslaved person's systematic subordination to the will of a master (and their white affiliates in a slavocracy), emancipation should secure the power to direct one's affairs without arbitrary interference.[20] Second slavery, instead, indicates that your political and economic fortunes are not subject to your democratic control or political influence. In contrast, positive power should be grounded in the public recognition of African Americans as free and equal persons with meaningful political power. Thus the ratification of citizenship by birthright in the Reconstruction Amendments is born of the abolition of slavery.[21] The prospect of black persons joining the modern American state as free and equal citizens is an *essential* component of "modernity in black." In the Americas, race determines – perhaps even unilaterally – who stands in or outside the circle of citizenship. The historian Martha Jones formulates the problem of citizenship as "the thorny problem of who belongs and by what terms."[22] The idea of free and equal citizenship for all must then constrain democratic will formation to delegitimize racist laws and public policies.

Du Bois's historiography of Reconstruction rejected white revisionist histories that black participation in federal government was an unmitigated catastrophe. The Reconstruction era set a precedent for an explosion of black participation in government that has seldom been matched since.[23] As news of the Haitian revolution arrived on American shores, US politicians worried that "too much of this newfangled French philosophy of 'liberty and equality' had found its way among them [the enslaved and free Blacks in the North]."[24] Du Bois noted their paradoxical worry that slaves might imagine themselves entitled to "French liberty," as had American revolutionaries against British occupation. (American revolutionaries invoked the notion of their "enslavement" to British colonial rule to stoke support for the Revolutionary War.)[25] The influence of the Haitian revolution on the abolition movement helped push African Americans into the circle of citizenship. "The wild revolt of despised slaves, the rise of a noble black leader, and the birth of a new nation of Negro freemen," observed Du Bois, "frightened the pro-slavery advocates and armed the anti-slavery agitation."[26] To the shock of the pro-slavery establishment, the modern American constitutional state became the vehicle of black emancipation:

> The first great goal of anti-slavery effort in the United States had been, since the [American] Revolution, the suppression of the slave-trade by national law. It would hardly be too much to say that the Haitian revolution, in addition to its influence in the years from 1791 to 1806, was one of the main causes that rendered the accomplishment of this aim possible at the earliest constitutional moment. To the great influence of the fears of the South was added the failure of the French designs on Louisiana, of which Toussaint L'Ouverture was the most probable cause.[27]

The Haitian revolutionary General Toussaint Louverture brought colonial France to its knees. Du Bois denied that the Haitian revolution and Reconstruction had "ruined" democracy in the New World. In fact, slave-led efforts in the Americas *actualized* the paragon of republican liberty. To wit, the principle of universal democratic self-determination remained an "abstract" republican ideal until black historical agents disrupted the prevailing institutional order in the Americas and rooted out the central contradiction between republics' racial realities and its republican self-definition.[28] Du Bois underlined the central paradox of American modernity: the struggle for freedom is spearheaded precisely by those groups often suppressed – and invisible – in modern American society. Ironically, their political victories tend to create a more rational social order that benefits *all* persons regardless of race inasmuch as it expands the socially recognized universal rights and privileges of citizenship. Conversely, for those with a monopoly on power, freedom often entails the systematic domination of others as its institutional condition, restricting the rights and privileges of citizenship to a select few. That is, whites seek the widest scope for the "free" exercise of their choice by restricting – and even suppressing, as in the case of slavery and Jim Crow – the moral right of non-whites to democratic self-determination in political and civil life as civic fellows.

This is not to say that black civic enfranchisement did not come with bloodshed. It was not lost on Du Bois that it took a civil war – and the arming of black soldiers, no less – to crush the Confederacy.[29] Nor did he ignore the bloodshed in St Domingue. Ironically, it often takes violence to blow open the legal circle of citizenship in order to foreground the public values of liberty and equality for all in a reconstituted interracial civic community.[30] Du Bois's defense of the Haitian revolution posited a positive role for modern constitutional states in successful slave revolts. Toussaint Louverture seized political power in Haiti and founded a new republican era. *In fine*, Du Bois's philosophy of the state defends the idea that modern constitutional states should be organized *for* and *by* black people. Du Bois thus envisioned a positive role for the state to complete the process of emancipation. Once subject to democratic control of a reimagined and reconstituted people, the modern constitutional state is a legitimate public institution. If the ideal of civic enfranchisement is suppressed, violence will break out to retrieve it.

American *Sittlichkeit*, or the modern state *in concreto*

For the remainder of the chapter, I revisit the ideal of civic enfranchisement and how it might deliver substantive freedom rather than mere formal or abstract legal standing in the transition of black standing from property to person in the postbellum United States. The Reconstruction Amendments failed to guide the reorganization of civil society to complete the transition from feudal agrarianism to a "free" labor society. Constitutional norms *underdetermine* the concrete public policies and initiatives that might advance substantive civic equality. Recall that for Du Bois civic enfranchisement is not reducible to legal enfranchisement inasmuch as it aims to build interracial social relations outside of the state and foster a substantive shared conception of the common good, such that each person recognizes the freedom of their civic fellows as the condition for their own freedom. I now turn to Hegel's philosophy of right to map with Du Bois a more substantive model of civic enfranchisement in the form of expansive participation in a social whole.

As I've already noted, the influence of Hegel's thought on Du Bois is a point of contention, with some scholars speculating about the usefulness of even making the comparison.

There are two dominant trends for establishing the Du Bois–Hegel connection, both of which I find lacking. In seeking to recover the integrity of black political thought, Adolph Reed rejects linking Du Bois to Hegel. He considers such a move an attempt to vindicate black thought by demonstrating its suitability for inclusion in the European philosophical canon.[31] Reed contends that one should instead interpret Du Bois's writing as a "historical artifact" whose relevance is determined by the sociohistorical *problématique* that frames his inquiry.[32] Unfortunately, Reed's view further isolates Du Bois's critique of nineteenth-century American society from philosophical debates about the nature of modern freedom. Moreover, historians agree that Du Bois's *problématique* engages Hegel's practical philosophy, such that at least some of his normative commitments share a Hegelian conception of modernity.[33]

Unlike Reed, Shamoon Zamir argues the Du Bois–Hegel connection is a promising avenue of research.[34] He focuses on the master–slave dialectic that Hegel outlines in the *Phenomenology of Spirit* in order to assess Du Bois's notion of double consciousness. Zamir argues that Hegel's master–slave dialectic models the relations between black and non-black citizens in the Jim Crow South and shows how racist judgment inhibits the flourishing of denigrated racial groups. As I will explore at greater length in chapter 7, double consciousness is "this sense of always looking at one's self through the eyes of others, of measuring one's soul by the tape of a world that looks on in amused contempt and pity."[35] If one belongs to a denigrated racial group, one is compelled to assume an objectifying, third-person stance on one's own self. The hostile white gaze is rendered the "measure" of the black "soul," against which a black person struggles to affirm a positive sense of self-worth.[36]

I am sympathetic with Zamir's account to the extent that

it highlights the importance of interracial social cooperation in a social whole. Overcoming double consciousness requires reconciliation with the will of one's fellow citizens without forgoing – indeed, by asserting – one's normative status as a "co-worker in the kingdom of culture."[37] However, I reject the master–slave dialectic for assessing racial exclusion and misrecognition. The master–slave dialectic cannot illustrate the structural conditions necessary for the successful self-determination of all as a black historical achievement in the wake of the Civil War.[38] On my view, the linchpin of Du Bois's political thought is his defense of the civic enfranchisement of former slaves as moral equals in the American civic community. Unlike his republican predecessor Frederick Douglass, who considered legal abolition to mark complete freedom for newly emancipated slaves, Du Bois stressed positive institutional conditions for integrating black freedmen into social, economic, and political life. In *The Souls of Black Folk* (1903) and in *Black Reconstruction* (1935), he pointed to the family, the conditions of free black labor in civil society, and former slaves' relation to the federal government. Taken together, the democratic reconstitution of this tripartite framework articulates the ideal institutional conditions of black civic enfranchisement. Du Bois's political thought thus asserts that inclusion in the basic structure of American society is crucial for advancing the promise of freedom for former slaves. A Hegelian conception of ethical community in a modern state (*Sittlichkeit*) allows us to rethink, with Du Bois, the ideal of civic enfranchisement under the principle of democratic self-determination. However, Du Bois scholars have yet to note that the family, civil society, and the state are precisely the institutions that constitute Hegel's conception of ethical life. Because both Du Bois and Hegel appeal to this tripartite institutional framework in their political philosophies, it is instructive to read them together on this point. It clarifies which institutions have historically played an important role in the black struggle for freedom and conveys its emancipatory potential for orienting future racial justice movements.

I restrict my analysis of the Du Bois–Hegel connection to the historical period of Radical Reconstruction in the United States. Before delving into the Du Bois–Hegel connection, I would like to note that my analysis does not rest on the philological question of whether or not Du Bois was thinking of Hegel's *Philosophy of Right* in developing his critique of Reconstruction, although historians confirm Du Bois's study of Hegel. Be that as it may, exploring the Du Bois–Hegel connection does not require ascribing to Du Bois a "conscious" or "unconscious" adoption of Hegel in his political critique. Rather, I aim to justify the institutions of the black family (as a sphere of freely chosen and expressed intimacy), dignified black labor, and the racially inclusive modern American state as crucial in advancing the struggle for black freedom and therefore establish that these institutions are essential features in the historical articulation of the concept of modern freedom in the United States.

Public reason in the circle of citizenship: on the self-conscious development of institutional rationality

Du Bois and Hegel both employ a philosophical methodology that responds to history, albeit they write in different historical contexts. Hegel developed his model of ethical life in the context of the Prussian empire. His formulation of the ideals of ethical life is oriented towards modern European history, offering an anti-democratic and Eurocentric defense of constitutional monarchy. He rationalizes the exclusion of significant sections of the population from government and public life.[39] Du Bois's political thought, on the contrary, defends universal civic enfranchisement on a democratic basis. Because Du Bois's notion of development has a democratic basis, he supports ordinary citizens' *self-conscious* collective judgment, grounded in the public values of freedom and equality. This form of judgment expresses the political demands for inclusion of former slaves, who lobbied for the federal protection of their democratic rights, labor, and families.[40] In this section, I sketch Hegel's model of objective spirit and show that – unlike Du Bois's political thought – he describes the modern European's relation to the universal as "unconscious" (*bewußtlose*) in the context of the family and in civil society. Drawing on Du Bois, we see that the "self-conscious" ideal of civic belonging precipitates the revision of institutional rationality *in* historical time, realizing more perfectly the universal, namely the "Idea of Freedom." In Du Bois's words, public reasoning on the basis of civic fellowship "teach[es] a nation the value of its own ideals," leading to the democratic development of the postbellum United States.[41]

Hegel writes that ethical life is a "rational system of the will's determination," encompassing a constitutional monarchy, a constrained capitalist free market, and the bourgeois nuclear family informed by gender hierarchy.[42] In the realm of actualized freedom, rational principles structure modern institutions, that is, their external, given aspect comprises objective freedom. A person wills the principles expressing institutional rationality as an instance of her own self-determination. Modern ethical life operationalizes the rights of moral subjectivity that Kant prizes, but "sublates" or "raises" (*aufheben*) them through concrete social practices. By partaking in ethical life, a person acts *through* a universal that has achieved the status of a legitimate expression of practical agency inasmuch as it successfully functions as an ideal of self-governance and normative mutuality.

The norms of self-governance that organize the family and civil society are unconscious, according to Hegel. That is, through individuals' pursuits of their immediate ends and desires, the universal end is inadvertently realized within an objective rational system that mediates the development and expression of subjective particularity. As a family member, a person honors a standard of behavior that is loving, a novel achievement for relations of mutual recognition. Historically, the institutional rationality of the family did not privilege the subjective experience of love or sexual autonomy. For moderns, however, love constitutes an essential rule for comportment qua membership in the family. There, an individual satisfies her immediate disposition towards sensuality and creates a family that is uniquely her own.[43] In the process, she alienates her immediate self-interest to constitute the shared interest of the family as a social entity, which then becomes the unified object of juridical and public respect. On Hegel's view, women's ethical personalities are identified with the family, which requires their subordination to reproductive activities in the household. Du Bois, however, defends the moral right of black families to juridical and social recognition without presupposing gender subordination to be an essential feature of intimate familial bonds. As I detail below, in the context of racial caste, the recognition of freely formed familial bonds is essential for actualizing black public standing as moral equals in the American civic community.

According to Hegel, the marriage contract is based on "the inwardness of subjective feeling," experienced by the individual as an "immediate ethical relationship."[44] The freely formed family achieves the status of "ethical substance" through the marriage contract. It then becomes an object of juridical protection and public respect, possessing "self-subsistent objective reality," which is legally recognized as a "person" with a distinct "right."[45] Hegel writes that the actual feeling of love must sustain a marriage, as there is no licit dictate that requires one to enter or remain in a loveless marriage. The crucial unconscious ethical function of the family is to prepare children to enter civil society, start their own families, and become responsible citizens.[46] In the best-case scenario, the marriage dissolves with the death of the partners who unwittingly achieve the infinite through the dignified lives of their children and the flourishing of their civic community. The family also stands as a bulwark against the chaotic forces of the free market and civil society.

Civil society is a "system of needs," where the selfish pursuit of needs simultaneously – and again, unconsciously – satisfies the needs of others through an endless series of free-market exchanges.[47] Under the influence of Adam Smith, Hegel asserts that in the institutional context of civil society individuals' pursuit of their self-interests inadvertently yields a greater good – the universal satisfaction of needs. However, aware of the dangers of capitalist free-market society, he posits state-supported, public auxiliary institutions, i.e., the Police (*Polizei*) and the Corporation (*Korporation*), to protect individuals against the chaos of a free-market economy.[48] The *Polizei* and the *Korporation* secure and actualize "the livelihood and welfare of individuals."[49] The police is "the state insofar as it relates to civil society."[50] As a public authority, it defends civil rights, private property, and social welfare; and it incorporates the universal to constrain pernicious free-market competition. The *Korporation* functions like a union or a community interest group, providing individuals with a sense of self-worth in their professional lives. The state-supported ethical integrity of civil society makes possible the economic self-determination of all, though Hegel never resolved how to maintain the ethical integrity of the capitalist economy as it splinters under competition and growing poverty.

Drawing on Du Bois's critique of Reconstruction, I offer three insights into how transformative public reasoning works to model the historical emergence of the ideal of normative mutuality in American civic life. These insights distinguish the normative character of a country and the people in it, that is, the "peculiar principle" that animates the spirit of the people, as it is objectified in public political culture. A self-conscious "substantial will" carries the historical legacy of a democratic people striving to be free.[51] For Du Bois, the aspiration to restructure modern American society tracks this form of public reasoning in the postbellum black community during Reconstruction.[52] To put it in Hegelian parlance, American *Sittlichkeit* is a historical achievement of spirit that distinguishes our specific capacity as Americans to respond to, and create, social institutions which, taken collectively, show Americans – and African Americans in particular – valuing universal freedom and equality as the object and product of the self-conscious substantial will.

To be clear, I am not interested in providing an account of ethical life that invokes what Ludwig Siep describes as "a strong identity of the spirit of the people" or Charles Taylor's communitarian conception of the good.[53] The appeal to the "strong identity" of a people does not demonstrate the normative significance of civic belonging as a historical achievement of spirit. As a historical achievement, spirit motivates praxis from One to Some to All acting under the idea of freedom. In other words, a sense of strong identity can just as well undermine as advance the prospect of all acting under the idea of freedom. Following Du Bois, I map social values that define a civic community, for they are the basis for public reasoning that impels the progressive transformation of American society.

Radical Reconstruction (1865–77): on the self-conscious development of institutional rationality in the postbellum United States

"The true significance of slavery in the United States to the whole social development of America lay in the relation of slaves to democracy."[54] In order to deliver this promise of emancipation, we must appreciate how slavery arrested the institutional rationality of antebellum American society and, in turn, public reason on the basis of civic fellowship advanced the institutional conditions of love and labor. The norms of romantic love and self-standing labor in public reason emerged as prominent social values guiding the democratic reconstitution of civil society. For Du Bois, the emergence of American modernity is spearheaded by, on the one hand, a people just emerging from slavery; and, on the other hand, it implicates a republic hostile or indifferent to the public values it proclaims in principle but imperfectly realizes in practice. He contended that black freedmen spurred America's "first blossoming into the modern age," where "human freedom would release the human spirit [...] and set it free to dream and sing."[55] "America thus stepped forward," he continued, "and added to the Art of Beauty, gift of the Renaissance, and to Freedom of Belief [...] a vision of democratic self-government: the domination of political life by the intelligent decision of free and self-sustaining men."[56]

On the family

Du Bois articulated the ethical significance of the family as a social institution and black freedmen's subjective particularity, expressed in the "freedom to love."[57] Since Du Bois, a rich literature has emerged about the black family in relation to the history of slavery.[58] In my remarks, I merely point out that Du Bois invoked the right of the black family against externality, which imposed a duty on the social world while reflecting freedmen's affective desire to reconstitute their families in the wake of the Civil War.[59] Unlike Hegel, Du Bois defended the expression of desire, sexual autonomy, and the enforcement of custodial rights without presupposing gender hierarchy. He rejects gender subordination for the internal organization of family life, though the transition from property to person incorporates black Americans' right to enter a legal marriage contract, if they so choose. As Lawrie Balfour points out, "Rather than arguing that black women, too, should be enthroned as queens of a tightly domestic sphere, he defends the importance of sexual freedom for any meaningful conception of women as free citizens."[60] In realizing the promise of emancipation, civic enfranchisement included the recognition of black dignity with respect to the social (and juridical) status attached to participating in freely constituted familial bonds. Du Bois thus underscored the social values motivating former slaves, which drove their claim for the social and juridical recognition of familial bonds.

Du Bois described slavery as a social system that viewed enslaved Africans as incapable of "human feelings" and of forming social bonds sustained by feelings of love.[61] In *Black Reconstruction*, he described the family unit in the antebellum period as "defenseless," highlighting its vulnerability on slave plantations.[62] Slaves "could be sold – actually sold as we sell cattle with no reference to calves or bulls, or recognition of family. It was a nasty business [b]ut it was a stark and bitter fact."[63] This is not to say that social relations among slaves did not emerge that were intimate and loving in spite of their harrowing circumstances. Rather, Du Bois accented the impact of economic markets on the social organization of slave plantations. In light of the absence of the public recognition of the rights of the family, which must be predicated on citizenship, the slave economy regularly destroyed families as family members were sold off to different owners; families were often only kept together by the capricious wishes of a slave-owner. These wishes typically asserted unbridled sexual license: women and girls were routinely purchased and kept for concubinage. Sexual slavery was enmeshed with slavery as a system for the extraction of value in productive labor. Du Bois also described the emergence of "breeding states."[64] When Congress outlawed the transatlantic slave trade in 1807, the price of slaves exponentially increased, bolstering slave-owners' economic incentive to "breed" and rape human beings.[65]

The ethical obligations generated by love were not only disrespected, but rendered criminal, as slaves often had to "steal their own bodies" to see loved ones.[66] The following are some newspaper notices reporting runaway slaves that Du Bois gathered. He demonstrated the ethical importance of love whose "rights" the slavocracy refused to recognize:

Fifty Dollar Reward – Ran away from the subscriber, a Negro girl named Maria. She is of copper color, between 13 and 14 years of age – bareheaded and barefooted. She is small for her age – very sprightly and very likely. *She states she was going to see her mother in Maysville.*

Committed to jail of Madison County, a Negro woman, who calls her name Fanny, and says she belongs to William Miller, of Mobile. She formerly belonged to John Givens, of this county, *who now owns several of her children.*

Fifty Dollar Reward – Ran away from subscriber, his Negro man Pauladore, commonly called Paul. I understand Gen.

R. Y. Hayne has purchased his wife and children from
H. L. Pinckney, Esq., and has them on his plantation at
Goosecreek, where no doubt, *this fellow is frequently lurking*.[67]

With respect to the last newspaper notice, Du Bois inter-
jected that, indeed, "[o]ne can see Paul 'lurking' about his
wife and children" on the Goosecreek plantation.[68] In the
slave-owning South, the desire for a black man to see his
own family is scorned. The actual manifestation of affection
is characterized pejoratively – in this case, as "lurking." Black
people, as property, were viewed as incapable of intimacy;
the intention to act according to the ethical ideal of love was
mocked or represented as bestial and irrational. The phenomenon continued into the Jim Crow era, when family
ties were disrespected and often merited violent reprisal, as
when black mothers were lynched for defending their children against hostile whites.[69] Du Bois anticipated some of
the arguments of prominent black feminist philosophers
such as Angela Davis who explores the gendered nature of
the denigration of black familial bonds.[70] To wit, the (white)
feminist philosophy tradition often calls for (white) women
to exit from, or abolish, the family; this call contrasts with
the black historical experience, where black women demand
entry into their own families and enforcement of their custodial rights.[71] To be sure, Du Bois never extolled the cult of
motherhood. In *Darkwater*, he writes "We cannot imprison
women again in a home or require them all on pain of death
to be nurses and housekeepers."[72] In criticizing the bourgeois
family, he observed, "only at the sacrifice of intelligence and
the chance to do their best work can the majority of modern
women bear children."[73] And yet his critique of the bourgeois family also asserted that a woman "must have the right
of motherhood at her own discretion."[74] Thus he affirmed
the moral rights of freely chosen, affective familial bonds,

while rejecting the inegalitarian structure of bourgeois family life. With the end of the Civil War, Du Bois noted freedmen's desperation to locate loved ones, a journey that would sometimes last many years and has become a recurrent theme of modern Africana literature. The democratic reconstitution and legal recognition of the family is a key gain of Reconstruction. It attests to freedmen's resilience and desire to be truly free. As Toni Morrison in her novel *Beloved* (1987) observes, "to get a place where you could love anything you chose – not to need permission for desire – well now, *that* was freedom."[75]

On emancipated black labor

In order to render freedom "substantive" and "actual," the federal government had to facilitate the universal satisfaction of needs, addressing the needs of emancipated black labor in particular and the fair adjudication of the terms of the wage contract. Such a provision was necessary to ensure that emancipated black labor became self-standing. According to Du Bois, the federal government – through the long defunct Freedmen's Bureau – undertook the "herculean" task of "the social uplift [. . .] of four million [former] slaves to an assured and self-sustaining place in the body politic and [in the] econom[y]."[76] In particular, the polity had to recognize the social value of the free economic self-determination of black (and white) laborers. In this section, I discuss the establishment of the Freedmen's Bureau, operating from 1865 to 1872, and show how it – much like Hegel's corporations and police – functioned to preserve the ethical integrity of civil society. Guiding the Bureau's intervention were black freedmen themselves who, in asserting their civic equality, helped direct, organize, and fund the Bureau's activities.[77]

Because freedmen "didn't even own the rags on their

backs," Du Bois claimed that federal intervention in civil
society had to disrupt the antebellum racial caste system and
secure the institutional conditions of dignified black labor.[78]
He asserted that the Bureau was an indispensable institution for the satisfaction of black labor's interests and those of
white refugees of the Civil War.[79] The Bureau administered
the transition from the "feudal agrarianism [of the slavoc-
racy] to modern farming and industry [of post-Emancipation]
civil freedom."[80] "An instrument of social regeneration,"
the Bureau was designed to make emancipated labor "self-
supporting."[81] He stressed that without economic rights the
black community would remain "enslaved in all but name."[82]
With emancipation, for the first time, black people in the
South assumed the social identity of civilian laborers and
became *legally entitled* to *payment* for their work and a wage
contract – a transition that the Freedmen's Bureau over-
saw. Their social identity as a civilian labor force was often
resented by white proprietors. Each dollar paid to a black
laborer was a dollar *fleeced* from the white community. To
suppose that black labor is free to choose its own ends and
becomes self-supporting was anathema.[83]

Without federal intervention, the occupations widely available to black laborers in the postbellum period were often
limited to farming, vocational and unskilled labor, and the
service industry. Such occupations facilitated the unbridled
economic exploitation and bolstered stereotypes about black
intelligence and talent that first emerged in the antebellum
period on slave plantations. African Americans thus remained
stigmatized by popular conceptions about one's "proper"
place in American society. The principle of fair equality of
opportunity required fighting against racist convictions about
the forms of employment that were considered "appropriate" for former slaves and their descendants.[84] That a black
laborer was even free to leave their place of employment to

choose a new employer worked against antebellum notions of black labor. In the absence of governmental support, black freedmen had limited access to the ballot, education, and fair employment opportunities.

According to Du Bois, in such circumstances it becomes the responsibility of the state to make economic rights "substantive" and "actual" for laborers.[85] Without federal support, freedmen's standing as rights bearers remained formal. They were subjected to the unrestrained interference of white proprietors, who exerted "a determined effort to reduce black labor as nearly as possible to a condition of unlimited exploitation and build a new class of capitalists on this foundation. The wage of the Negro worker [...] was to be reduced to the level of bare subsistence by taxation, peonage, caste and every method of discrimination."[86] To prevent this, through the Freedmen's Bureau, "the United States government assumed charge of the emancipated [slave] as the ward of the nation."[87] Countering "practical re-enslavement," the Bureau created the "social conditions" for "the improvement, protection, and employment of refugee freedmen, as well as for their "general welfare."[88] In his view, the Bureau was "the most extraordinary and far-reaching institution of social uplift that America has ever attempted."[89]

Du Bois asserted that the Bureau's primary responsibility was to "see that freedmen were free to choose their employers and help mak[e] fair contracts for them."[90] Pro-slavery politicians complained that the abolition of slavery was an "unconstitutional" intervention in states' rights.[91] The federal oversight of the institutional conditions of free labor stipulated the following: no beating, harassment, or intimidation in the workplace; white employers must *pay* black workers without withholding earnings; black labor has the right to *choose* employers and *leave* offices of employment at will without being forced to labor under any condition not of their choosing; black labor was *entitled* to and *received* judicial standing in civil courts, including the right to *sue* former employers; and *all* wages were taxed.[92] With tax monies, a public school system was established for the first time in the South.[93] The Freedmen's Bureau thus subordinated the accumulation of capital to the needs of labor.[94] One Southern politician at the time complained with respect to the federal government's efforts, "That is more than we do for white men!"[95]

The complaint ignored the political reality: white refugees of the Civil War received aid and support from the Bureau as well.[96] Although the Reconstruction Amendments aimed to ease the plight of black freedmen, the Bureau also helped poor whites who lacked adequate access to basic resources and were excluded from meaningful job opportunities. Moreover, it compelled their cooperation with, and the expression of goodwill towards, black laborers. The Bureau, nonetheless, was perceived as an intrusion into Southern plutocracy for the exclusive benefit of black persons. Resistance to the Freedmen's Bureau Bill was exemplified by President Andrew Johnson (in office 1865–9), who declared that it was unconstitutional, unnecessary, and extra-juridical and suppressed the rights of "all citizens." In other words, an organization that protected against wage theft, fought for fair wage contracts, secured black property rights, and advocated interracial social cooperation was perceived as *infringing upon* whites' civil rights.[97] Du Bois responded that historical conditions required securing the ethical integrity of civil society as a system for the universal satisfaction of needs. "The [US] government must have [the] power to do what manifestly must be done."[98] He posited: the right to a fair wage should be a privilege of American citizenship as such, white or black, and must therefore be protected by the modern American state.[99]

The backlash against the expansion of federal power to protect civilian labor and social welfare led to the dismantling of the Freedmen's Bureau. As the backlash prevailed, economic rights were left unprotected. A racial caste system was reaffirmed and interracial social cooperation in any sphere became increasingly rare. With the dismantling of the Freedmen's Bureau, states passed the Black Codes and endorsed the ascendancy of the Ku Klux Klan. Poor whites reasserted the privilege and license of racial whiteness in the rise of Jim Crow. But they lost the opportunity to exercise meaningful economic rights, which is only possible through a cooperative alliance with non-white labor.

Why Du Bois is neither an elitist nor an assimilationist

I have argued that Du Bois's critique of Reconstruction illustrates that American *Sittlichkeit* transforms, as black freedmen asserted – and redefined – the term of American civic belonging. Public reasoning affirmed the social values of racial plurality, love, and self-standing labor and functioned as the normative basis for the critique of the postbellum United States. As a result, the federal government administered justice with respect to the institutional conditions of love and of labor for black freedmen and white refugees of the Civil War. Du Bois identified the development of American modernity with the reconstitution of the black family, civil society, and the federal state, with black freedmen playing a central role. Black freedmen publicly assumed social identities as family members and civilian laborers, demanding the recognition of their families and labor, as well as basic civil and political rights. Each of these components is necessary and, for Du Bois, form an interlocking system that is the institutional basis of universal civic enfranchisement. In this regard, the Hegelian-inflected conception of ethical life is normatively gripping for his critique of Reconstruction. He thus held that freedmen were responsible for America's "first blossoming into the modern age."[100]

By way of concluding, I would like to address two objections to my presentation of Du Bois's critique of Reconstruction. First, one might object that I have only restated a long-standing consensus that Du Bois is an assimilationist. Second, the objection might continue, Reconstruction failed, so why invoke democratic self-determination through the modern American state, which does not have a good record of protecting black interests? With respect to the first objection, I submit that Du Bois's guarded affirmation of modern American society does not warrant his long-standing reputation as an elitist snob or an assimilationist with regard to "the constitutive norms of modernity."[101] Strictly speaking, one cannot "assimilate" to the norms of modernity, if one conceives modernity as the emergence of the institutional conditions of democratic self-determination. In presenting the Hegelian dimension of his critique of Reconstruction, I have stressed the normative basis of black agency, which served as the impetus for the development of the American republic during a major episode of American history. In a time of crisis, with the breakdown of intersubjective relations of recognition, new social values must achieve the status of institutional norms to guide anew institutional rationality. The emergence of new institutional norms results from conflict; and conflict is often racial in character in the United States. The struggle for which norm should count as rationally obligatory for all diagnoses a crisis, but it also paves the way forward for a more integrated and rational social whole. The uncharitable label of assimilationist thus distorts Du Bois's view of the relation of slaves to American democracy. Former slaves were not judging *themselves* unworthy in light of democratic ideals. Rather, they judged the polity as *falling short of its own ideals*, which were accepted in principle but seldom realized in practice.

With respect to the second objection, given his emphasis on the state-supported transition of black chattel slavery to free labor, Du Bois shifted responsibility for the ultimate failure of Reconstruction onto the shoulders of the federal government. He maintained that, *ideally*, the state ought to have alleviated the burden placed on disenfranchised American citizens. Unlike most of his contemporaries, he did not blame black historical actors for a lack of resourcefulness and democratic literacy for the failure of Reconstruction. Instead, he observed that once the federal government withdrew its support of the Reconstruction policies and defunded the Freedmen's Bureau, which Du Bois believed should have been made a permanent federal institution, "At least eight million Negroes [were] left without effective voice in government, naked to the worst elements of the community."[102] Though he never called for the reestablishment of the Freedmen's Bureau, he continued to call for the realization of the full value of the promise of civic equality. My account of Du Bois's political thought establishes that future racial justice movements remain *justified* in appealing to the social values of love and self-standing labor to guide the substantive meaning of civic enfranchisement.

Finally, although hostile reactionary forces prevailed with the dismantling of Reconstruction policies, Du Bois emphasized the importance of appreciating the political gains of the period. "The attempt to make black men American citizens was in a certain sense a failure, but a splendid failure."[103] He added that the "rebuilding" of American democracy, "whether it comes now or a century later, will and must go back to the basic principles of Reconstruction."[104] There is therefore much that philosophers and the American public alike have to learn from Du Bois's critique of Reconstruction, which shows the challenges and the triumphs of creating a democratic society that is truly free and equal for all.

The contemporary implications of a "second slavery"

Since Reconstruction, the federal government has left laborers unprotected against the vagaries of the free market. The idea of the dignity of labor has hardly functioned as a constraint on the institutional conditions of labor from the twentieth century till today. After the Civil War, the federal government has made few attempts to recreate a *racially* inclusive social safety net for laborers. Though the New Deal created some relief for labor after the Great Depression, its social welfare policies did not benefit the majority of black, brown, and migrant laborers, whose predominant occupations as farmers and domestic workers were excluded from federal qualification guidelines.[105] Du Bois still welcomed the New Deal, citing the need for the federal government to control the free market:

> It seems to me that the Roosevelt administration [1933–45] has recognized that unless capitalism [. . .] is more and more curbed by government action in the interest of the consumer, that private initiative will disappear. [. . .] I, therefore, see Mr. Roosevelt as the distinct champion of the man who has an income sufficient for decent living and can exercise his freedom to work, think and dream as he will, uncoerced by hunger and threat of unemployment.[106]

Be that as it may, powerful private interests have gradually destroyed the social welfare state in the last fifty years.

Industry, commercial banks, and corporations are hardly regulated or taxed. Social security and Medicaid benefits established under the Great Society programs of the New Deal are under the ax.[107] During the Clinton administration, a democrat imposed draconian work measures on welfare recipients, dropping the eligibility rates and real benefits of the program.[108] Poverty in the United States grew exponentially. Income inequality has reached its highest level since the Census Bureau began tracking the data fifty years ago.[109] For a child born into poverty today, chances are they will never escape their economic bracket as adults.[110] Of my five siblings, three were able to pay for and finish college; two, including myself, entered the middle class. A class caste system is firmly in place that locks millions of Americans into soul-crushing poverty.

These economic trends are compounded by the racial realities of the market. Lack of federal oversight has had a particularly devastating impact on black, Latinx, Asian-American, and immigrant laborers, who are more likely to be poor and underpaid. According to the 2018 census, one in eight Americans lives below the official poverty line – US$25,465 for a family of four. At 20.8%, the black poverty rate is more than double the white poverty rate (10.1%); 45.8% of young black children (under age six) live in poverty, compared to 14.5% of white children.[111] A capitalist political economy trends towards lowering the remunerative value of labor for increased profits, but this general trend leaves black and brown laborers especially vulnerable to poverty, un- and underemployment, and exploitation. For workers of color still lack *social recognition* as equal persons (or civic fellows) entitled to become self-standing laborers in the first place; and this misrecognition, in turn, translates to worse pay and working conditions and occupational segregation. To be sure, in terms of absolute numbers, whites far outpace the absolute number of Americans living in poverty today. According to 2017 national averages, there were seventeen million whites living below the poverty line, compared to nine million African Americans.[112] Yet since the attack on the welfare state began in the 1970s, the racialized and stigmatized image of the welfare recipient has made a lasting impression on the American public. During his 1976 presidential campaign, Ronald Reagan had invoked the myth of the black "welfare queen" buying a Cadillac with government checks as a pretext to roll back the social safety net, plummeting poor whites into deep poverty as collateral damage.[113]

In thinking with Du Bois about the concept of second slavery, my goal is not to make overgeneralizations about the politics of race and labor today. Rather, it is to show that the racially denigrating social values that first emerged in the antebellum period still influence the organization of labor markets and the de facto scales of wage rates. As Lebron aptly puts it, in understanding "socially embedded" racist values that result in racist misrecognition of the value of productive labor, "we get a clearer, theoretically valuable picture of institutional recalcitrance, as well as a nuanced understanding of how racial norms transmitted over time distinctly serve to mark out social spaces and the normative values accorded those spaces."[114] The afterlife of slavery has at least two important implications for the politics of race and labor today with respect to prison labor and Walmart and Amazon workers.[115]

Mass incarceration and prison labor

In her acclaimed book, *The New Jim Crow*, Michelle Alexander details the explosive growth of the prison system in the United States in the aftermath of Jim Crow.

More African American adults are under correctional control today – in prison or jail, on probation or parole – than were enslaved in 1850, a decade before the Civil War began. The mass incarceration of people of color is a big part of the reason that a black child born today is less likely to be raised by both parents than a black child born during slavery.[116]

Alexander sketches the consequences of mass incarceration on black men's life prospects:

More black men are disenfranchised today than at any other moment in our nation's history. More are disenfranchised today than in 1870, the year the fifteenth amendment was ratified prohibiting laws that explicitly deny the right to vote on the basis of race. Young black men today may be just as likely to suffer discrimination in employment, housing, public benefits, and jury service as a black man in the Jim Crow era – discrimination that is perfectly legal because it is based on one's prison record.[117]

Mass incarceration in the United States provides a legal cover for the systematic disenfranchisement of black and brown Americans, resulting in a racialized loss of rights comparable to the de jure racial caste systems of the past. The United States leads the world in incarcerating its population, but African Americans are five times more likely to be incarcerated in state prisons than whites; in twelve states *more than half* of the prison population is black.[118] Racialized assumptions about criminality funnel people of color into prisons at an extremely high rate, and there they endure literal bondage in forced prison labor. The sole exception to the Thirteenth Amendment that outlawed involuntary servitude is imprisonment. The prison system provides perhaps the most evocative illustration of the racial reality of a "second slavery" today.

The prison system dramatically influences the overall institutional conditions of black labor, inside and outside of prisons. Outside of prison, formerly incarcerated persons are hyper-exploited through low wages, un- and underemployment, and suffer legalized exclusion from formal job markets and the voting franchise. In prison, the institutional conditions of labor are de jure slavery. Not only has the federal government failed to provide a racially inclusive social safety net to protect laborers. As in the antebellum period, it facilitates literal black re-enslavement through a booming for-profit prison industry. In the postbellum era, in the country's first "prison boom," the federal government coerced disproportionately black prison laborers for public works projects and "leased" prisoners to "the highest private bidder."[119] The rise of private prisons today has made mass incarceration into big business, parasitic on taxpayer dollars, with a financial interest to imprison more and more people.[120]

Transnational corporations exploit the burgeoning for-profit prison system for free or almost free labor – housed, clothed, and fed by tax dollars. Through modern-day slavery of prison labor, the state is in effect subsidizing private corporations. Today in the United States, prison labor produces commodities and services, including furniture, license plates, jeans, the American flag, and Victoria Secret lingerie; prisoners fight wildfires in California and pack Starbucks coffee into paper bags in Washington, often for just a few cents an hour.[121] Undoubtedly, the politics of race serves to cloak and legitimize these labor practices, which align with the antebellum conviction that "the slave plantations of the American South were no worse than the industrial factories of the North."[122] That is, white capitalists assert their prerogative to exploit a racial caste system to their advantage, except now they use the state as the principal means to warehouse defenseless laborers "naked to the worst elements" of the market and civil society.[123]

To be sure, racial caste is not merely an instrument of profit; it is driven by the sustained misrecognition and marginalization of people of color as moral equals and civic fellows; and this racist misrecognition has injurious implications apart from economic institutional arrangements. Yet sustained racial denigration enables black "re-enslavement" in civil society through their overrepresentation in the prison system. In 2018, prison laborers in seventeen states went on strike to end their modern-day slavery, holding work stoppages and hunger strikes to raise awareness about their working conditions.[124] Stuck in an institution that disenfranchises and degrades them, prison laborers undergird our capitalist economy but are often removed from the public eye. In direct collaboration with organizers of the prison strike, the group Jailhouse Lawyers Speak issued a press release outlining key demands that pressed for the end of slave labor in prisons.[125] Without safe working conditions or medical compensation for injuries, their penitence wages do not provide enough for ex-prisoners to build a life after prison, thereby facilitating their eventual return into the devouring colossus of the prison system.

On Walmart and Amazon: the two largest employers in the private sector

Walmart today is America's largest private-sector employer, "with 1.3 million US employees – more than the population of Vermont and Wyoming combined."[126] Aggressive union-busting has stagnated the growth of wages, averaging US$11/hr. A Walmart employee as part of a family of four lives below the poverty line and qualifies for food stamps.[127] Like the prison system, Walmart leans on the state to satisfy the basic needs of their employees whose low wages aren't enough to buy enough food for their families. Though a better-paying employer than Walmart, America's second-largest employer, Amazon, has made headlines because of its poor labor conditions. The CEO of Amazon, Jeff Bezos, is the richest person *in the world*, whereas his employees suffer uncompensated workplace injuries and daily abuse. They must hit a target speed of scanning a new item every eleven seconds to meet the company quota or risk being penalized or fired.[128] Many workers are disciplined for walking too slowly across the warehouse floor to the bathroom and resort to peeing in bottles to meet corporate fulfillment demands.[129] "Seventy-four percent of workers avoid using the toilet for fear of being warned they had missed their target numbers."[130] Presumably the situation is worse for women who can't pee in a bottle.

These general trends of contemporary capitalism are exacerbated by racial caste. Of Walmart employees, 42% are people of color and 21% are black, making Walmart the largest employer of black labor outside the public sector in the United States.[131] Four out of five part-time black, Latinx, and Asian workers describe themselves as "involuntarily part-time" and therefore unable to qualify for medical benefits, pensions, or bonuses.[132] In 2001, Walmart employees filed the largest class-action lawsuit in the nation, alleging gender-based discrimination in compensation. The case is ongoing. Amazon's workforce is nearly 25% black. In Minnesota, a group of predominantly black Amazon workers protested working conditions, holding signs evoking the BLM movement: "We are humans, not robots!"[133] Like Walmart, Amazon attacks and destroys workers' efforts to unionize.

Building an interracial labor movement

Du Bois advocated that African Americans and communities of color must become self-standing laborers, "giving the Negro the right to sell his labor at a price consistent with his own welfare."[134] After the failure of Reconstruction, Du Bois imagined that the ballot would protect the interests of black labor. Black voters could then reshape the general political will for all Americans to fight inequality and poor labor conditions together. An interracial labor movement might thus become a central feature of democratic politics.[135] For this to be possible, the polity must recognize black laborers as civic fellows with equal moral value, whose concerns and interests pose a legitimate constraint for the market and civil society.

The system of racial caste, rooted in the antebellum period, persisted in denigrating the conditions and compensation of black labor; achieving true equity for all would be impossible without foregrounding the influence of racial caste in the organization of the market. The idea of second slavery thus tests the bounds of interracial civic fellowship in the labor movement. To guard against their collective exploitation, all laborers must care enough about black and brown laborers to recognize them as civic fellows and to work together to address *each aspect* of their shared economic realities. That is, white workers too would have to fight against racial disparities in the workplace, even if they, in the short term, risk losing their jobs or wages. The labor movement must include black labor, building an interracial alliance with Latinx, immigrant, and low-wage white laborers.

Unfortunately, the recent mobilization of retail and service workers has avoided focusing on the politics of race, even though people of color disproportionately fill the retail service and fast-food sectors and receive the lowest wages.

The reluctance to focus on race is a missed opportunity for building a strong interracial labor movement:

> While recent street actions by fast-food and Walmart workers have aimed to highlight industry conditions writ large, in many cities the faces of protest have been notably brown and black. Their presence reflects the disproportionate concentration of Latinos and African-Americans – about 40 percent – in entry-level retail and service jobs. In places like St. Louis, Detroit, New York and Durham, N.C., African-Americans have come to symbolize low-wage labor, a role typically filled by immigrants. Yet in contrast to campaigns for domestic workers, janitors and car *washeros* that connect workers' rights to immigrant rights, the fast-food and retail movements have shied away from a racial-justice framework. Beyond analogies to the March on Washington, speeches by civil rights leaders and Walmart worker caravans inspired by the Freedom Riders of yore, race has not been on the agenda.[136]

Without a politics of race, it is difficult to address in a concrete way the influence of racial caste in the organization of labor markets and wage compensation. Such organization also overlooks the local communities of which workers are members. The local support of communities of color can buoy the protracted struggle against the retail, service, and fast-food sectors.

Drawing on Du Bois, the activist Ebony Slaughter-Johnson writes: "'So long as the Southern white laborers could be induced to prefer poverty to equality with the Negro,' Du Bois lamented, 'a labor movement in the South [was] impossible.' Though similarly exploited by white elites, economically disenfranchised whites and blacks 'never came to see their common interest.'"[137] In other words, poor whites' historical failure to recognize their common interest with non-whites *exacerbated* their own economic insecurity. So, even in developing a labor movement that focuses on the material conditions of economic inequality, we must return to the political task of cultivating a shared sense of political fate, where every laborer comes to see that the freedom of each is the condition of the freedom of all. A shared sense of interracial civic fellowship must undergird an effective labor movement.

The power of the idea of second slavery in labor politics today is that it encourages us to remember that an obstacle to abolition was the failure of poor whites to make common cause with slaves. In *Black Reconstruction*, Du Bois noted that the institution of slavery required the allegiance of millions of poor whites who acted as an armed "police force" for slavocracy. Their purpose was "to keep Negroes in slavery and to kill the black rebel."[138] Although the system of slavery kept the vast majority of white Southerners poor, they willingly enforced it. Their version of the American dream was to own their own slaves one day. Though they were expropriated by slave-owners, they did not question the political economy of slavery.[139]

The failure to cultivate a shared sense of political destiny across the color line remains the same obstacle to the formation of a powerful labor movement today. Rather than rally together with black and brown laborers against their common exploitation through an interracial labor effort, whites often struggle to perceive the dignity of black persons as a legitimate object of their concern. Oftentimes, as a result, a reactionary ethno-nationalist politics sweeps through poor white communities to rationalize a system where the select (white) few amass boundless wealth, as if one day *they* too might join that corporate elite, a dream that racial whiteness helps make plausible. Trump's "America first" is a euphemism for "white people first." The result is more or less the same: the formation of white power movements and the demise of interracial labor movements.

The "solution" to white poverty requires a politics of race that puts whites into solidarity with black, brown, and immigrant labor and addresses racialized forms of social denigration that persist in the creation of racial disparities in the market. That is, it requires the cultivation of a sense of interracial civic fellowship in the labor movement. The upshot is that union leaders and poor, rural whites must agitate in interracial coalitions for economic justice. "But beyond all this must come the Spirit – the Will to Human Brotherhood of all Colors, Races, and Creeds," wrote Du Bois. "Perhaps the finest contribution of the current of Socialism to the world is neither its light nor its dogma, but the idea back of its one mighty word – Comrade!"[140]

6

Du Bois on Sex, Gender, and Public Childcare

Du Bois was an advocate of women's suffrage and a pioneer in the history of American feminist thought. Admittedly, he sometimes rationalized sexist ideas about sexual purity and marriage.[1] Neither his writings nor his life offer an unblemished record of feminist commitment. As an activist and scholar, Du Bois nonetheless considered gender to be central in his conception of the politics of black self-assertion. He demonstrated that gender was both a platform and an obstacle for African-American women to seize political power behind the color line. In this chapter, I show that Du Bois's contributions to American feminist thought involve his defense of (1) women's suffrage, including the right to vote for women of color, (2) women's moral right to become mothers and (3) their right to become civic leaders in segregated African-American communities, and finally (4) women's contribution to rethinking childcare as a public good, reconceived as a legitimate universal right of American citizenship.

The Du Bois household

Du Bois's checkered relationship with women has received renewed scrutiny.[2] His career was bolstered by his first wife Nina Gomer, who maintained their household, while Du Bois focused on his career and periodic dalliances. He met Gomer at Wilberforce University in Xenia, Ohio, his first job after returning from Germany. Gomer was an undergraduate student and he a professor. Evidently, dating an undergraduate student troubled neither him nor university administrators. He wrote little about Gomer and their long relationship. They were married in 1896 and remained married until her death in 1950. There is little evidence that Du Bois considered Gomer an intellectual equal or a formidable participant in the life of the mind, as he would the young women whom he later mentored and with whom he had extramarital affairs. Gomer was a housewife, solely responsible for domestic labor, including assuming primary responsibility for childcare. Her devotion to the family was the pillar on which Du Bois built his studious and self-absorbed habits. Before departing for a day's work, ever the meticulous planner, Du Bois would leave her a grocery list and an allowance, which practically amounted to housekeeping instructions for his young wife.[3]

Du Bois was no less controlling in his relationship with his daughter, Yolande. He suggested she go to college "for furnishing topics of conversation in the long years to come" in a future marriage.[4] He forced her to leave a partner whom she loved to marry the poet Countee Cullen because, in his eyes, Cullen had more social prestige and better fitted his vision of the illustrious future of black America. Their marriage was brief and unhappy. Cullen had affairs with men, having entered the marriage under pressure to conform to a narrow and

stultifying heterosexual ideal of black masculinity.[5] Yolande
eventually became a teacher, remarried, and had a daughter,
settling into a life in Baltimore that broke the suffocating con-
fines of her father's dreams for her to be the prized wife of the
black upper crust. Du Bois spent a lifetime instructing Nina
and Yolande on the virtues of marriage and domesticity, all
the while stepping outside his own marriage and neglecting
them; he would later express regret for his absence from their
lives but made no apologies for his hypocrisy.[6]

Du Bois's inegalitarian disposition towards women was also
manifest in his professional relationships. He had an uneven
record of backing black women intellectuals who were his
peers, including Jessie Fauset, Pauline Hopkins, and Anna
Julia Cooper.[7] He failed to recognize Ida B. Wells-Barnett's
critical role in the founding of the NAACP and sidelined her
from its committees, even though she had *mentored* him and
campaigned for the Anti-Lynching Bill in Congress while he
was still a student in Germany.[8] In his reportage on lynching,
he drew on Wells-Barnett's work without acknowledging
it. Yet he supported the careers of young women artists
during the Harlem Renaissance. He likely cultivated friend-
ships with young women writers, activists, and artists to have
extramarital affairs. Alas, the support of powerful men often
has this repulsive condition.

Du Bois and the women's suffrage movement

The reality of Du Bois's personal life clashes with his lifelong public advocacy for women's rights, issues, and feminist
political thought. At a time when it was still unpopular, he
was a vocal champion of women's suffrage. Many scholars
have noted that his advocacy for women's right to vote has
received comparatively little attention.[9] He wrote numerous

editorials in *The Crisis* to garner the African-American community's support for women's suffrage while also challenging the women's rights movement to represent black and brown women. The politics of race impacted the alliances that were forged and broken among suffragists. The Reconstruction amendments had limited the extension of the ballot to black men. The exclusion of women from the ballot incited white suffragists to attack black political enfranchisement. Their attack was not provoked by the fact that black women remained politically disenfranchised. Rather, white suffragists resented black men getting the right to vote before they did and took black suffrage as a *threat* to the advance of their political rights. "White suffragists argued that the principle of equal suffrage prevented them from supporting the [Reconstruction] amendments, and many turned to racist and sexist arguments to demonstrate that Black men should not be enfranchised."[10] The influential white suffragist Susan B. Anthony proclaimed that she would rather cut off her right arm than work for the black vote.[11] She kept both her arms and her distance from the African-American community. What is more, white suffragettes prodded white men to join them in targeting black enfranchisement as anti-woman.

This early phase of the women's suffrage movement deeply alienated the African-American community and left a rift between black and white suffragists. After the dismantling of Reconstruction policies, the rift intensified as white suffragists pursued "the Southern Strategy." In return for the South's backing of women's suffrage, white suffragists condoned the rise of de jure racial segregation. Some Southern white women entered the struggle for the ballot just to have legal protection against the perceived menace of black criminals and rapists, thus aligning themselves with the scourge of lynching as a means to promote their political power.[12] Some white women joined the suffrage movement just to have the chance to elect white supremacist ideologues. Women's struggle for political power sometimes functioned as a white-power movement.

In the context of this tense and toxic political scene, Du Bois strove to include African-American communities in the fight for women's suffrage by affirming black women as equal citizens. He asserted that their inclusion was pivotal for the success of the movement in that it built a broad-based interracial coalition for women's suffrage that was impossible for the federal government to ignore.[13] In particular, he empowered black women's voices in *The Crisis*, which "published many articles by women, about women, and about women's issues. [. . .] In doing so, Du Bois provided a national platform to highlight the work of Black women suffragists and Black women throughout his tenure as editor."[14] Once women got the right to vote with the passage of the Nineteenth Amendment in 1920, he remained engaged with feminist political thought as he had throughout his career. An original feature of his feminist thought was reimagining the democratic agency of black women in the fight against the color line, often in innovative ways.

Right to motherhood outside the nuclear family

The task of achieving the civic equality of black women as free and equal American citizens, for Du Bois, opened new avenues for feminist theorizing. Lawrie Balfour explores the power of Du Bois's feminist thought in his essay, "The Damnation of Women," published in 1910 in *Darkwater*.[15] In imagining black women as free and equal citizens, Du Bois articulated in "Damnation" their historical experiences and needs, which were often sidelined in the predominantly white women's movement. The history of slavery, in particular, looms large in his account of the intersection of the politics of race and gender: "The crushing weight of slavery fell on black women. Under it there was no legal marriage, no legal family, no legal control over children."[16] As we've seen in the previous chapter, the legal recognition of the black family, in part, marked the "revolutionary refounding" of the republic in the aftermath of the Civil War. Yet Du Bois had an expansive conception of sexual freedom in the light of the history of the violent sexual abuse of black women, foregrounding their institutionalized rape on slave plantations. He noted that he "will never forgive [the South's] wanton and continued and persistent insulting of the black womanhood which it sought and it seeks to prostitute to its lust."[17] Just as he upheld the legal recognition of marriage and parental rights, he also asserted the moral right of motherhood *outside* of marriage and of the heterosexual ideal of the nuclear family.[18]

In *Darkwater*, his rendering of the politics of self-assertion continued to affirm that the love and intimacy that sustain black familial bonds is a key feature of the exercise of black practical agency and should be nurtured, even if it does not conform to Puritan and bourgeois ideals of chastity before marriage. He thus defended what he called the "sex freedom" of black women "to have and raise children regardless of their marital circumstances."[19] His direct treatment of unmarried women's sexuality assailed the hypocrisy of dominant gendered norms. "All womanhood is hampered today because the world on which it is emerging is a world that tries to worship both virgins and mothers and in the end despises motherhood and despoils virgins."[20] Both married and unmarried women are undervalued as self-determining agents, whose economic health and social status is determined by their relationship with men.

Du Bois instead underlined the importance of "women

existing for themselves, [not] for men."[21] In his view, "the right of motherhood at her own discretion" is a critical way for women in general and black women in particular to assert themselves as self-determining agents: "I see more of a future promise in the betrayed girl-mothers of the black belt than in the childless wives of the white North, and I have more respect for the colored servant who yields to her frank longing for motherhood than her white sister who offers up children for clothes."[22] The refusal to strike up an economic bargain with men or to give up a "frank longing for motherhood" showcased black women's agency and resolve to control their own fate.

Du Bois's defense of the right to motherhood avoided upholding the cult of domesticity that locks women into the household and disables their pursuit of labor and a public life. Women must have the power to assert themselves, as mothers, as participants in the labor market, and as democratic agents in the public sphere. He highlighted that most women sacrifice "their intelligence and the chance to do their best work" to become mothers.[23] The challenge of democratic politics then as now is to foreground the experiences and needs of women such that no woman is driven back into the home nor must forgo family life against her will.

The black church and women as civic leaders behind the color line

From *Souls* to *Black Reconstruction*, Du Bois defended an institution that some political philosophers might regard as an unlikely source of civic spirit: the black church.[24] As a major institution in the segregated black community in the twentieth century, he argued that the black church functioned as a "government of men" that pressed for the recognition – and the actualization – of black moral equality.[25] Under the conditions of de jure segregation, not only did it spearhead the black struggle to achieve freedom and equality but its efforts promoted the democratic development of modern American society by realizing the implicit moral principles and public values of US constitutional democracy.[26]

His comment about the church being a "government of *men*" notwithstanding, Du Bois highlighted *women*'s crucial role in the black church for cultivating habits of democratic citizenship. He thus established the centrality of black women's democratic agency as civic leaders for rethinking and advancing the ideal of civic enfranchisement. He underscored that even though they often lacked formal public recognition, their grassroots initiatives prepared a generation of black youth to assume political power under conditions of extreme duress, and he lobbied within the walls of the church for informal social welfare policies. Balfour contends that for Du Bois the normative reconstruction of the moral value of American citizenship demonstrates that black women "were critical to the development in churches of newspapers and magazines, schools at a range of academic levels, and an expansive array of social welfare programs."[27] With black women at the center of the historical reconstruction of the moral value of civic belonging, a new bundle of social goods emerges as possible rights and privileges of American citizenship.

Du Bois described the black church as a social settlement that assailed the "dead weight of social degradation" through grassroots initiatives for "social regeneration."[28] It "reproduced in microcosm, all that great world from which the Negro is cut off by color-prejudice and social condition."[29] The black church did not simply encourage democratic discussion, it actualized black moral equality through the public distribution and administration of material resources. The activities showcasing its civic function include efforts to establish and support a public school system in the South in the aftermath of Radical Reconstruction.[30] It combated illiteracy through bible circles and makeshift schoolhouses, financing schooling at all levels. It established orphanages, hospitals, and retirement homes, as well as rudimentary public programs for childcare and poverty relief. It provided meal and clothing subsidies.[31] The noted historian Evelyn Brooks Higginbotham observes that the black Baptist church conventions ran committees that issued statistical reports about children's nutrition, mortality and life expectancy rates, and the prevalence of various diseases (including an open and frank discussion of venereal disease). Additionally, it pioneered methods for teaching and rearing children.[32] The church thus shouldered the responsibility of *enacting* the privileges morally appropriate to citizenship, which the federal government did not even recognize as legitimate entitlements of citizenship, black or non-black.

Du Bois's novel account of democratic agency captures the process of how the principle of political legitimacy democratically expands the rights and privileges of citizenship, which are recognized as morally appropriate through a struggle for public legitimation. He showcases the potential moral power of democratic agents to transform the organization of the basic structure and of the federal government. He thus substantiates the idea of the democratic public sphere by framing it within the moral ideal of citizenship, which aims to institutionalize improved norms and redistribute social and political power fairly.[33] The black church's support of the democratic public sphere strives to legitimate new material resources as public goods, expanding the public infrastructure of twentieth-century American society in the process. These are developments from which *all* citizens benefit, such as the establishment of public school systems in the South, first widely championed in the postbellum black community.[34]

If my analysis is correct, then what qualifies as a material resource that should become a public good protected by justice reflects ongoing democratic contestation about what should count as a legitimate right and privilege of citizenship in the first place; and a public process articulating the full normative value of citizenship is more likely to have a fair outcome if it *foregrounds* the claims that segregated and vulnerable social groups advance in the name of civic equality.[35] In the case of Jim Crow, black women's claims had a distinct normative power to redefine the moral meaning of civic belonging because they did the difficult work of protecting the political and economic integrity of the segregated black community. Equitable integration requires, then, that the federal government *alleviate* the burden that was assumed by black women in the black church and thereby protect the economic interests and basic needs of the segregated black community, if the federal government is to fulfill its responsibility to recognize *and* actualize the moral equality of all. In other words, "The needs of African Americans ought ultimately to be met by American, not African American, institutions."[36] In the absence of public institutional intervention, basic needs will simply go unmet, limiting access to capital, education, healthcare, and childcare, to name just a few major material resources that the black church informally distributed and administered overseen by women.[37] As Du Bois stressed, the challenge of democratic politics is whether whites are prepared to reject the wanton privileges of racial caste, recognize black moral equality, *and* share the resources of a "great world" – the accumulation of which originated with the violent dispossession and subjugation of non-white peoples. Until the white-controlled polity is willing to acknowledge the historical legacy, and the continued

existence, of the color line, even a modest conception of economic justice is insecure.[38] In a white-controlled polity, that
any social good from which people of color genuinely benefit
attains political legitimacy is a significant accomplishment.

Furthermore, women's civic activities within the black
church confirm the egalitarian promise of Du Bois's model
of democratic leadership. Grassroots social-welfare initiatives were funded by an informal tax system that was made
possible by the sacrifices of ordinary people, who donated
labor and resources, although many hardly earned enough
for their own subsistence.[39] Their principled enactment of
the moral ideal of citizenship assisted the worst off, and a
minimal basis of the common good was thus maintained.
The organizers were both professional and working-class
people – preachers, regular churchgoers, ministers, washer-
women, and schoolteachers – who became "ethical and social
leaders."[40] In *Souls*, Du Bois refers to the preacher and the
teacher as sorts of "politicians" in the "social, intellectual,
and economic centers" of their communities.[41] In *Darkwater*,
he writes:

> Black women (and women whose grandmothers were black)
> are today furnishing our teachers; they are the main pillars
> of those social settlements which we call churches; and they
> have with small doubt raised three-fourths of our church
> property. If we have today, as seems likely, over a billion
> dollars of accumulated goods, who shall say how much of it
> has been wrung from the hearts of servant girls and washer-
> women and women toilers in the fields.[42]

As a volunteer labor force, women "reproduced in microcosm" a "great world."[43] Tellingly, the material resources
that they asserted should become public goods, rather than
the "natural" or "contingent" advantages that the lucky few

possess, alleviated the private burdens typically shouldered by them, such as childcare and education. Unfortunately, rarely did their sacrifices receive public recognition. Unlike the idea of education at public expense, their reinterpretation of the common good as also including childcare at public expense did not result in its federal recognition as a legitimate entitlement of US citizenship. And yet, like the defense of public school systems, childcare at public expense remains a critical ideal for the democratic expansion of the rights and privileges morally appropriate to a version of American citizenship that includes women of color; and public childcare is an ideal that is, at least in part, historically rooted in black women's struggle for justice for themselves and their children.[44]

Childcare: actualizing the value of the civic equality of black women

In 2019, Tucker Carlson, the vitriolic talking head of Fox Five News, wrote in an opinion piece: "Is it more virtuous to devote your life to some soulless corporation than it is to raise your own kids?"[45] Suddenly inspired to attack corporate America, Carlson reasserted the virtue of women who retreat into the cult of domesticity to undertake unpaid childcare. In identifying childcare with "virtue," Carlson insinuates that reproductive labor lacks economic value. He thus ignores the fact that the absence of quality and affordable childcare locks middle-class mothers into economic dependence on male breadwinners and depletes the wages of black and brown women for whom such matronly "virtue" is not a viable option because their households rely on their income. Of course, it is unlikely that Carlson was thinking of African-American women as virtuous mothers walking away from corporate jobs; historically, black and brown women's economic reality barred them from the traditional gender role of the Victorian housewife and pushed them into hyper-exploitative, low-wage jobs.[46] Drawing out the implications of Du Bois's feminist politics, I propose that childcare at public expense remains key for dramatically advancing women's civic enfranchisement. It is a public good that would especially benefit black and brown women laborers and enable them to become "self-standing" laborers. In fact, as we've seen, it is a political goal that emerges in part from the legacy of black feminist struggle in the early and mid-twentieth century.

A recent poll conducted by the Center for American Progress asked women of color in so-called "battleground" states what they considered to be the most important political issue. One in four replied access to affordable childcare.[47] Perhaps this finding would be less shocking if we considered the economic reality of black households in America today. "The average annual cost of center-based child care for an infant and a four-year-old is nearly $18,000, which amounts to 42 percent of the median income for a typical African American family."[48] And yet the issue of childcare seldom appears in public policies debates. Some companies have expanded access to much-needed parental leave for new parents, though the United States falls far behind most developed countries in extending parental leave. The issue of protracted care that does not fall into private hands but under public control is all but invisible. And that invisibility in part continues to reflect the lack of political will to address the concrete needs of women of color and to guide their substantive civic enfranchisement as self-standing "free" laborers.

To enter the labor market without sacrificing "the chance to do their best work," most mothers require extensive aid to help raise their children. Oftentimes, childcare is a private burden shouldered by women. If a woman has strong family and community ties, she can sometimes lean on those social networks for help. In most cities across the United States, the cost of childcare is prohibitive for most single- and two-parent households; and it is simply not an option for families slipping into deep poverty, struggling to pay rent, medical bills, and utility bills. As a result, families are burdened with arranging private childcare; and that task often falls to women. To this day, "the burdens of concrete emotional and physical caring tend to fall on individual women alone and disproportionately on women of color."[49] Historically, women of color have dominated domestic work, taking care of white affluent children and struggling to arrange quality care for their own children.

Access to affordable and quality childcare liberates women, and women of color in particular, to pursue a career and prevent them from temporarily dropping out of the workforce to raise children. Exiting the workforce results not just in the loss of an income. It exacerbates economic insecurity in the long term, a phenomenon that disproportionately impacts the economic well-being of black and brown households. Re-entry into the workforce is extremely difficult after an extended departure; and it is often more difficult for low-paid service sector jobs.

As the US public resists publicly subsidized childcare, only *18 percent* of Americans believe that both parents should work full time outside the home.[50] And so, to echo Carlson, the vast majority still implicitly counts on the "virtues" of full-time parenting, often done by women. A political climate that does not even value the independence of women from the domestic sphere or their right to make a living is unlikely to shore up public support for public childcare, and it is even less likely to consider the dire consequences for black and brown women. Indeed, the vicious attack on abortion rights and the push to repeal *Roe v. Wade* is a terrifying indication of public reinvestment in the cult of motherhood, subjecting women and their children to the vagaries of the free market and their romantic partners.

With foresight, in 1984 bell hooks wrote:

> Because women are doing most of the parenting, the need for tax-funded public child care centers with equal numbers of non-sexist male and female workers continues to be a pressing feminist issue. Such centers would relieve individual women of the sole responsibility for child-rearing as well as help promote awareness of the necessity for male participation in child-raising. Yet this is an issue that has yet to be pushed by masses of people. Future feminist organizing (especially in the interests of building mass-based feminist movement) could use this issue as a platform. Feminist activists have always seen public child care as one solution to the problem of women being the primary child-rearers.[51]

By concretely addressing the disproportionate hardships faced by black women and women of color, a radical feminist politics today can expand what should even count as a social good protected by the state and thereby relieve the burden placed on millions of working mothers of all races. Nearly thirty years after hooks's initial call – and more than a century after Du Bois's original formulation of black women's power and imagination as leaders – the republic is still putting off a feminist "future" that would secure public childcare as a legitimate universal right.

Part III

Despair

7

Du Bois on Self-Segregation and Self-Respect: A Liberalism Undone? (1934–1951)

[T]he black man is tired of begging for justice and recognition from folk who seem to have no intention of being just and do not propose to recognize Negroes as men.

W. E. B. Du Bois[1]

Reporting on the destructive impact of the Great Depression on segregated black communities, a newfound sense of urgency prompted Du Bois to rethink his earlier approach to democratic politics. As he began to doubt the willingness of the US federal government to end Jim Crow segregation, in the mid-1930s he penned a series of articles in *The Crisis* that defended voluntary black self-segregation and targeted for criticism the NAACP.[2] In effect, he fell into a despair from which, arguably, he had no respite until his death: "There seems no hope," he wrote, that the white American "in our day will yield in its color or race hatred any substantial ground and we have not physical nor economic power, nor any alliance with other social and economic classes that will force compliance with decent civilized ideals in Church, State, Industry, or Art."[3]

The board of directors at the NAACP protested that Du Bois's defense of voluntary black self-segregation violated the liberal ideals on which the organization was founded. Its mission was to fight for equal civil and political rights and to pressure federal and state government to redress black political disenfranchisement. The board of directors held that advocating voluntary self-segregation violated their principles as a civil rights organization and, in essence, signaled black acquiescence to de jure segregation. Such a program would, in effect, signify the victory of the Ku Klux Klan and keep de jure segregation intact.

Du Bois rejected the criticism that his proposal was anti-liberal or disempowered segregated black communities. In an acrimonious break from the NAACP, on July 1, 1934, he resigned from the organization over the dispute and returned to teaching full time at Atlanta University in Georgia. Forced to retire from teaching, he briefly returned to the NAACP ten years later, 1944–8, before departing again over another bitter dispute, this time permanently.[4] He was again forced to resign in 1948 in part because of his support of Henry A. Wallace for president on the Progressive Party ticket. He had a dispute with Walter White, then head of the NAACP, over a UN petition for "minority rights" that was critical of the Truman administration and which Du Bois had written. In Du Bois's eyes, White appeared to cozy up to Truman when he refused to support the petition and accepted instead an invitation from the US federal government to serve as a special consultant for the US delegation to the UN in Paris later that year. White's acceptance of the position in effect served to quell international scrutiny of Jim Crow violence in the United States. Du Bois's petition was dead in the water. Even as he approached his eightieth birthday, he did not shy away from controversy.

The decisive shift in Du Bois's political thought after his initial departure from the NAACP combined elements that, at first blush, do not appear compatible. He synthesized liberal, black nationalist, and Marxist considerations to formulate a unique program for black mobilization. He began to theorize more systematically black self-respect and economic welfare in a hostile and violent anti-black world. Consider a short excerpt from his resignation letter in 1934 that explained the reasons for his departure:

> [N]o matter what the Board [. . .] says, its actions toward segregation has got to approximate, in the future as in the past, the pattern it followed in the case of the separate camp for Negro officers during the World War and in the case of the Tuskegee Veterans' Hospital. In both instances, we protested vigorously and to the limit of our ability the segregation policy. Then, when we had failed and knew we had failed, we bent every effort toward making the colored camp [. . .] the best officers' camp possible, and the Tuskegee Hospital, with its Negro personnel, one of the most efficient in the land. [. . .] The only thing, therefore, that remains for us is to decide whether we are openly to recognize this procedure as inevitable, or be silent about it and still pursue it. Under these circumstances, the argument must be more or less academic, but there is no essential reason that those who see different sides of this same shield should not be able to agree to live together in the same house.[5]

He asserted that black self-segregation is consistent with political liberalism, believing it was possible for him to live "in the same house" as the NAACP and that their disagreement was "more or less academic." In fact, in the past, in cases where the federal government refused to desegregate, the NAACP supported segregated institutions to ensure that black workers' needs were met. For example, once it became clear that their employers would not do so, the organization equipped black officers and hospital personnel with the basic tools of their trade.

Likewise, by the mid-1930s, Du Bois exhorted the board members to accept that "we have failed and we know we had failed." They should focus, instead, on providing alternative arrangements to better protect segregated black laborers, launching black business initiatives and workers cooperatives to ensure that the needs of black laborers were met. He maintained that the NAACP "finds itself in a time of crisis and change, without a program, without effective organization."[6] In line with his wide-ranging experimentation with methods, he called upon it to "reorganize itself according to the demands of the present crisis."[7] After decades, the desegregation effort had not mitigated the injurious effects of de jure segregation on black communities. Moreover, the NAACP had no response to the devastating impact of the Great Depression on the economic well-being of segregated black communities. The failure of desegregation had caused untold harm: African Americans had waited since the end of the Civil War for the promise of freedom, enduring mob violence and stultifying poverty. The strategy of voluntary self-segregation might be more effective, at least temporarily, to protect their social and economic interests. Du Bois took for granted that African Americans must work together to help each other, rather than wait for white Americans to listen to their better angels. In his view, the NAACP was ready to sacrifice the welfare of another generation of African Americans for the arrival of those far-flung angels. Once he accepted that the color line would not disappear any time soon, a new political program was required to ensure black survival *and* flourishing in the Jim Crow era.

In this chapter, I examine Du Bois's shift to support voluntary black self-segregation from 1934 to 1951. In *Dusk of Dawn* and a series of short articles published between 1934 and 1951, he linked self-segregation to a program of economic readjustment for black social welfare. He developed a serious interest in Marxian philosophy and sympathies for the Soviet Union and Maoist China. However, his defense of voluntary black self-segregation was not just motivated by economic considerations. He argued that African Americans were morally entitled to self-segregate to assert their *self-respect* as equal moral persons. He thus combined black nationalist and Marxian thought to offer a unique defense of black self-segregation that remained at least nominally grounded in the public values of freedom and equality. His proposal, I submit, remained *consistent* with the ideal of black civic enfranchisement in that it highlighted the weak will of the American public to live up to its own democratic ideals.

In the first section below, I present Du Bois's black nationalist and Marxian commitments from the mid-1930s onwards in his changing political affiliations and the ideal of civic enfranchisement which remained important in his political thought. In the following two sections, I revisit the concept of double consciousness from the early Du Bois. Although he first formulated the concept in *Souls*, it sheds light on why he came to support voluntary black self-segregation in the 1930s, for the concept shows why racist misrecognition undermines self-perception. Through an exposition of the concept of double consciousness it becomes easier to track the theoretical continuity of his early and late thought. Finally, I conclude with a discussion about the viability of the politics of self-segregation today.

Du Bois's black nationalism and Marxism: economic grounds for voluntary self-segregation

While Du Bois embraced his first close study of Marx in the 1950s, he had been sympathetic to socialism since his student days. In fact, by 1904, he already considered himself a "socialist."[8] In light of his emphasis on black separatism during this period, there are at least two questions for us to consider. First, in what sense does Du Bois remain committed to the ideal of black civic enfranchisement? Second, how does black economic welfare couple with a black separatist politics? To answer these questions, we must confront his dissatisfaction with *both* conventional liberal *and* communist approaches to the "Negro Problem." Though he eventually joined the Communist Party USA in 1961, it was with hesitation, outlining in a letter his reasons for doing so. In essence, Du Bois believed that liberals and socialists were too optimistic about the prospect of reaching common ground with white labor during the Jim Crow era. He grew skeptical of the possibility of forging a meaningful interracial workers' alliance, at least at that particular historical moment, although he believed that, ideally, all laborers *should* come together to build an interracial labor movement. He was just reconciling himself to the fact that they would not any time soon. He did not give up on the hope that eventually white laborers would cooperate with people of color in the United States and around the globe. Hence, he remained committed, at least in principle, to the normative ideal of a racially pluralistic polity, an ideal that is crucial to liberal political thought. He did not believe, however, that, in the interim, such a laudable ideal was achievable in any nonideal circumstances where anti-black animus was as intense as it was during Jim Crow.

What's left of the liberal ideal of civic enfranchisement?

Let's tackle the first question about what to make of Du Bois's black "radical" liberalism from the mid-1930s onwards. Given the shift in his political affiliations and strategies for political mobilization, it is difficult to determine what is left of Du Bois's political liberalism or what notion of democratic politics he continued to uphold. To illustrate the sense in which he remained theoretically invested in the ideal of black civic equality, it is worth briefly revisiting his polemic with the "accommodationist" Booker T. Washington. Du Bois had shot into national prominence because of his disagreement with Washington's acceptance of de jure segregation. Washington's political philosophy shared the black nationalist commitment that African Americans must close ranks in response to the reality of Jim Crow segregation. Washington aimed to unify African-American business to promote the economic welfare of the community. In Du Bois's view, Washington neglected to affirm the moral value of equal black citizenship. His disagreement with Washington came down to Du Bois's endorsement – and Washington's rejection – of the possibility of racial justice in America. Du Bois held that the state is ultimately responsible for redistributing rights and resources to all persons on the basis of the moral value of free and equal citizenship. And to the extent that the state fails to complete its responsibility towards African Americans as free and equal citizens, it must be subject to public scrutiny and more inclusive democratic control.

To be sure, though Du Bois's polemic with Washington takes place before the 1930s, their exchange provides insight into Du Bois's evolving program for black freedom. In an essay published in 1944, Du Bois claimed, "By 'Freedom' for Negroes, I meant and still mean, full economic, political, and social equality *with American citizens*, in thought expression

and action, with no discrimination based on race and color."[9]
Recall that Washington lent legitimacy to the segregationist
policy of "separate but equal." In response to black disenfranchisement, Washington advocated self-reliance through the
adoption of the virtues of thrift and hard work by the working poor. To this end, he favored vocational training to make
black labor skilled or semi-skilled, as well as the formation of
a black business league that would invest capital into black
neighborhoods. But Du Bois had rejected Washington's
acquiescence to de jure segregation. He asserted that civil
and political rights were inalienable, and their loss should
neither be provisionally accepted nor tolerated. He never
gave up on the ideal that African Americans *ought* to have
formal standing in public American institutions, even when
he had the sober realization – some three decades after his
bitter polemic with Washington – that public institutions
might not recognize black equal standing any time soon.
As Du Bois claimed in *Dusk of Dawn* (1940), "This plan of
action would have for its ultimate object, full Negro rights
and Negro equality in America."[10]

In consideration of black economic distress, Du Bois conceded that it was imperative for black business leaders and
worker cooperatives to protect black labor interests, which
would otherwise remain unmet in the white-controlled
polity.[11] In *Dusk of Dawn*, he stressed that a program of self-
segregation is the most effective means for "a planned and
intelligent agitation for political, civil and social equality." In
considering how his program differed from Washington's
policy of thrifty self-reliance, it is instructive to quote Du
Bois at length here:

> [What] lately I have been [. . .] advocating can easily be mis-
> taken for a program of complete racial segregation and even
> nationalism among Negroes. Indeed it has been criticized as

such. This is a misapprehension. First, [. . .] I have stressed the economic discrimination as fundamental and have advised concentration of planning there. We need sufficient income for health and home; to supplement our education and recreation; to fight our own crime problem; and above all to finance a continued, planned and intelligent agitation for political, civil, and social equality. How can we Negroes in the US gain such average income as to be able to attend to these pressing matters? The cost of this program must fall first and primarily on us, ourselves. It is *silly* to expect any large number of whites to finance a program which the overwhelming majority of whites fear and reject.[12]

Noteworthy is his list of basic social goods whose administration he advised should be the objective of public "planning." Presumably, then, self-segregation is a means to acquire and administer public goods effectively. Note that Du Bois did not consider that it was *impossible* for whites to develop a sense of racial justice. Rather, given how toxic the public sphere had become during the Jim Crow era, it was "silly" to expect whites to support policies that would benefit African Americans. He remained invested in the idea of civil and political rights and the expansion and centralization of the federal government into something akin to a democratically controlled welfare state; these public institutional developments, he believed, should eventually ease the undue economic burden placed on black communities to have to acquire and administer basic social goods.

And so Du Bois's critique of American democracy and political economy tackled the peculiarly stubborn recalcitrance of de jure and de facto racial segregation. He did not accept that white supremacy was inevitable or irremovable from the polity. Under extreme duress, the African-American community should *temporarily* – not permanently – "close ranks" behind the color line to protect their social welfare.[13] The strategy of black strategic self-segregation behind the color line can sometimes better actualize black welfare and political interests when official institutions of political power are saturated by white supremacist ideology. If the polity at large manifests a stubborn – and unreasonable – resistance to racial justice, he holds that vulnerable racial communities are entitled to form black alliances within domestic borders and in the context of a cosmopolitan pan-African movement.[14]

Perhaps, in the end, his difference with Washington is merely terminological. For, in substance, they came to support similar separatist programs for black economic self-determination at the height of the Jim Crow era. They just invoked different justifications for their separatist programs. But Du Bois was never one to play down the significance of subtle theoretical differences in the development of political strategies. Indeed, those differences fertilized the bitter polemics against which Du Bois defined his evolving political program for black freedom. "Through voluntary and increased segregation," Du Bois said in 1934, "by careful autonomous and planned economic organization [. . .] 12 million men can no longer be refused fellowship and equality in the United States."[15] He thus championed a strain of black nationalist thought, defending black organizational autonomy behind the color line, without forgoing the ideal of eventual equitable integration into the polity at large on the moral basis of free and equal citizenship.

Du Bois's dissatisfaction with the Communist Party

A meaningful response to the Great Depression required a modified Marxian analysis that concentrated on the material reality of the working class. Unions had facilitated upward mobility and fair wage contracts, but Du Bois noted that their protection was limited to white people. He heatedly criticized the trade union movement in the twentieth century for closing ranks along white lines and thus forgoing the ideal of interracial civic fellowship that is necessary to galvanize an interracial labor movement. Ironically, in doing so, the strategy drove down the average compensation of white workers. Though their compensation was still much higher than that of a non-white worker, it was only better relative to the latter's low threshold for compensation. The "slavery and semi-slavery of the colored world" domestically and globally would continue to drive down wages overall.[16] Were unions to have formed an interracial labor alliance, they would have been able to extract a greater amount of income and real benefits and might have secured the permanent political influence of unions, which has been in decline in the United States since the mid-twentieth century.

Du Bois was never naive about how difficult it would be to bring together laborers to form an interracial alliance. His defense of voluntary self-segregation reflected his sense of the actual disposition of the white workers to organize with non-whites. In 1933 in *The Crisis*, Du Bois targeted white laborers and white capitalists alike for exacerbating black economic insecurity:

> Slowly but surely I came to see that for many years, perhaps many generations, we could not count on any such [i.e., white] majority; that the whole set of the white world in America, in Europe and in the world was too determinedly against racial equality, to give power and persuasiveness to our agitation. Therefore, I began to emphasize and restate certain implicit aspects of my former ideas. I tried to say to the American Negro: during the time of this frontal attack which you are making upon American and European prejudice, and with your unwavering statement

and restatement of what is right and just, not only for us, but in the long run, for all men; during this time, there are certain things you must do for your own survival and self-preservation.[17]

In *Dusk of Dawn*, he defended black consumer cooperatives for building black-run economic institutions. Black purchasing power, he thought, though small, could make inroads against poverty without relying on white cooperation.

As Adolph Reed notes, it is not clear what Du Bois, then, means by "socialism" or "Marxism," given his idiosyncratic proposals and criticism of the Communist Party.[18] How one defines the "true" meaning of socialism and communism tends to depend on how one characterizes a viable Marxian politics in its relation to the democratic self-determination of a people. Du Bois had argued that capital should be subordinated to the interests of labor, positing that "industry" should be "guided according to his wants and needs and not exclusively with regard to the profit of the producers and transporters."[19] For him, the political economy has a social form, such that the organization of production and consumption should be guided by democratic control. In his late period, he still believed in the promise of democratic reform, which was grounded in his elemental faith in "reason" and nonviolence as the principal means for enacting change.[20] He still hoped to "abolish poverty by reason and intelligent use of the ballot."[21] Du Bois did not reject the modern American state as a mere instrument for capital accumulation that can offer no viable political solution to poverty. In "The Negro and Social Reconstruction" (1936), he asserted that he was: "convinced of the essential truth of Marxian philosophy and believed that eventually land, machines and materials must belong to the state, that private profit must be abolished, that the system of exploiting labor must disappear, that people who work must have essentially equal income and that in their hands the political rulership of the state must eventually rest."[22]

He consistently advocated for public control of capital and the conditions of labor and hoped that a worker-run "industrial democracy" would eliminate poverty. He thus hoped to "socialize" the economy by "inaugurat[ing] a welfare state."[23] In sum, then, his radical break from political liberalism is not such a radical break after all. He admitted that he was building on the "essential rightness of what we have been asking for a generation [with respect to] political, civic, and social equality."[24]

In nonideal circumstances, where federal and state government fail to protect the ideal of black civic enfranchisement, the political mobilization of the segregated black community must protect, in the short term, their own immediate interests and welfare. Because Du Bois conceded that the state would not desegregate any time soon, he advocated for black citizens to invest in their own communities to counteract their political and economic disenfranchisement. His appeal to a black cooperative commonwealth showcased that it is not even always necessary to close ranks along racial lines in nonideal circumstances.

It [i.e., a black cooperative commonwealth] can see to it that not only no action of this inner group is opposed to the real interests of the nation, but that it too works for and in conjunction with the best interests of the nation. It need draw no line of exclusion *so long as the outsiders join in the consensus.* [. . .] Its great advantage is that it is no longer marching face forward into walls of prejudice. If the wall moves, we can move with it; and if it does not move it cannot, save in extreme cases, hinder us.[25]

As he had in *Souls*, he still assumed the capacity for whites to refine their moral sensibility and "join in the consensus" to support racial justice. His justification for black self-segregation thus dovetailed more broadly with the justification of a constitutional democratic republic. It is in the "interest" of the state to promote free and equal citizenship for all. To the extent that small organizations in civil society are working towards civic equality, they are also working towards the realization of the objective of just republican governance. Until major public institutions substantively transform their existent structure, he wanted the segregated black community to form a powerful bulwark against "the walls of prejudice." The final step of his program for black emancipation is "scientific investigation and organized action among Negroes, in close cooperation, to secure the survival of the Negro race, until the cultural development of America and the world is willing to recognize Negro freedom."[26]

His defense of voluntary self-segregation brings us, then, to the problem of recognition – and racist misrecognition – in his critique of American democracy. The harm posed by the "walls" of prejudice is not limited to economic harm. In *Souls*, Du Bois described the walls of prejudice as "unscalable," rising over the "sons of night" whose psychological well-being and very sense of self suffer as a consequence. Anti-black prejudice mediates the judgment that a person of color forms about the value of their very self – who they are as unique individuals and their worth as persons. Racist judgment and the circulation of racist social values and denigrating images of black life constitute a danger to black psychological well-being. With time, Du Bois noted, it is very difficult *not* to believe these disgusting things about yourself. Du Bois thus added distinct moral considerations in favor of voluntary black self-segregation. He challenged political theorists and activists to define what it means to cultivate and assert black self-respect in a hostile anti-black environment. Though I cannot in this chapter lay out the full power of that challenge, I now turn to consider why his proposal for voluntary black self-segregation is a way of *cultivating* and *asserting* black self-respect.

A closer look at double consciousness as an effect of the color line

In presenting Du Bois's moral considerations in favor of voluntary black self-segregation, I revisit the concept of double consciousness, which I briefly sketched in chapter 1. The concept of double consciousness showcases the importance of recognition – and racist misrecognition – in the formation and disintegration of one's sense of self. Recall that the way whites *perceive* African Americans – that is, misrecognize and disvalue blacks as a racial group – is the origin of the so-called "Negro Problem." And Jim Crow America exposed African Americans to hostile, mocking, or indifferent whites. Du Bois defended blacks' moral right to mitigate their exposure to white people, that is, to avoid risky, potentially violent, or humiliating confrontations with whites. He believed that through avoidance – by "closing ranks" behind the color line – one *asserted* one's self-respect. Avoiding whites did not signify acquiescence to segregation. Self-segregation prevented one from "facing almost universal disparagement," so that one can "keep one's soul."[27]

Recall that, in *Souls*, Du Bois meditated on what it means to "keep" one's soul in the face of racist hostility. He suggested the metaphor of a "veil" to capture the way blacks are judged (and misjudged by others), reflecting on the "strange meaning" of being black in Jim Crow America.[28] As an African American, he was "shut out from the world by a vast veil," and yet in approaching "their" (i.e., the white-controlled) world, he did so by way of the veil, that is, by way of the racist misrecognition of black humanity.[29] The judgment of the white world ensnared one "in a complex network of degrading and dehumanizing fictions."[30] Kirkland adds, "the strangeness [of] the meaning of being black is that to say or represent what is or is not the case about being black" is not controlled by the black person being judged.[31] Disrespectful and denigrating forms of recognition surround you like "the walls of a prison-house."[32]

As an effect of the color line, double consciousness produces two options: either conform or reject the white-controlled world. Engagement with the world leads to repeated confrontation with anti-black prejudice and ill will; and it exposes a person to the risk of violence and humiliation. In the pursuit of basic opportunities, a person of color must assume the perspective of hostile whites – to measure one's own soul by the "tape" of the white world. With time, this pressure proves disorienting, as one is made to feel that success requires apologizing for or distancing oneself from one's race. Constant confrontation with prejudice, ill will, and the threat of violence undermines one's self-esteem: "The facing of so vast a prejudice could not but bring the inevitable self-questioning, self-disparagement, and the lowering of ideals which ever accompany repression and breed in an atmosphere of contempt and hate."[33] But the rejection of the (white-controlled) world forces one to abandon the pursuit of the good life altogether, leaving intact the color line that devalues black life and "doubles" consciousness in the first place.

With his first experience of the color line as a child, Du Bois grew resolved to "wrest [. . .] prizes and opportunities" from "the other world."[34] He detailed his ambivalent feelings about his resolution, which contempt had motivated, and

juxtaposed it with those of other black children for whom
"the strife was not so fiercely sunny":

> [T]heir youth shrunk into tasteless sycophancy, or into silent
> hatred of the pale world about them and mocking disgust
> of everything white; or wasted in a bitter cry, Why did God
> make me an outcast and a stranger in mine own house? The
> shades of the prison-house closed round us all: walls strait
> and stubborn to the whitest, but relentlessly narrow, tall,
> and unscalable to sons of night who must plod darkly on
> in resignation, or beat unavailing palms against the stone,
> or steadily, half hopelessly, watch the streak of blue [sky]
> above.[35]

He confided to his reader that even his own "fiercely
sunny" strife did not lift him outside of "the walls of the
prison-house." In noting the "tasteless sycophancy" of the
other children, he did not fault them with moral failure for
being too weak or cowardly to assert themselves against
the "walls of prejudice." Instead he placed all the "sons of
night" inside the walls of the prison-house, including himself
with his exuberance to "beat his [white] mates at examina-
tion-time, or beat them at a foot-race, or even beat their
stringy heads."[36] He traced resignation, sycophancy, and
his own "fiercely sunny" strife to a spectrum of attitudes
within double consciousness, identifying them as the subjective effects of racial exclusion through the color line. The
important point was to understand that the veil encroaches
on black self-consciousness without slipping into resentment
or always feeling like one has to prove oneself.

For Du Bois, the black experience of double consciousness
should impress upon the reader of *Souls* that whites' habits
of judgment *about* the deontic status, i.e., equal moral standing, of non-whites *causes* the problem of the color line.[37] If

they had been responsive to the judgment of black practical agents, then the color line would not exist in the first place. Whites must, therefore, develop a moral sensibility that enables them to discern their role in the establishment of the color line and recognize the moral equality of others across it. For all his misgivings about white people, Du Bois was not content to give up the world to them. In the early work *Souls*, he defended the ballot and the principle of fair equality of opportunity for the segregated black community and was optimistic that white moral sensibilities could change over time. By the mid-1930s, his optimism flagged and, in despair, he took precautions to mitigate black exposure to the white world in order to protect black psychological and economic well-being.

An orthodox liberal approach: Kant on self-respect

Du Bois's illustration of the black experience of double consciousness poses a challenge to common ways in which moral philosophers think about self-respect.[38] The idea of double consciousness illustrates the crucial role that the judgment of others plays in the development of our self-perception. If the judgment of others is consistently negative, Du Bois suggested that fighting them warrants *avoiding* exposure to their judgment in the first place. Black self-segregation, in his mind, is then an assertion of black self-respect.

In contrast, a popular conception of self-respect in moral philosophy offers what I characterize as a "battering ram" approach to self-assertion. What I mean by a "battering-ram" approach is the view that it is always morally correct to confront those who devalue you, regardless of the consequences for your own life and well-being. The battering-ram approach to asserting self-respect is linked, I submit, to a romantic vision of "fighting the good fight" that is popular in the white liberal imagination. Images of unarmed African Americans facing down a white mob are engrained in the popular historical memory of the civil rights movement and are often invoked as a paradigm of democratic virtue and black self-righteous defiance against impossible odds. Du Bois was irked by this convenient narrative for thinking about what it means to assert self-respect for members of a vulnerable racial group. Such a narrative does not address the danger or the cost of facing down a mob by actual black persons, who should not be considered mere caricatures of fearless virtue. Du Bois thus raised a difficult and delicate theoretical question: is it always a show of self-respect to confront hostile whites, such that the failure to do so is a moral failure that entails a lack of self-respect? Or do you better assert the equal moral value of the self by *avoiding* such risky confrontations?

An important philosopher who has often been used to justify the battering-ram approach to asserting self-respect is Kant, whose work I have already discussed in connection with Du Bois. In the context of the systematic institutional failure of the state, as exemplified by Jim Crow America, Kant's practical philosophy is unclear about what it means to assert self-respect. Kant does not focus on the grave obstacle that systematic misrecognition might cause in the development and exercise of moral agency.

According to Kant, we have a perfect duty to avoid the destruction of, and damage to, our rational nature, as well as an imperfect duty to develop a moral personality. He defends the moral obligation to resist the denigration of moral personhood as (private) moral agents and as a matter of (public) rightful honor (*honeste vive*).[39] This follows from his formulation of the categorical imperative as the principle of humanity: "Act so that you treat humanity, whether in your own person or in that of another, always as an end and never as a means only."[40] He explains, "every rational being exists as an end in himself and not merely as a means to be arbitrarily used by this or that will. He must in all his actions, whether directed to himself or to other rational beings, always be regarded at the same time as an end."[41] To exercise moral autonomy, one must not allow oneself to be used as a "mere means" for others' pursuit of their arbitrary ends. That is, one must stand up for oneself to assert one's moral value if others are using you as a "mere" means.

To clarify what kind of a moral failure a lack of self-respect amounts to, the Kant scholar Thomas Hill distinguishes between two dimensions of self-respect in Kant's moral philosophy. Basic self-respect, Hill writes, establishes that the moral law is authoritative for all rational practical agents capable of following it; and basic self-respect isolates the will as the author of the moral law to establish the intrinsic moral value of rational humanity. Jacqueline Mariña suggests conceptualizing the irremovable binding authority of the moral law on the will by "speaking of a graced nature. [T]his feature of our nature cannot be lost; Kant notes that we are 'never able to lose the incentive that consists in the respect for the moral law, and were we ever to lose it, we would also never be able to regain it.' "[42] In *Religion*, Kant identifies this "incentive" or "interest" of practical reason as "the predisposition to personality," which is the subjective ground for the formulation of maxims or the freely chosen "ends" of our action.[43] Our predisposition for personality confirms *both* the spontaneity of practical reason to legislate unconditional moral laws and that the "goal" of moral development is to cultivate habits of autonomous moral judgment that increasingly elicit a goodwill: "the goal of the human being is to become what in some sense she already is, that is, to develop out of herself that which is in some sense already within."[44] In this case, there is no duty to self-respect as such, only the self-conscious awareness of the transcendental authority of the moral law, which is "in some sense" already within us.

Hill contrasts basic self-respect with moral self-regard:

> [It] is something that all moral agents ought to have, though many do not. To have it is to choose to live in a self-respecting way, expressing proper regard for one's humanity in one's acts (e.g., preserving and developing one's rational capacities) and one's attitudes (e.g., readiness to affirm and honor one's moral status of dignity and equality as a person).[45]

Kant's account of self-respect requires that we express "proper" regard for the innate value of our humanity by "choosing to live in a self-respecting way." This is where the trouble begins because it is not always clear what it would entail to live in a "self-respecting way" in a dysfunctional polity. Kant holds that persons should act on the *intention* to respect the moral law and interact with others in a way that asserts their deontic status as a moral equal.

Kant's commitment to an intention-based view of morality is evident in his conception of servility. Servility "[w]aives any claim to moral worth in oneself, in the belief that one will thereby acquire a borrowed worth."[46] He describes the vice of servility as a deliberate self-instrumentalization with the aim of wresting a conditional end, such as power or money. As Cynthia Stark puts it, for Kant, "failures of self-respect are deliberate or involve a kind of self-deception."[47] Stark elaborates: "they involve either the intentional ignoring of one's moral worth when one knows better [. . .] or a kind of mental subterfuge [. . .] whereby one rationalizes or neglects to undergo a proper degree of self-scrutiny."[48] Through self-deception, one rationalizes servility as consistent with the moral law by convincing oneself that one's servility does not really constitute servile behavior. One thereby allows oneself to be used as a mere means for someone else's ends.

But are all injuries to self-respect – or the most troubling kind – the result of a deliberate self-instrumentalization for a conditional end or self-deception? Kant does not consider that apparent servility might wrest not a conditional end, such as power or money, but might be elicited from persons in hostile circumstances that threaten them with violence and death. If others refuse to recognize – on racist principle – one's deontic status as a moral equal, social intercourse with them exposes one to a radically evil will that might destroy or seriously damage one's life and community. The Kantian model overlooks that vulnerable racial groups often invite excessive risk to their lives and well-being by cultivating goodwill towards hostile whites.[49] "Proper" moral self-regard demands a person defend herself against the devaluation and destruction of her rational humanity. But in circumstances where others express ill will and racial animus, does moral self-regard warrant one to engage or limit interaction with those who are deaf to one's deontic status as a moral equal?[50]

In the *Critique of Practical Reason*, Kant famously writes that even those threatened with death by a tyrant are "free" to refrain from violating the moral law by refusing to give false testimony.[51] He acknowledges that the prospect of death would discourage many from following the moral law, but he upholds truth-telling in the face of death as a powerful example of moral courage. And yet this example offers a misleading characterization of the overall structure of his practical philosophy. For he does not believe that modern moral life should demand ongoing extraordinary self-sacrifice as part of the condition for the exercise of autonomous practical agency. In fact, his idea of the highest good holds the opposite view: that the virtuous ought to find happiness in proportion to their virtue. Those who respect the moral law ought not to suffer random acts of violence. If moral goodness were always rewarded with capital punishment and an excruciating death, then one would be incapable of developing a sense of moral agency in the first place inasmuch as the causality of practical reason would appear to be ineffective in the world. Moral life would seem to be just an illusion. The idea of the highest good is a principle that should motivate the establishment of an inclusive and just republican state and an international cosmopolitan federation of peaceful states. In other words, Kant assumes the historical development of stable and functional modern states to buttress the moral development and standing of individuals. A functional legitimate state mitigates the chaos and unpredictability of random acts of violence. He thereby hopes to facilitate the convergence of virtue and happiness through a just state exacting punishment and recognizing citizens' innate right to freedom.[52] That is, good people should find their happiness in proportion to their moral goodness – they should not have to face excessive risk in their lives. Unfortunately, Kant does not consider the complications of the moral life in a profoundly unjust or nominally liberal state, where entire sections of the population are treated as if they are still in the state of nature with "no rights which the white man is bound to respect," as the US Supreme Court ruled in the Dred Scott case of 1857.

A modern constitutional state that systematically disrespects and denigrates persons of color creates a condition where their expressions of moral self-regard, even as they aim to change nonideal circumstances, expose them to a radically evil will. Such is the political order that black and brown Americans encountered in the Jim Crow South. The exercise of moral self-regard should not require a person to *always* be prepared to risk their lives and the very existence of their communities to try to win the respect of hostile white others. The shortcoming of Kant's model of self-respect is that it overlooks the potentially devastating impact that the indefinite struggle to wrest moral recognition from hostile others can have on a person's life and their sense of self. In aiming to avoid injury, and death – and the constant defense of one's moral worth to indifferent others – in a white supremacist society, one might publicly (and temporarily) give up endless confrontations, although one has *not* given up one's sense of oneself as a moral equal. Instead, as Kirkland puts it, one puts one's ideals into "abeyance," that is, one temporarily sets the end aside to avoid the destruction of one's rational humanity in particular instances.[53]

Double consciousness reconsidered: Du Bois's defense of black self-segregation as black self-respect

Let us consider again the phenomenon of double consciousness. I have argued that the phenomenon is experienced in the context of the color line, as a black citizen attempts to exercise practical agency in a racial caste society. A recurrent theme in Du Bois's writing is the interaction between black and non-black citizens. Let us consider, then, the example of a black citizen yielding the sidewalk to a white gentleman in the Jim Crow South. In this example, the person who yields needs not have relinquished the unconditional value of her rational humanity. Indeed, she may subjectively cling to the authority of the moral law and recognize that she is nevertheless a moral equal to this hostile white person. But she nonetheless acts in accordance with a white supremacist system of social values and practices that disrespects and denigrates her: she steps aside. She experiences double consciousness inasmuch as she judges herself through the derogatory values of a hostile other. She need not endorse those values, but she must learn to acknowledge them and anticipate their consequences. Otherwise, she will not grasp an obstacle to the exercise of her practical agency. She must decide which circumstances merit publicly forgoing her ends and which are safe enough that it is unnecessary to do so. The picture is further complicated because she casts off her ends *for the sake of the intrinsic value of her rational humanity, which the white citizen refuses to recognize and who will face no legal repercussion if he destroys her body.* For the Jim Crow state is a dysfunctional state that would not punish a white murder of a black person. In the last instance, then, what is the moral worth of her action? Has she acted on the basis of the intrinsic value of her rational humanity, characterizing her wish not to see it destroyed and all her future life projects vanquished? Or has she exhibited servility by avoiding a confrontation with this white gentleman? In other words, has she failed to assert "proper" moral regard for the moral value of her humanity?

I maintain that it is not clear on the Kantian model whether the young woman has violated the moral law to respect the rational humanity in her own person by stepping aside. In this case, neither deliberate self-instrumentalization for some conditional end, such as money, nor self-deception characterizes her apparent servility, given her plain intention to respect herself as a moral equal to her antagonist. Moreover, neither confronting nor avoiding the white gentleman is obviously the right thing to do to assert her moral self-regard. The battering-ram approach does not obviously seem to be the right call. In any case, in pursuing either option she exposes herself to devaluation and violent reprisal and may be blameworthy for failing to *protect* the intrinsic value of her rational humanity. Du Bois explains:

> Some people seem to think that the fight against segregation consists merely of one damned protest after another. That the technique is to protest and wail and protest again, and to keep this up until the gates of public opinion and the walls of segregation fall down. The difficulty with this program is that it is physically and psychologically impossible. It would be stopped by cold and hunger and strained voices, and it is an undignified and impossible attitude and method to maintain indefinitely.[54]

And yet because the young woman in the example above does indeed step aside, her intention to respect the moral law has not found spatiotemporal expression. Her practical ideal is, instead, put in "abeyance" – also an "undignified and impossible attitude and method to maintain indefinitely." So we are left once again with the problem of racist misrecognition that emerges as an *obstacle* to asserting one's self-value. For it is not enough to focus on *her* intentions (or the intentions of oppressed peoples) to determine the nature of the moral injury to the self-respect that the young woman has sustained, one that she has not inflicted on herself through her own moral failure. Rather, the example above shows *the moral responsibility of others* to cultivate goodwill and a sense of civic fellowship towards vulnerable racial groups to ensure that major recognitive social relations increasingly confirm the moral equality of all.

The young woman should *not* have been expected to step aside in the first place. The polity at large has a moral responsibility towards *her* to ensure that major recognitive relations acknowledge black moral personhood in civil and political life.[55] As Barbara Herman explains, "to be a moral agent in a community of equals is to know that you may claim (some) space for your (permissible) pursuits and that you may have to leave a space for others."[56] She adds, "a conception of oneself as a moral agent among others [is] the condition of human agency."[57] At the very least, the public institutional recognition of the moral equality of persons must dismantle the color line, which undermines black public standing and renders confrontations exceedingly *risky* for one group.[58] Although Kant does not believe that modern constitutional states are perfect, he takes for granted that they are inclusive and reciprocal in the appropriate fashions because they are not in the state of nature, failed states, or profoundly dysfunctional states.[59]

The phenomenon of double consciousness illustrates a more troubling issue than the theoretical problem of characterizing the moral worth of an oppressed person's actions. It shows that even in holding tight to the intention to assert one's equal moral value, one nevertheless suffers a moral injury because one is coerced into yielding to the arbitrary ends of another. For public conditions do not give one an opportunity to act in a fashion that is consistent with one's deontic status as a moral person with an innate right to freedom. In experiencing double consciousness, one finds that others consistently refuse to leave a "space" for one's "permissible pursuits." One ultimately experiences self-estrangement from the ends that one would otherwise freely endorse and publicly act on. Inevitably, there is a cost to forgoing one's ends in the anticipation of the bad behavior of others: Du Bois describes this moral injury as the strain of the sustained deferral – or abeyance – of one's ideals.[60] Over a prolonged period of time, cynicism and apathy can infect moral subjectivity.[61] The outcome of double consciousness is that the world begins to appear as a "prison-house" that extracts a "bitter cry" from the bodies it shackles: "Why did God make me an outcast and a stranger in mine own house?"[62]

In the example above, the young woman could have risked it and refused to yield. If she had held her ground, her action might have contributed to the disruption of a racial caste society. Indeed, Radical Reconstruction and the civil rights movement reconstituted the standing expectations for public engagement and interracial social cooperation in the United States. *Or*, she might have endured public humiliation, economic destabilization, arrest, sexualized torture, and a slow, excruciating death, which was the fate of countless black Americans whose striving and untimely deaths are not recorded in history books.[63] To be sure, ultimately, the public refusal to yield is necessary to galvanize social change. However, given the pernicious effects of the color line, any particular vulnerable individual's action must be uplifted by a moral community prepared to publicly defend her unconditional moral worth (and the moral righteousness of her public refusal to yield), when the polity at large refuses to do so.[64] This is why racial justice movements in the United States in the nineteenth and twentieth centuries were often led by marginalized racial communities that shored up the moral resilience of an oppressed people, affirming their positive normative self-understanding and publicly mourning the black lives lost to white supremacist violence, when no other political or civil associations chose to do so.

Du Bois's reservation about the desegregation of schools

Overcoming double consciousness requires that the predominant racial group respond appropriately to the valid claims of historically marginalized and disempowered racial groups, "according each other appropriate attention, concern and respect."[65] The power of Du Bois's account of the black experience of double consciousness is that even the most resilient and courageous spirit can eventually be crushed by the unflagging hostility of the world if it does not find a moral community to defend and uplift it, recognizing one's unconditional moral worth. Du Bois was aware that building a new political order – and, by extension, transforming attitudes in a white-controlled polity at large – takes time. Reform is often slow and piecemeal, as many whites resist giving up the privileges of racial caste. In the context of de jure and de facto racial exclusion, he recommended that the black community provisionally self-segregate to *assert* its self-respect as a community. He argued that as a moral community behind the color line, African Americans should continue to engage whites in calculated political efforts to dismantle the color line.[66] But they have the moral right to shield themselves from exposure to a radically evil will and to develop civil associations that recognize their positive normative self-understanding as free and equal human beings, as well as to satisfy their immediate economic needs. He thus contended that the black community – out of self-respect and self-defense – has the moral right to *avoid* confrontations that might spill over into overt displays of anti-black racial animus and violence.

In fact, Du Bois stated that in extreme nonideal circumstances moral suasion can be self-deprecating, as one tries to convince ill-disposed and potentially violent others that one is "worthy" of their recognition:

> We have got to renounce a program that always involves humiliating self-stultifying scrambling to crawl somewhere where we are not wanted; where we crouch panting like a whipped dog. We have got to stop this and learn that on

such a program [we] cannot build manhood. No, by God, stand erect in a mud-puddle and tell the white world to go to hell, rather than lick boots in a parlor.[67]

He builds on his reservations expressed here to develop a controversial critique of the desegregation of schools. The push for desegregation would become a marker for the success of the racial justice movement in the United States. Yet he feared that the ideal of integration would be a Pyrrhic victory – it would come at such a great cost to black America as to hardly constitute a victory at all. He was especially concerned about damaging the healthy social and psychological development of black children in integrated schools, where the majority of white students, teachers, and residents of the neighborhood do not welcome them. Without the cultivation of goodwill and interracial civic fellowship of a white majority, integrated public spaces would leave African Americans – and children in particular – "crucified":

> If the public schools of Atlanta, Nashville, New Orleans, and Jacksonville were thrown open to all races tomorrow, the education that colored children would get in them would be worse than pitiable. It would not be education. And in the same way, there are many public school systems in the North where Negroes are admitted and tolerated, but they are not educated: they are crucified.[68]

Two decades before the *Brown v. Board of Education* decision, in the essay "Separation and Self-Respect" (1934), Du Bois cautioned against sending black children to integrated schools "where white children kick, cuff, or abuse [them], or where teachers openly and persistently neglect or hurt or dwarf [their] soul[s]."[69] In the context of Jim Crow segregation, he was aware of the crucial importance of limiting black children's exposure to the ill will of hostile whites. He was not inclined to sacrifice black children to make an abstract point about the promise of political liberalism in the United States. He states: "Let us not affront our own self-respect by accepting a proffered equality which is not equality, or submitting to discrimination simply because it does not involve actual and open segregation."[70] In circumstances where whites show no goodwill towards members of the black community, Du Bois held that the de jure desegregation effort *upholds* de facto racial caste. Changing the law would not necessarily result in better treatment from actual members of the white community. The overturning of segregation law must be accompanied by a dramatic shift in the attitudes of whites to ensure that future generations of black children are not terrorized in their legally enforced daily contact with whites. He writes: "We have by legal action steadied the foundation so that in the future segregation be by wish and will and not law, but beyond that we have not made the slightest impress on the determination of the overwhelming mass of white Americans not to treat Negroes as men."[71]

By promoting voluntary black self-segregating, he hoped to mitigate the needless exposure of black children to anti-black prejudice, humiliation, and the threat of violence, which would undermine healthy psychological development and self-esteem. According to Du Bois, segregated black schools protected black children from circumstances that would have compelled them to accept a debased view of themselves and to defer to hostile whites in their day-to-day lives. In conjunction with the black church, segregated black schools often strove to inculcate into children the democratic literacy and the civic virtues necessary for a lifetime of navigating – and struggling against – a racial caste society.[72] In black-run schools, children thus found black teachers who recognized their value as moral persons *and* as knowers. Du Bois stressed none has a "right to sneer at the 'Jim Crow' schools of South Carolina, or at the brave teachers who guide [children] at starvation wages."[73] These teachers, who were typically educated at historically black colleges, recognized and celebrated the humanity and talent of black children when few others beyond the color line did so. They exemplified that it is a *"privilege* to work with and for Negroes."[74]

In contrast, the 1954 Supreme Court ruling *Brown v. Board of Education* suggested that it is an intrinsic good for black children to be in the company of white children, as if the exclusive company of black students automatically makes them feel inferior. Du Bois believed, on the contrary, that the support of the black community is often the principal source of well-being and self-esteem for black children since only white people believe that black skin color is a stigma. He did not place a premium on the recognition of white people for their healthy social and psychological development. He did, however, emphasize the crucial importance of a welcoming local community and, ultimately, a quality education for persons to form a positive sense of self.

Echoing Du Bois's reservations, Derrick Bell writes of the unforeseen consequence of *Brown v. Board of Education*:

> The implementation of the court orders that I helped obtain resulted in the closing of black schools and the dismissal of thousands of black teachers and administrators. When the black children who were the beneficiaries of those court orders were admitted previously to all white schools, they often faced hostility, and only infrequently found a teaching environment that was conducive to their needs.[75]

In the face of a recalcitrant color line, the black community has the moral right, provisionally, to self-segregate to develop black civil associations that offered positive social recognition in the black community on a local scale. Positive social recognitive relations among blacks fostered a positive normative self-understanding as free and equal persons, when the white world refused to even consider African Americans as moral equals.

Contemporary implications: the politics of self-segregation today

To be clear, Du Bois remained opposed to de jure segregation and upheld interracial civic fellowship as an ideal of domestic and cosmopolitan justice where all can coexist under institutional conditions of mutual respect, esteem, and reciprocity. He explained that segregation:

> is the separation of human beings and separation despite the will to humanity. Such separation is evil; it leads to jealousy, greed, nationalism, and war [and yet] without it, the American Negro will suffer evils greater than any possible evil of separation: we would suffer the loss of self-respect, the lack of faith in ourselves, the lack of knowledge about ourselves, the lack of ability to make a decent living by our own efforts and not by philanthropy.[76]

His departure from the NAACP raised crucial questions about optimal anti-racist organizing tactics. In bringing Du Bois's spirit to bear on the current world, in a post-civil rights era that has witnessed the resurgence of white-power nationalist movements, one wonders whether a black separatist politics or interracial political coalitions are more viable? Or would some combination of these two approaches work?

In voicing his objection against *Brown v. Board of Education*, Du Bois asked what "with all deliberate speed" actually meant.[77] In the essay, published in 1957, he conducted a historical overview of civil rights legislation in the United States that was rendered inconsequential and ineffective because of ordinary white citizens' reluctance to recognize black civic equality, which would come to translate into state and local governments breaking away from the enforcement of federal legislation or exerting pressure to change federal laws. He began his survey with the Reconstruction era's progressive legislation that was soon countermanded by the rise of black codes in the South. Invariably, a lack of goodwill among white majorities undermines legislation that aims to reconstitute the polity along more racially inclusive lines. And so, he asked again, how long is it permissible to ask a community to wait and to endure the injurious effects of segregation before alternative measures are called for to ensure black survival and welfare?[78]

For Du Bois, "all deliberate speed" is an empty promise that some sixty years later has yet to be delivered, much like the promise of black civic enfranchisement itself. Recent trends have shown that the reluctance to comply with desegregation laws and civil rights legislation plagues the nation as a whole. The African-American community continues to suffer prolonged disenfranchisement along de facto segregated lines. At the K-12 level, it is illegal to establish all-black schools using federal monies, which would stand in opposition to the 1954 Supreme Court ruling. But the viability of the strategy of voluntary self-segregation continues to play out on the campuses of historically black colleges and universities (HBCUs). Though many campuses are diversifying and enrolling non-black students, the mission of an HBCU remains, at the very least, to ensure the quality college education of black children and the successful completion of their degrees.

In the context of rising hate crimes across college campuses, providing a welcoming and nurturing environment to students of color remains vital. Recently the *Michigan Daily*, a student-run newspaper at the University of Michigan, ran the headline: "Frequent bias incidents affect campus mental health, experts say."[79] The author Maya Goldman reports that an increase of racist incidents on the University of Michigan, Ann Arbor campus correlates with a decrease in the academic success and well-being of the targeted students. In the reported incidents, students of color received death threats and were subject to racial slurs; and posters appeared in dormitories that read "Make America White Again" and "Free Dylann Roof," the white supremacist who pleaded guilty to the murder of eight black parishioners and the pastor of the Emanuel A. M. E. Church in Charleston, South Carolina in 2015. Goldman describes "the physical and mental wear-and-tear" that leads to "alarming occurrences of anxiety, stress, depression and thoughts of suicide, as well as a host of physical ailments like hair loss, diabetes and heart disease."[80] In the aftermath of these incidents, supportive resources on campus were crucial for students to cope with and complete their degrees.

Unwittingly echoing Du Bois, Goldman's report demonstrates that the lack of recognition of black moral equality significantly impacts social and psychological development. The way others treat you affects the goals you set for yourself and your sense of your capacity to achieve them. Ultimately, misrecognition can diminish your sense of self as having unconditional value and a moral entitlement to pursue a conception of the good life in the first place. Understandably, some black students at the University of Michigan who were the targets of racial harassment transferred to an HBCU. At least in part, the future of HBCUs is to provide an outlet for students of color to shield them from white supremacy, as well as to launch their careers as young professionals. So much the loss for the University of Michigan.

The bright future of HBCUs suggests that nurturing institutional spaces explicitly designed to recognize black moral equality, history, and genius still serves a vital role in the nation. Until whites express goodwill towards people of color, Du Bois maintained that it is *consistent* with liberal ideals and an assertion of black self-respect to limit black exposure to hostile whites whenever possible. Such is "the sobering realization of the meaning of progress."[81]

Conclusion

The Passage into Exile: The Return Home Away from Home (1951–1963)

To this day, the town of Great Barrington refuses to erect a statue in honor of Du Bois because the local, predominantly white townsfolk protest the memorialization of a communist sympathizer.[1] In the town itself, there is little to carry the memory of its most famous son. Only the foundation of his childhood home remains, over which stands a small sign with some biographical information about Du Bois. If you follow a footpath from a small parking lot into the forest, you can find the foundation of the house and read the little sign. Du Bois's life and legacy has been poorly understood and even more poorly remembered and honored. And in the last decade of his life, no doubt, Du Bois acutely felt the shock and pain of being alienated from his first homeland, America. One could almost feel the afterlife of his sense of alienation still lingering in his hometown.

In the twilight of his life, a sense of despair, combined with an unwavering intellectual drive, led him to continue exploring political strategies that preserved and mobilized

black racial solidarity. While he had pioneered black nationalist thinking to motivate the African-American community
to close rank within US national borders, by the end of
his life he focused on strengthening black transnational
networks that could resist a global color line and further
distanced himself from conventional models of governance
and reform promoted by western liberal democracies. To be
sure, even as a young scholar and activist, he had pursued his
late mentor Alexander Crummell's pan-African philosophy,
organizing the first Pan-African Congress in Paris in 1919
and others again in 1921, 1923, 1927, and 1945.[2] The idea
of continental Africa as an ancestral home had been important to Du Bois since his first visit to Africa in 1923, and he
had hoped that a pan-African congress would be held in an
African nation rather than in the United States or Europe.[3]
In his final decade, his anti-imperialist and anti-colonial politics reflected a global perspective that centered on national
African and Asian independence movements. His renewed
vision of progress called upon the oppressed colored people
of the world to unite in a concerted political action against
a global color line. He could not accept that nations with
white majorities might lead the effort to realize a peaceful and egalitarian global order. Anglo-European nations
had benefited so much from endless war and conquest. He
called upon formerly colonized peoples to take the initiative to establish a cosmopolitan global community where
all persons would stand as equal citizens of the world. He
criticized the unrestrained economic growth of the West at
the expense of developing nations and denounced a global
order that robbed developing nations of their right to political and economic self-determination. He eventually went
into exile and died in Accra, Ghana, on August 27, 1963 at
the age of 95. Although Du Bois was a newly naturalized
Ghanaian citizen, President Nkrumah organized an ornate

state funeral attended by thousands, while crowds gathered at the Washington Monument, DC, to listen to Martin Luther King and to step into an uncertain era without the figure who for so long was the guiding star of liberation.

In this chapter, I follow the events and reasoning that precipitated Du Bois's passage into exile. I reintroduce the themes of the book and reexamine the ideal of civic enfranchisement in the context of a cosmopolitan pan-African philosophy. I also raise the interpretive issue of the significance of Du Bois's legacy today. I trace the lines of theoretical continuity in his oeuvre, while reflecting on a new era in global and US domestic politics in the wake of the Cold War and de-colonial struggles for independence.

Du Bois's life, scholarship, and activism in his last decade (1951–1963)

I hope you will not either over-stress that earlier part of my career or forget that latter part. There seem to be a considerable number of persons who think I died when [Booker T.] Washington did[.][4]

The 1950s was a turbulent decade for Du Bois and his family, marked by personal loss and unexpected new beginnings. In 1950, his first wife, Nina Gomer, died. He buried her in Great Barrington, Massachusetts beside the grave of their infant son, Burghardt, who had died decades earlier. Recollecting their lives together, he admits that his careerism made him an unideal partner in 54 years of marriage: "I was not, on the whole, what one would describe as a good husband. The family and its interests were never the center of my life. I was always striving to guide the world and certainly the Negro group, so that always I was ranging away in body and in soul and leaving the home to my wife."[5] Du Bois married Shirley Graham in 1951 with whom he would later move to Accra, Ghana in 1961 and whom he would widow in 1963. Graham was a prominent playwright, biographer, and activist close to the Communist Party. In 1945, she was one of the first African-American women to win the prestigious Guggenheim Fellowship.[6] A formidable intellectual in her own right, Graham not only provided much needed support to her aging husband, who was 29 years her senior, but steadied his life in its turbulent final years. After burying his first wife, Du Bois quickly resumed his focus on work and politics. In broad strokes, transnational activism, pacifism, and his growing interest in communist and labor politics were three features that distinguished his last decade. In my view, however, it is difficult to identify a comprehensive set of principles that informed the normative basis of his critique of domestic and global politics in his last decade.

In 1950, Du Bois ran unsuccessfully for United States Senator on the American Labor Party ticket. He had grown disenchanted with the two-party system. He did not believe he had a shot at winning the senate seat. Rather, he used the campaign as a platform to give speeches and radio broadcasts across the United States on what he considered the pressing issues of the time that were misrepresented by Cold War propaganda. He advocated for denuclearization, peace, and labor rights. He was stunned to win 4 percent of the vote, 15 percent of which came from Harlem residents of New York City.[7]

He also aligned himself with countries that he believed posed a genuine alternative to colonial imperialism and global capitalism. He became a vocal apologist for the Soviet Union and Maoist China in the 1950s. Du Bois had visited China and the Soviet Union several times between 1926 and 1959 and backed their policies in leftist weeklies, even after news surfaced of mass arbitrary detention and state-supported murder.[8] A departure from his usual unsparing attitude, he wrote a flowery eulogy at the death of Stalin in 1953, writing "Joseph Stalin was a great man [. . .] He knew the common man, felt his problems, followed his fate."[9] He appeared to accept the official state-spun narratives of communism's bold and triumphant step into the future. He won the Lenin Peace Prize from Nikita Khrushchev in 1959 for "promoting relations of stable friendship and cooperation among all peoples of the world."[10]

It is noteworthy that as Du Bois was losing influence in the United States, he was warmly welcomed by the Soviet Union and China. Both countries hosted him for many months at public expense. Countries in the Eastern Bloc were translating his works and awarding him various honors. In contrast, his position in the United States was increasingly uncertain. At the height of the Cold War, he was targeted in a harassment campaign by the federal government. Briefly, he stood as an indicted criminal in federal court, charged with acting as a foreign agent for the Soviet Union.

Du Bois's involvement with the pacifist group, Peace Information Center, led to a criminal indictment.[11] Board members of the NAACP believed that the Soviet Union covertly funded the Peace Information Center. In short, neither the NAACP nor the American Civil Liberties Union rallied to his defense. He later described the experience: "I have faced during my life many unpleasant experiences: the growl of a mob; the personal threat of murder; the scowling distaste of an audience. But nothing has so cowed me as that day, November 8, 1951, when I took my seat in a Washington courtroom as an indicted criminal."[12]

Ironically, it was Du Bois's activism for peace that pitted him in a chaotic battle with the US federal government. The most extreme action that the Peace Information Center had taken was to promote the Stockholm Peace Appeal "to abolish the atom bomb."[13] In the convoluted logic of the Cold War, peace activism was perceived as a communist front to cripple US military defenses against a looming Soviet invasion. Du Bois and three of his fellow peace activists dissolved the Peace Information Center in the hope that it would bolster their defense against the indictment.

So late in life he was prosecuted by the same country for whose democratic ideals he had so passionately fought. To his deep disappointment, he was deserted by many prominent civil rights leaders and organizations during his trial, many of whom had been lifelong friends and allies. During this chapter in American history, American public figures, writers, and teachers routinely had their careers ruined and their lives destroyed by the House of Un-American Activities. Like so many others, Du Bois and Graham were blacklisted. Presses refused to publish their books.[14] A celebration for his 83rd birthday had been planned before the indictment, but the Essex House Hotel in Manhattan suddenly refused to host the event and numerous prominent guests made their excuses for their inability to attend. An alternative celebration was planned in Harlem by Du Bois's closest friends.[15] "I can stand a good deal, and have done so during my life," wrote Du Bois, "but this experience was rather more than I felt like bearing, especially as the blows continued to fall. I had meantime been finger-printed, handcuffed, bailed, and remanded for trial."[16] Once Albert Einstein agreed to testify on his behalf, the Department of Justice feared that Du Bois would emerge as a sympathetic figure during public testimonies. The charges against him were eventually dismissed by a federal judge.

After being victimized by the Red Scare, his future and even the reception of his legacy after his death in the United States suffered. Even after his victory against the Department of Justice, he remained alienated from the political establishment. He was isolated and ostracized in institutions that had once welcomed him as a forebear. Universities rescinded their invitations for him to speak at their campuses. Black newspapers were wary of printing his essays. The campaign against him left him nearly penniless and a de facto stateless person, precipitating his exile to Ghana under Nkrumah's sponsorship. In 1961, in a final defiant gesture, perhaps tinged with indignation, he officially joined the Communist Party USA, just months before his permanent departure from the United States later that same year.

It is not clear what ultimately drove Du Bois at the age of 93 to leave the United States behind after a lifetime of battling its recalcitrant political forces. But it is reasonable to suppose that he was exhausted and despondent as a result of the persistent disrespect he faced so late in life. "I just can't take any more of this country's [America's] treatment," he wrote in a letter to Grace Goens on September 13, 1961. "We leave for Ghana October 5th and I set no date for return . . . Chin up, and fight on, but realize that American Negroes can't win."[17]

His despair in his last years suggested that racial justice in the United States is impossible. I believe that we can have compassion for his cruel treatment and understand his reasons for leaving the United States, without going so far as to follow him into despair. There is still good reason to hold onto the democratic ideals, for which he had spent a lifetime advocating. Clearly, by the time Du Bois had written to Goens, he was looking for a new political vision and a new ideal to fight for, one that left the United States receding into oblivion.[18] And, anyway, Du Bois came to stress that the United States was not the only player in the black diasporic struggle. Moreover, he sensed that the rising figures of the new era of the civil rights movement, many of whom he publicly supported, including Martin Luther King Jr, were emerging as better positioned to carry on the domestic struggle for racial justice.[19] Lastly, it was particularly painful for Du Bois to outlive his only surviving child, and this fueled his conviction that the few ties he had left to America were severed. Yolande suffered a heart attack and died in 1961. He buried his daughter in the family plot in Great Barrington in March; he departed for Ghana in October of that year.

Between domestic justice and cosmopolitanism: the pan-African movement in the black diaspora

Du Bois's interest in Africa and African politics can be traced back to early in his career. He made his first trip to Africa in 1923. In *Dusk of Dawn*, he recounted that formative experience: "When shall I forget the night I first set foot on African soil? [. . .] The long arm of the bay enveloped us and then to the right rose the twinkling hill of Monrovia [present-day Liberia], with its crowning star."[20] Charting the relation of US politics – and the African-American community – to the African diaspora marked a recurrent theme in his political thought. The idea of Africa also came to increasingly define his sense of personal identity. He would sometimes refer to himself as an "African" or a "son of Africa" and to Africa as a "homeland" or "motherland."[21] In 1930, he published two books on Africa, *Africa, Its Geography, People, and Products* and *Africa – Its Place in Modern History*. Just as he had illustrated the transformative agency of enslaved Africans in spearheading emancipation and Reconstruction in the United States, he too aimed to illustrate the centrality of Africa in the development of world civilizations. His works illustrated the effective practical agency of black African historical actors who are seldom represented as making any relevant contributions to world history. He argued that one cannot conceptualize the historical development of the world without acknowledging its interpenetration with African affairs. He also posited that future political progress will be in the hands of colored nations in general and of Africa in particular. And so he wrote about Africa with a sense of urgency to seize a political moment that could galvanize de-colonial efforts and usher in a new global era, one that is both peaceful and economically egalitarian for all persons in the world reconceived as equal cosmopolitan citizens.

Du Bois described the special importance of Africa in his moral and political imagination:

> Since the concept of race has changed so much and presented so much of a contradiction that as I face Africa I ask myself: what is it between us that constitutes a tie which I can feel better than I can explain? Africa is, of course, my fatherland. Yet neither my father nor my father's father ever saw Africa or knew its meaning or cared overmuch for it. My mother's folk were closer and yet their direct connection, in culture and race, became tenuous; still, my tie to Africa is strong. On this vast continent were born and lived a large portion of my direct ancestors going back a thousand years or more. The mark of their heritage is upon me in color and hair. These are obvious things, but of little meaning in themselves; only important as they stand for real and more subtle differences from other men. Whether they do or not, I do not know nor does science know today.[22]

Du Bois's avowed personal connection to Africa was not mere rhetorical flourish. He aimed to illustrate the ties of black racial solidarity that might provide a shared basis for black political mobilization in the light of a global color line. He believed that Africa could lead the world into a cosmopolitan condition of peace and universal flourishing inasmuch as newly independent African republics assumed positions of global leadership. He knew that it was a difficult task to confront the obstacles imposed by global capitalism and white supremacy; and so he advocated for nations of the so-called Third World to lean on each other to achieve economic and political growth independent of western influence. This vision of concerted political action on the basis of global racial solidarity, in part, defined his pan-African philosophy.

Du Bois accepted the position of chairman of the Council on African Affairs in 1948, after publishing *The World and Africa* (1947). His seat at the Council on African Affairs was his first public institutional affiliation after his final ousting from the NAACP in 1948. The objective of the Council was to advance de-colonial efforts and basic civil rights, and to resist colonial apartheid in Africa. Du Bois's work on the Council deepened his engagement with African politics. President Nkrumah solicited his advice after Ghana won its independence from the United Kingdom in 1957. A socialist and pan-African dissident, Nkrumah became the first president of the republic of Ghana after suffering years of political persecution and incarceration for contesting English colonial rule. Nkrumah had been educated abroad in the United States and the United Kingdom and had likely already met Du Bois through their joint participation in the Pan-African Conference held in Manchester, England in 1945. Nkrumah's Convention People's Party (CPP) worked to promote workers' rights and the end of British occupation of Ghana. With his unprecedented political victory, which saw him rise from a jail cell to the most important public office in the country, he welcomed Du Bois and Graham to their adopted homeland. He was keen to create an ideal political community where influential black writers and intellectuals could find fellowship and escape the racial provincialism of their native countries. Nkrumah and the Du Boises shared a sense of urgency to seize a historical moment that could realize their shared ideal of a utopian, black-led global future.[23]

By accepting an invitation from Nkrumah, Du Bois dedicated his remaining intellectual energy to completing a final project, *Encyclopedia Africana*.[24] He had first imagined the encyclopedia in 1909 as a systematic account of African and Afro-descended peoples around the world. He may have been inspired by the publication of *Encyclopedia Judaica* in 1907.[25] His various attempts to fund the project through the decades were unsuccessful. He jumped at the opportunity to fulfill a lifelong dream, just when he was otherwise losing support in the United States for his political and intellectual ambitions. As a way of enticing Du Bois to resettle in Ghana, Nkrumah offered generous funding and the assistance of a cadre of scholars at the newly founded Ghana Academy of Arts and Sciences. Unfortunately, Du Bois died before completing the project, joking that, ideally, it would take him ten years to finish each volume of the encyclopedia he envisioned.[26] It was later completed by the prominent Africana scholars Henry Louis Gates Jr and Kwame Anthony Appiah in 1999. In their introduction to the first edition of the encyclopedia, Gates and Appiah explain:

[Du Bois] envisioned a comprehensive compendium of "scientific" knowledge about the history, cultures, and social institutions of people of African descent: of Africans in the Old World, African Americans in the New World, and persons of African descent who had risen to prominence in Europe, the Middle East, and Asia. Du Bois sought to publish nothing less than the equivalent of a black *Encyclopaedia Britannica*, believing that such a broad assemblage of biography, interpretive essays, facts, and figures would do for the much denigrated black world of the twentieth century what *Britannica* and Denis Diderot's *Encyclopédie* had done for the European world of the eighteenth century.[27]

Du Bois's pursuit of the project invoked the scientific ideal of his early years as a rising social scientist: Knowledge is a crucial means for fighting anti-black prejudice and a systematic account of the diversity and complexity of black life could be a potential source of self-esteem for African and Afro-descendant peoples. He strove not only to establish the significance of Africa in world history but to provide an unprecedented comprehensive account of the government, culture, and the arts of continental Africa and its sons and daughters.

Just as Du Bois acknowledged the importance of Africans to be the main agents in their political affairs, he too hoped that the encyclopedia would primarily be written for and by African scholars: "I propose an Encyclopedia edited mainly by African scholars. I am anxious that it be a scientific production and not a matter of propaganda. [. . .] I want the proposed Encyclopedia to be written mainly from the African point of view by people who know and understand the history and culture of Africans."[28] Du Bois had some pushback for being an African-American scholar leading the project; and it may be why the project stalled for so long. In his first proposals for the project, he had also to defend himself against the inclusion of so many white scholars. He would come to share the worry that scholarship on Africa was becoming dominated by white academics who had no special interest in the development of a pan-African identity that could resist a global color line and global capitalism. His final proposal showed that he considered it crucial that scholars from newly independent African republics should have the primary role in telling their own histories and defining their own futures. So it is no surprise that he rekindled the project – and it became a feasible endeavor – only in the context of a successful pan-Africanist movement that centered Africa in global politics. The completion of such a formidable intellectual project raised the prospect of a political future that was defined by a pan-African coalition of united and free African republics. In his mature conception of pan-African philosophy, he too cautioned against African Americans presuming to be leaders of continental Africa, thereby recreating a colonial attitude towards indigenous Africans as "backward" or "premodern."[29]

For Du Bois, the encyclopedia was an example of a cultural artifact that provided something akin to a positive normative self-understanding for citizens of African republics, fostering a sense of greater political unity across the continent. The neglect and denigration of the African historical experience, Du Bois agreed, had to be counteracted by a certain kind of scholarship – and, ultimately, concerted political action – spearheaded by Africans themselves. As the philosopher Katrin Flikschuh explains, there is a form of racism, which she identifies as "philosophical racism," that devalues persons as equal participants in philosophical discourses and in the formation of sociocultural and epistemic practices. Flikschuh argues that "philosophically racist forms of thought and beliefs" share "unstated background assumptions about which contexts and domains of human experience are or are not worthy of philosophical reflection."[30] Africa and the African historical experience had for too long been omitted as unworthy of philosophical reflection and systematic "scientific" study. The formation of free African republics in the wake of de-colonialism was an opportunity, as Du Bois saw it, for Africans to define themselves on their own terms as practical and epistemic agents. Thus a pan-African project of political and economic self-determination should include the collective effort of cultural self-definition. For other nations to learn to recognize historically excluded and derided persons as equal participants and addressees of discourses in science, culture, and politics would indicate a true cosmopolitan interracial civic fellowship. And it would illustrate "a common search for true universals" among all peoples of the world.[31]

The project of the encyclopedia, in part, aimed to redefine the nature of African modernity and its intersection with, but ultimate divergence from, the historical development of America and Europe. Du Bois intended to highlight the distinct history and practices that represent the free purposive agency of Africans. In part, the project raises the question of what it means for a people to be "modern" and "civilized" in the first place. A viable notion of modernity cannot simply demand external conformity to standards of social and political comportment that are imposed by outsiders. Such an approach, for Du Bois, had sanctioned the elision of African history and western intervention for regime change, slavery, colonialism, and economic exploitation that had rendered continental Africa dependent on – and subjugated by – the West. Slavery, colonialism, and apartheid had been rationalized as a means to impart liberal "civilized" norms to a "backward" people who prima facie did not seem to meet some sociocultural threshold of human development.[32] Formulating a conception of African modernity required a context-sensitive account of African life-worlds that showcased the complexity and purposiveness of indigenous African sociocultural and epistemic practices. As the Du Bois scholar Chike Jeffers puts it, a "viable cosmopolitanism" must "validate the indigenous non-Western grounds for concepts of universal application [and is] essential to an anti-Eurocentric cosmopolitanism."[33]

To be sure, Du Bois was *not* a relativist. Nor did he

endorse the notion of "alternative modernities" that rendered Africa somehow permanently "outside" the historical development of the West, as if Africa followed an idiosyncratic line of historical development that could share nothing with other peoples and states.[34] Rather, in his works on Africa, he upheld the *universal ideals of democratic self-determination* and *sovereign nation-building* (likely, a keen topic of conversation for Nkrumah).[35] His approach to African history aimed to highlight the indigenous sociocultural and epistemic practices that illuminated the positive role that Africans have yet to play in refining their own constitutional republic and in advancing a global cosmopolitan condition. Irony was a favored narrative tool for Du Bois: for he held that Africans are better positioned – and far more likely – to actualize the democratic ideals and a cosmopolitan condition that a violent and imperialistic West has nominally endorsed for centuries. But Africa must actualize these ideals on its own terms and independent of the destabilizing patronage, neocolonial subjugation, and intervention of the West.

In *Color and Democracy*, Du Bois asked, "How far are we working for a world where the peoples who are ruled are going to have effective voice in their governments? We have stated and reiterated that this democratic method of government is going to be applied in the future as widely as possible."[36] The pan-African movement defended the national sovereignty of African republics in the aftermath of the de-colonial struggle. His defense of the sovereignty of African states complements his pointed critique of western imperial power. Namely, he linked western demilitarization to the struggle for the political and economic self-determination of former colonies.[37] The fight against the military aggression of the West would facilitate the rise of independent African republics.

In his early essay, "The African Roots of the War" (1915),

he outlined the economic incentives of western states to establish hegemony over Africa using extreme violence. The scramble to mine African resources resulted in World War I.[38] He elaborated that "the ownership of materials and men in the darker world is the real prize that is setting the nations of Europe at each other's throats today."[39] Western interest in the economic exploitation of the "darker world" created a special obstacle in the cultivation of ties of interracial fellowship between Africa and white-majority states. Du Bois explained:

> [T]he white workingman has been asked to share the spoil of exploiting "chi**s and ni**ers." It is no longer simply the merchant prince, or the aristocratic monopoly, or even the employing class, that is exploiting the world: it is the nation; a new democratic nation composed of united capital and labor. The laborers are not yet getting, to be sure, as large a share as they want or will get, and there are still at the bottom large and restless excluded classes. But the laborer's equity is recognized and his just share is a matter of time, intelligence, and skillful negotiation. Such nations it is that rule the modern world. Their national bond is no mere sentimental patriotism, loyalty, or ancestor-worship. It is increased wealth, power, and luxury for all classes on a scale the world never saw before. Never before was the average citizen of England, France and Germany so rich, with such splendid prospects of greater riches. Whence comes this new wealth and on what does its accumulation depend? It comes primarily from the darker nations of the world – Asia and Africa, South and Central America, the West Indies and the islands of the South Seas.[40]

The white worker in England and France was inclined to rationalize imperial power with the promise of a raised national standard of living. The "new democratic nations" were bolstered by a global economic hegemony that undermined the aspirations of republican sovereignty of non-western states.[41] Du Bois highlighted the *contradiction*, pointing out that democratic self-determination, taking root in a particular domestic context, cannot then serve to destroy the economic and political foundations of other nations to be masters of their own fate. His pan-African philosophy thus aimed to render the ideal of democratic self-determination a true universal across the globe.

Du Bois's critique of US and European imperialism was grounded in the universal ideals of democratic self-determination and sovereign nation-building for an independent Africa. He viewed the promotion of domestic justice and nation-building as a *means* to advance a cosmopolitan condition. Recall that the cosmopolitan condition, according to Du Bois, would usher in a period of global peace and economic egalitarianism, where no country would be subjugated by another to mine its resources or wealth, especially at the expense of colored nations for the benefit of the West. But the feasibility of cosmopolitanism *presupposes* the formation of free black republics, which Du Bois envisioned would serve as the primary political agents for advancing global peace and economic justice. This means that the cosmopolitan citizens of a pan-African movement must both assert their moral status as free and equal citizens within their respective national borders and "reenvision themselves as part of a transnational collective."[42] What David Levering Lewis describes as Du Bois's "diasporic nationalism" is consistent with and catalyzed by an ideal of civic enfranchisement in manifold concurrent schemes of domestic justice in republics across the globe.[43]

Du Bois drew on George Padmore, a communist and a secretary of the pan-African Congress, to define pan-Africanism: "In our struggle for national freedom, human dignity, and social redemption Pan-Africanism [. . .] [the movement] rejects both white racialism and black chauvinism. It stands for racial co-existence on the basis of absolute equality and respect for human personality."[44] This definition of pan-Africanism can be further illuminated by considering the concrete goals that Du Bois attached to the movement. Below are the goals that he listed at the Pan-African Conference held in New York City in 1927:

> Negroes everywhere need:
> 1. A voice in their own government.
> 2. Native rights to the land and its natural resources.
> 3. Modern education for all children.
> 4. The development of Africa for the Africans and not merely for the profit of Europeans.
> 5. The reorganization of commerce and industry so as to make the main object of capital and labor the welfare of the many rather than the enriching of the few.
> 6. The treatment of civilized men as civilized despite differences of birth, race, or color.[45]

These goals, I submit, are only feasible in a functional constitutional state whose national sovereignty is respected by other states. Some three decades later, in 1956, Du Bois would repeat roughly the same goals in restating the aims of the pan-African movement.[46] Note, too, that the "social revolution" of Reconstruction, which I detailed in chapter 5, reflected the pursuit of comparable goals in the postbellum African-American community, which called upon the emergence of a racially pluralistic and centralized US federal government in the aftermath of the Civil War to guarantee the legal rights of black citizenship to equal representation, resources, and education.

Apart from regional partnerships in continental Africa, Du Bois also advocated for the establishment of "pan-African" alliances of all "colored" nations, hoping that Africa and China would unite to create a bulwark against western intervention. An alliance between China and Africa could appeal to what he imagined to be a transnational basis for racial solidarity of colored nations against global white supremacy.[47] Thus he surmised that forging intercontinental alliances was key to the success of the pan-African movement; regional partnerships had the power, he hoped, to expel corporate private interests and western imperial power.

Additionally, Du Bois often equated the idea of pan-Africanism with "pan-African socialism."[48] His pan-African philosophy called on rising sovereign African republics to mitigate economic dependence on the West through regional and global partnerships. The young African republics could bolster the economic self-determination of workers and guarantee workers' rights to determine the allocation of wealth, income, and resources. Du Bois defended what he sometimes referred to as the "welfare state" in Africa to nationalize resources and to create public institutions that subordinated the accumulation of capital to the interest of labor. He warned against borrowing capital at high interest rates from western nations. The economically egalitarian dimension of his cosmopolitanism presupposed the ideal of the sovereign republic that guaranteed the satisfaction of workers' needs and extended their democratic control over production.

Du Bois explained in a speech delivered by his second wife (on his behalf) at the All-African Conference in Accra, Ghana in 1958:

Pan-African Socialism seeks *the Welfare State in Africa*. It will refuse to be exploited by people of other continents for their own benefit and not for the benefit of the peoples of

Africa. It will no longer consent to permitting the African
majority of any African country to be governed against its
will by a minority of invaders who claim racial superiority or
the right to get rich at African expense. It will seek not only
to raise but to process the raw material and to trade it freely
with all the world on just and equal terms and prices.[49]

In this way he hoped that "African states [. . .] can take
their place among the nations of the world."[50] A cosmopolitan condition can, then, create a global federation of states
to include diverse republics that each upholds the ideal of
democratic self-determination that enables the flourishing of
distinct life-worlds. Jeffers notes that "a viable cosmopolitanism" would thus be a "rooted" cosmopolitanism: it must
not force integration into a world state but attend instead to
asymmetries of power that undermine the cultural, economic,
and political integrity of historically oppressed peoples.[51] Du
Bois posited that the ideal of sovereign African republics was
a crucial means for advancing peace and abolishing poverty.[52]

While Du Bois held a global concern for colored peoples
and their struggles, his pan-African cosmopolitan orientation
is compatible with an emphasis on the constitution – and
reconstitution – of particular civic communities delineated
by national constitutions. How does pan-African thought
intersect with the democratic ideals of civic enfranchisement
in a particular imperfect constitutional republic? Echoing
Balfour, I affirm that Du Bois's understanding of the reconstruction of American democracy, and the historic lessons of
the advance of democratic ideals, can inspire democratic politics globally.[53] In fact, he hoped that a pan-African movement
could aid the African-American struggle for racial justice in
the future as the Haitian Revolution had inspired slave revolts
and abolition in the United States. The idea of cosmopolitan
citizenship can enhance domestic justice, resulting in the uni-

versal extension of inalienable civil, political, and economic rights. In fact, pan-African cosmopolitanism *requires* a legitimate public authority to institutionalize the terms of civic belonging and thereby approximate a cosmopolitan condition.[54] I thus submit that Du Bois's pan-African philosophy is compatible with his defense of the ideal of civic enfranchisement in his early thought. The creation of modern states in the de-colonial effort must press on African modernity as testing – just as in the postbellum United States – the ideal of a democratic government that is truly free and open to all.

Not long after Du Bois's death, Nkrumah was overthrown in a violent military coup in 1966; he died in exile in 1972. One can only speculate what could have become of Du Bois under a military dictatorship of the National Liberation Council, which succeeded Nkrumah's pan-African socialist party. The tragedy attests to the fact that no place on earth eschews the formidable task of establishing free and open democratic government.

I would like to end this section with a poem that Du Bois wrote in 1960 and dedicated to Nkrumah. As if summoned by a dream, "Up from hell / a land had leaped," and it called to him to make Ghana a new home. There he lies buried. Perhaps he still hears the call.

"Ghana Calls"

And then it came: I dreamed.
I placed together all I knew
All hints and slurs together drew.
I dreamed.

I made one picture of what nothing seemed
I shuddered in dumb terror
In silence screamed,
For now it seemed this I had dreamed;

How up from Hell, a land had leaped
A wretched land, all scorched and seamed
Covered with ashes, chained with pain
Streaming with blood, in horror lain
Its very air a shriek of death
And agony of hurt.

[. . .]

Here at last, I looked back on my Dream;
I heard the Voice that loosed
The Long-looked dungeons of my soul
I sensed that Africa had come
Not up from Hell, but from the sum of Heaven's glory.

I lifted up mine eyes to Ghana
And swept the hills with high Hosanna;
Above the sun my sight took flight
Till from that pinnacle of light
I saw dropped down this earth of crimson, green and gold
Roaring with color, drums and song.[55]

After exile: Du Bois's legacy today

Upon his conviction for corrupting the youth of Athens, Socrates was given the choice to depart Athens or drink hemlock. He chose death rather than exile. A Socratic gadfly, the United States would not tolerate Du Bois's relentless prodding, and he was not inclined towards martyrdom. And so he departed, for he still had much work to do. His departure raises the question of what to make of his complicated legacy today. Does his vision of a racially pluralistic America make sense, given the troubling experiences of his last decade? We can approach this question from two perspectives: that of justified ideals and that of what Du Bois saw as a justified ideal.

There will thus always be a divergence between how readers today should evaluate the merit of Du Bois's ideas and
how Du Bois himself judged their merit. The first approach
is fundamentally philosophical in that it focuses on offering
independent justifications for a historical figure's changing
views. The second approach is intellectual history that simply
tracks a historical figure's changing views. I propose that the
power and richness of Du Bois scholarship is that it allows
us to pursue both options at once – a tactic that I have pursued in this book. Both approaches yield novel insights about
political theory and strategy. As the historian Shawn Leigh
Alexander aptly puts it, the best way to honor Du Bois's life
and legacy is to "examine the totality of his thought and
actions, to not limit one's examination and analysis to one
part of his life or one phrase of his written or spoken words.
Amid all the tragedy in the world, Du Bois believed in progress and hope for the future."[56]

Perhaps the one through line in Du Bois's writings is his
faith in the still-to-be-born future that can redeem a world
disfigured by racial violence, war, and poverty. On his 83rd
birthday, he declared:

I am a native-born citizen of the United States as my fore-
fathers on both sides have been for two hundred years. I
have in my life loyally done my full duty as a citizen as I saw
it. I have obeyed my country's laws even when I thought
some of these laws barbarous. I have tried to make this
nation a better country for my having lived in it. It would
not be true for me to say that I "love my country," for it
has enslaved, impoverished, murdered and insulted my
people. Despite this I know what America has done for the
poor, oppressed and hopeless of many other peoples, and
what indeed it has done to contradict and atone for its sins
against Negroes. I still believe that some day this nation will

become a democracy without a color line. I work and shall work for an America whose aim is not solely to make a few people rich, but rather to stop War, and abolish Poverty, Disease and Ignorance for all men.[57]

The struggle for justice often elicits incredible sacrifices from those most vulnerable who heed its call. Du Bois himself grew weary of the howling hostility or indifference of the white world. And yet so much of his historiography attests to the resilience of the human spirit in an intergenerational phenomenon. When one person departs, the vision that inspired them remains. And it is difficult for any future movement to find its identity apart from the legacy of those who came before. In a show of belated thanks, the US polity must honor and understand Du Bois's life and thought. For each new component that Du Bois developed to fight anti-black prejudice reflects each new tentacle, horn, and antenna that white supremacy grew to suffocate democracy and communities of color. Confronting Du Bois's complicated legacy is an opportunity for the United States to confront itself for all its moral failure and hypocrisy.

By promoting an expansive vision of black racial solidarity that drew on transnational solidarity, global in scale, and by foregrounding economic inequality, in his last decade Du Bois remained absorbed with the same recurring questions that defined his storied life: How can the promise of a brighter future be delivered to African and Afro-descendant peoples? What does it mean for a formerly enslaved and colonized people to be free?

"du bois in ghana"

at 93, you determined to pick up and go –
and *stay* gone. [. . .]

[. . .] dr. du bois, i presume
you took the climate in stride, took to it,
          looked out your library's louvered windows
onto a land you needed
neither to condemn nor conquer,
and let the sun tell you what you already knew:
          this was not a port to pass on. [. . .]

[. . .] your memory,
          your tireless radiant energy, calls me

to my work, to my feet, insisting
that somewhere on the earth, freedom is
learning to walk, trying not to fall,
          and, somewhere, laboring to be born.[58]

Notes

Introduction

1 James Baldwin and Margaret Mead, *A Rap on Race*, Philadelphia and New York: J. B. Lippincott Company, 1971, p. 3.

2 For an incisive critique of Coates, see Melvin L. Rogers, "Between Pain and Despair: What Ta-Nehisi Coates Is Missing," *Dissent*, July 31, 1995, online.

3 Ta-Nehisi Coates, *Between the World and Me*, New York: Random House, 2015, p. 69.

4 Susan Neiman notes that a major difference in the twentieth-century political history of Europe and North America is that Europe was willing to confront its atrocities and genocide – at least with respect to the Holocaust – and thus attempted to atone for the past, whereas the United States has never really tried. See her *Learning from the Germans: Race and the Memory of Evil*, New York: Farrar, Straus, and Giroux, 2019.

5 In contrast, the "Afropessimist" intellectual movement posits that anti-black racism is almost an unstoppable, permanent, and quasi-natural force in US history. See Frank B. Wilderson III, *Afropessimism*, New York: Liveright, 2020.

6 Africana philosophy is an umbrella term that categorizes philosophical inquiry centrally focused on the experiences of African and Afro-descendant peoples. For an overview of the subfield, see Lucius T. Outlaw, "Africana Philosophy," in Edward N. Zalta (ed.), *The Stanford Encyclopedia of Philosophy* (Summer 2017 edn), https://plato.stanford.edu/archives/sum2017/entries/africana/

7 See Aldon Morris, *The Scholar Denied: W. E. B. Du Bois and the Birth of Modern Sociology*, Oakland: University of California Press, 2017.

8 Charles W. Mills, "W. E. B. Du Bois: Black Radical Liberal," in Nick Bromell (ed.), *A Political Companion to W. E. B. Du Bois*, Lexington: University of Kentucky Press, 2018, pp. 19–56.

9 W. E. B. Du Bois, *The Souls of Black Folk*, New York: Penguin, 1989, pp. 3–4.

10 W. E. B. Du Bois, "The Development of a People," in N. D. Chandler (ed.), *The Problem of the Color Line at the Turn of the Twentieth Century: The Essential Early Essays*, New York: Fordham University Press, 2015, p. 244.

11 Christopher Lebron, *The Making of Black Lives Matter: A Brief History of an Idea*, New York: Oxford University Press, 2017, p. xx.

12 W. E. B. Du Bois, *In Battle for Peace: The Story of my 83rd Birthday*, New York: Oxford University Press, 2007, p. 82.

13 Chike Jeffers, "Appiah's Cosmopolitanism," *The Southern Journal of Philosophy* 51(4) (2013): 488–510; Chike Jeffers, "The Cultural Theory of Race: Yet Another Look at Du Bois's 'The Conservation of Races,'" *Ethics* 123(3) (2013): 403–26; Ines Valdez, *Transnational Cosmopolitanism: Kant, Du Bois, and Justice as a Political Craft*, New York: Cambridge University Press, 2019.

14 Juliet Hooker, *Theorizing Race in the Americas: Douglass, Sarmiento, Du Bois, and Vasconcelos*, New York: Oxford University Press, 2017, pp. 113–54.

15 In my view, it is not plausible to hold that Du Bois became an anarchist who rejected the legitimacy of the modern state or an anti-democratic who favored strong-man leaders like Stalin and Chairman Mao. He did, however, write several opinion pieces in support of the latter.

16 Mills, "Du Bois: Black Radical Liberal," pp. 49–50.

17 Du Bois, *Souls*, pp. 3–4.

18 Du Bois, *Souls*, p. 142.

Chapter 1 Du Bois and the Black Lives Matter Movement: Thinking with Du Bois about Anti-Racist Struggle Today

1 K. A. Appiah, *Lines of Descent*, New York: Norton, 2014, p. 21.

2 W. E. B. Du Bois, *The Souls of Black Folk*, New York: Penguin, 1989, p. 3.

3 Hannah Arendt, *Eichmann in Jerusalem*, New York: Penguin, 2006, p. 273.

4 The transcript of Zimmerman's 911 call is available online.

5 Resnick Gideon, "Zimmerman Taunts Trayvon Martin's Parents," *The Daily Beast*, April 13, 2017, online.

6 Du Bois, *Souls*, p. 166.

7 Du Bois, *Souls*, p. 193. See also W. E. B. Du Bois, *Darkwater: Voices from Within the Veil*, Mineola: Dover, 1999, p. 29.

8 W. E. B. Du Bois, *Dusk of Dawn: An Essay Toward an Autobiography of a Race Concept*, New York: The Library of America, 1986, p. 75.

9 Du Bois, *Dusk of Dawn*, p. 34.

10 Cf. James Baldwin, *The Cross of Redemption: Uncollected Writings*, New York: Pantheon Books, 2010.

11 Ramsey Orta, a friend of Garner's who recorded his murder on his cellphone, is the only person at the scene that day to have faced jail time. The journalist Chloe Cooper Jones writes: "'Someone will have to pay for this,' Orta thought, looking at his phone, not realizing that someone would be him." See Chloe Cooper Jones, "Fearing for His Life," *The Verge*, March 13, 2019, online.

12 Amy Goodman, *Democracy Now! Independent Global News*, August 20, 2019, online.

13 Interview Democracy Now, online: https://www.democracynow.org/2019/8/20/emerald_garner_daniel_pantaleo_nypd_firing

14 Christopher Berg, "About Blue Lives Matter," *Blue Lives Matter*, May 14, 2017, online.

15 Natasha Lennard, "Call Congress's 'Blue Lives Matter' Bills What They Are: Another Attack on Black Lives," *The Intercept*, May 18, 2018, online.

16 Du Bois, *Souls*, p. 3.

17 Du Bois, *Souls*, p. 3.

18 Du Bois, *Souls*, p. 5.

19 Du Bois, *Souls*, p. 5.

20 Du Bois, *Souls*, p. 5.

21 Du Bois, *Souls*, p. 5.

22 Paul C. Taylor, "W. E. B. Du Bois," *Philosophy Compass* 5(11) (2010): 904–15, 912.

23 Du Bois, *Darkwater*, pp. 131–2.

24 Du Bois, *Souls*, p. 5.

25 W. E. B. Du Bois, *Black Reconstruction in America, 1860–1880*, New York: The Free Press, 1992, pp. 325–79; David R. Roediger, *The Wages of Whiteness*, New York: Verso, 2007.

26 Du Bois, *Souls*, p. 8.

27 Linda Alcoff, *Visible Identities: Race, Gender, and the Self*, New York: Oxford University Press, 2006, pp. 248–9.

28 Du Bois, *Souls*, p. 172; W. E. B. Du Bois, *The Autobiography of W. E. B. Du Bois*, New York: Oxford University Press, 2007, p. 281.

29 Du Bois, *Souls*, p. 173.

30 Alcoff, *Visible Identities*, pp. 205–8.

31 Baldwin, *The Cross of Redemption*, p. 48.

32 Keeanga-Yamahtta Taylor, *From #BlackLivesMatter to Black Liberation*, Chicago: Haymarket Books, 2016, p. 154.

33 Keeanga-Yamahtta Taylor, *From #BlackLivesMatter to Black Liberation*, p. 154.

34 Melvin L. Rogers, "The Fact of Sacrifice and Necessity of Faith: Dewey and the Ethics of Democracy," *Transactions of the Charles Pierce Society* 47(3) (2011): 274–300, 275.

35 Paul Laurence Dunbar, "The Debt," *The Poetry Foundation*, online.

Chapter 2 Student Days, 1885–1895: Between Nashville, Cambridge, and Berlin

1 David Levering Lewis, *W. E. B. Du Bois: Biography of a Race, 1868–1919*, New York: Henry Holt, 1993, p. 16.

2 W. E. B. Du Bois, *The Souls of Black Folk*, New York: Penguin, 1989, p. 4.

3 W. E. B. Du Bois, *Dusk of Dawn: An Essay Toward an Autobiography of a Race Concept*, New York: The Library of America, 1986, p. 567.

4 Du Bois, *Dusk of Dawn*, pp. 631–2.

5 W. E. B. Du Bois, *Darkwater: Voices from Within the Veil*, Mineola: Dover, 1999, p. 5.

6 Lewis, *W. E. B. Du Bois: Biography of a Race*, p. 11.

7 Lewis, *W. E. B. Du Bois: Biography of a Race*, p. 14.

8 Lewis, *W. E. B. Du Bois: Biography of a Race*, p. 29.

9 Du Bois, *Darkwater*, p. 3; W. E. B. Du Bois, *The Autobiography of W. E. B. Du Bois*, New York: Oxford University Press, 2007, p. 56.

10 Du Bois, *Dusk of Dawn*, p. 566.

11 Du Bois, *Autobiography*, p. 65.

12 Du Bois, *Darkwater*, p. 9.

13 Du Bois, *Dusk of Dawn*, pp. 569–70.

14 Du Bois writes that he became James's "devoted follower" in his *Autobiography*, p. 83.

15 Lewis, *Du Bois: Biography of a Race*, p. 93.

16 Lewis, *Du Bois: Biography of a Race*, p. 139.

17 Du Bois, *Autobiography*, pp. 107–8.

18 Scholars often treat Du Bois as a central figure in various philosophical traditions. Cornel West and Paul C. Taylor argue that Du Bois is an American pragmatist. Frank M. Kirkland, Shamoon Zamir, and Stephanie Shaw consider Du Bois a Hegelian. Gooding-Williams contends that Du Bois is influenced by Max Weber's conception of charismatic rule and Wilhelm Dilthey's philosophy of social science. My own view stresses that if a philosophical tradition gives insights into an important feature of the normative basis of his political thought, then it is helpful to explore it.

19 This point was first established by Melvin L. Rogers who defends the idea of democratic development in Du Bois's *Souls*. See Melvin L. Rogers, "The People, Rhetoric, and Affect: On the Political Force of Du Bois's *The Souls of Black Folk*," *The American Political Science Review* 106(1) (2012): 188–203; Lewis, *Du Bois: Biography of a Race*, pp. 93–4; K. A. Appiah, *Lines of Descent*, New York: Norton, 2014, pp. 29–33.

20 My presentation of normativity is unrelated to its use in popular culture or postmodern theory. For example, Judith Butler calls gender "normative" in the sense that it "normalizes" gender conventions. Given my account of the is/ought distinction, her use of the term "normative" is, actually, descriptive. It describes conventions and their effects on gender identity.

21 W. E. B. Du Bois, "Sociology Hesitant," in Nahum Dimitri Chandler (ed.), *W. E. B. Du Bois: The Problem of the Color Line at the Turn of the Twentieth Century*, New York: Fordham University Press, 2015, p. 277.

22 This chapter deals with the Du Bois–Kant connection. Subsequent chapters address Du Bois's relation to Hegel and Marx. Charles W. Mills, "W. E. B. Du Bois: Black Radical Liberal," in Nick Bromell (ed.), *A Political Companion to W. E. B. Du Bois*, Lexington: University of Kentucky Press, 2018, pp. 19–56; Charles W. Mills, *Black Rights/White Wrongs: The Critique of Racial Liberalism*, New York: Oxford University Press, 2017, pp. 201–15; Charles W. Mills, "Black Radical Kantianism," *Res Philosophica* 95(1) (2018): 1–33.

23 Robert Gooding-Williams, *In the Shadow of Du Bois: Afro-Modern Political Thought in America*, Cambridge: Harvard University Press, 2009, p. 3.

24 Gooding-Williams, *In the Shadow of Du Bois*, p. 3.

25 Mills, "W. E. B. Du Bois: Black Radical Liberal," p. 33.

26 Mills, "W. E. B. Du Bois: Black Radical Liberal," pp. 34–5.

27 Mills, "W. E. B. Du Bois: Black Radical Liberal," p. 40.

28 Gooding-Williams, *In the Shadow of Du Bois*, p. 78.

29 Du Bois, *Souls*, p. 8.

30 Du Bois, *Souls*, p. 5.

31 Though Mills's interpretation of Kant is unique, he is not alone in turning to Kant to develop an anti-racist political critique. See Mills, *Black Rights/White Wrongs: The Critique of Racial Liberalism* pp. 209–15; Charles W. Mills, "Black Radical Kantianism," pp. 13–30; Pauline Kleingeld, "Kant's Second Thoughts on Race," *The Philosophical Quarterly* 57(229) (2007): 573–92; Lucy Allais, "Kant's Racism," *Philosophical Papers* 45(1–2) (2016): 1–36; Thomas Hill and Bernard Boxill, "Kant and Race," in Bernard Boxill (ed.), *Race and Racism*, New York: Oxford University Press, 2001, pp. 448–71.

32 Christopher Lebron, *The Color of Our Shame*, New York: Oxford University Press, 2008, p. 45.

33 Christopher Lebron, *The Making of Black Lives Matter: A Brief History of an Idea*, New York: Oxford University Press, 2017, p. 11.

34 W. E. B. Du Bois, *Black Reconstruction in America, 1860–1880*, New York: The Free Press, 1992, p. 694.

35 L. K. Bright, "Du Bois' Democratic Defence of the Value Free Ideal," *Synthese* 195(5) (2018): 2227–45.

36 Manning Marable, *W. E. B. Du Bois: Black Radical Democrat*, Boulder: Paradigm Publishers, 2005, p. ix.

37 Du Bois, *Dusk of Dawn*, p. 151.

38 See the Pew Research Report, "Race in America," *Pew Research Center: Social & Demographic Trends*, April 9, 2019, online.

39 A recent study noted that history textbooks widely differ in each state. Laura Isenee, "How Textbooks Can Teach Different Versions of History," *National Public Radio*, July 13, 2015, online.

40 W. E. B. Du Bois, "Criteria of Negro Art," in *W. E. B. Du Bois: Writings*, New York: The Library of America, 1986, pp. 993–1002.

41 Due to space constraints, I cannot discuss at length Du Bois's rich philosophy of art. See Davarian L. Baldwin and Minkah Makalani, *Escape from New York: The New Negro Renaissance Beyond Harlem*, Minneapolis: University of Minnesota Press, 2013.

42 For example, blues and hip-hop records impart black pain, desire, and loss, thereby preserving blacks' sense of their own humanity. Cultural production and consumption provide a strong sense of self that might withstand the shocks from a world that hates and neglects black lives.

43 Du Bois, *Souls*, p. 8.

44 Given Mills's claim that nonideal theory is "centrally focused" on the social and political organization of white supremacy, nonideal theory can characterize just about any figure in Afro-modern political thought, since a defining feature of the Africana tradition is theorizing modernity in light of the historical legacy of anti-black racism. Thinkers as disparate as Douglass, Wells-Barnett, and Baldwin then qualify as nonideal-theory liberals; and so, should we accept a broad cross-section of Africana philosophy as nonideal theory? What would this add to our understanding of racial justice or Africana philosophy?

45 See *Darkwater*, ch. 6.

46 Danielle S. Allen, *Talking to Strangers: Anxieties of Citizenship since Brown v. Board of Education*, Chicago and London: Chicago University Press, 2004, p. 55.

47 Gooding-Williams, *In the Shadow of Du Bois*, p. 16.

48 Allen, *Talking to Strangers*, p. 55.
49 Allen, *Talking to Strangers*, p. 5.
50 Gooding-Williams, *In the Shadow of Du Bois*, pp. 15–17.
51 Gooding-Williams, *In the Shadow of Du Bois*, p. 4.
52 Gooding-Williams, *In the Shadow of Du Bois*, p. 17.
53 Allen, *Talking to Strangers*, p. 18.
54 Carole Pateman and Charles W. Mills, *Contract and Domination*, Cambridge: Polity, 2007, pp. 96–9.
55 Joan Walsh, "The Radical MLK We Need Today," *Salon*, January 20, 2014, online.
56 Du Bois, *Souls*, p. 175.
57 Du Bois, *Souls*, p. 9.
58 James Baldwin, *The Cross of Redemption: Uncollected Writings*, New York: Pantheon Books, 2010, p. 45.
59 W. E. B. Du Bois, *The Suppression of the African Slave-Trade*, New York: Oxford University Press, 2007, pp. 197–8.
60 K. M. Bruyneel, "Creolizing Collective Memory: Refusing the Settler Memory of the Reconstruction Era," *Journal of French and Francophone Philosophy* 25(2) (2017): 36–44; and "Happy Days (of the White Settler Imaginary) Are Here Again," *Theory & Event* 20(1) (2017): 44–54.
61 I do not believe Bruyneel's objection picks out for any distinctive reason Du Bois's work, rather than, say, Dewey or Rawls, who each assert the legitimacy of the modern American state and so appear to invoke "settler memory" in the democratic redistribution of rights and resources. Though I cannot go into detail here, please note that Bruyneel's argument against Du Bois obtains for every new immigrant, asylum seeker, and white American in the United States as much as it obtains with respect to black freedmen's fight for inclusion in the republic. And his criticism of Reconstruction applies just as much to the Women's Rights, the Civil Rights, and the Black Lives Matter movements.
62 Bruyneel, "Creolizing Collective Memory," pp. 39–40.
63 Dale Turner, *This is Not a Peace Pipe: Towards a Critical Indigenous Philosophy*, London: University of Toronto Press, 2006, p. 4.
64 Turner, *This is Not a Peace Pipe*, p. 4.
65 Cf. Rogers's helpful "aspirational' notion of "the people" in Melvin L. Rogers, "The People, Rhetoric, and Affect: On

the Political Force of Du Bois's *The Souls of Black Folk*," *The American Political Science Review* 106(1) (2012): 188–203, 188–93.

66 See chapter 6 of Du Bois's *Darkwater*.

67 W. E. B. Du Bois, "The Development of a People," in N. D. Chandler (ed.), *The Problem of the Color Line at the Turn of the Twentieth Century: The Essential Early Essays*, New York: Fordham University Press, 2013, p. 256.

68 Walsh, "The Radical MLK We Need Today," online.

Chapter 3 The Emergence of a Black Public Intellectual: Du Bois's Philosophy of Social Science and Race (1894–1910)

1 Mitch Keller, "The Scandal at the Zoo," *New York Times*, August 6, 2006.

2 Ian Frazier, "When Du Bois Made a Laughing Stock of a White Supremacist," *The New Yorker*, August 19, 2019.

3 Robert Bernasconi argues that Kant developed the modern race concept, which is the view that racial differences are heritable and fixed in racial biology: "Who Invented the Concept of Race? Kant's Role in the Enlightenment Construction of Race," in R. Bernasconi (ed.), *Race*, Oxford: Blackwell, 2001, pp. 11–36.

4 Manning Marable, *W. E. B. Du Bois: Black Radical Democrat*, Boulder: Paradigm Publishers, 2005, p. 29; W. E. B. Du Bois, *Philadelphia Negro*, New York: Oxford University Press, 2014.

5 W. E. B. Du Bois, *The Autobiography of W. E. B. Du Bois*, New York: Oxford University Press, 2007, pp. 218–19.

6 Nathalie Baptiste, "Trump Is Trying to Deport Haitian Immigrants. They're Fighting Back," *Mother Jones*, December 3, 2018, online.

7 Eric Turkheimer, Kathryn Paige Harden, and Richard E. Nisbett, "There's Still No Good Reason to Believe Black–White IQ Differences are Due to Genes," *Vox*, June 17, 2017, online; Angela Saini, *Superior: The Return of Race Science*, Boston: Beacon Press, 2019, p. 392.

8 Saini, *Superior*, p. 391.

9 D. L. Lewis, *W. E. B. Du Bois: Biography of a Race, 1868–1919*, New York: Henry Holt, 1993, p. 153.

10 W. E. B. Du Bois, *Darkwater: Voices from Within the Veil*, Mineola: Dover, 1999, p. 11.

11 Lewis, *W. E. B. Du Bois: Biography of a Race*, p. 180.

12 Lewis, *W. E. B. Du Bois: Biography of a Race*, pp. 190–1.

13 Based at the University of Chicago in the early twentieth century, the Chicago School of Sociology is credited with developing urban sociology. The establishment of *The American Journal of Sociology* and the publication of *The Polish Peasant in Europe and America* (five volumes published from 1918 to 1920) by Florian Znaniecki and William I. Thomas are considered foundational texts. For further discussion, see Aldon Morris, *The Scholar Denied: W. E. B. Du Bois and the Birth of Modern Sociology*, Oakland: University of California Press, 2017, pp. 112–18.

14 W. E. B. Du Bois, "Sociology Hesitant," in Nahum Dimitri Chandler (ed.), *W. E. B. Du Bois: The Problem of the Color Line at the Turn of the Twentieth Century*, New York: Fordham University Press, 2015, pp. 272–6.

15 G. W. F. Hegel, *Introduction to the Philosophy of History*, Indiana: Hackett, 1988, p. 79.

16 Du Bois, "Sociology Hesitant," p. 272.

17 Du Bois, "Sociology Hesitant," p. 276.

18 W. E. B. Du Bois, "The Development of a People," in Chandler (ed.), *W. E. B. Du Bois* p. 247.

19 Julie Bosman, "Obama Sharply Assails Absent Black Fathers," *New York Times*, June 16, 2008.

20 Saini, *Superior*, p. 14.

21 Hegel, *Introduction to the Philosophy of History*, p. 65.

22 Hegel, *Introduction to the Philosophy of History*, p. 67.

23 Hegel was a virulent racist in his model of the historical development of world spirit.

24 Du Bois, *Autobiography*, p. 93.

25 In every major work, Du Bois averred to the "striving" of the black race.

26 Du Bois, "Sociology Hesitant," p. 277.

27 Du Bois, "Sociology Hesitant," p. 278.

28 Du Bois, "The Development of a People," p. 244.

29 Du Bois, "The Development of a People," p. 249.

30 Du Bois, "The Development of a People," p. 255; Du Bois,

"The Study of the Negro Problems," in Chandler, *The Problem of the Color Line*, pp. 78–81.

31 Robert Gooding-Williams, *In the Shadow of Du Bois: Afro-Modern Political Thought in America*, Cambridge: Harvard University Press, 2009, p. 47.

32 W. E. B. Du Bois, "On the Conservation of Races," in *W. E. B. Du Bois: Writings*, New York: The Library of America, 1986, pp. 817–19; cf. Paul C. Taylor, "W. E. B. Du Bois," *Philosophy Compass* 5(11) (2010): 908; Kimberly Ann Harris, "W. E. B. Du Bois's 'Conservation of Races': A Metaphilosophical Text," *Metaphilosophy* 50(5) (2019): 670–87; Chike Jeffers, "W. E. B. Du Bois's 'Whither Now and Why,'" in Eric Schliesser (ed.), *Ten Neglected Classics of Philosophy*, Oxford: Oxford University Press, 2017, pp. 222–55.

33 Du Bois, "On the Conservation of Races," p. 817.

34 Du Bois, "On the Conservation of Races," pp. 816–17.

35 Du Bois, "On the Conservation of Races," p. 818.

36 See Appiah's *In My Father's House: Africa in the Philosophy of Culture*, New York: Oxford University Press, 1992, pp. 28–46. See also: Lucius T. Outlaw, "On W. E. B. Du Bois's 'The Conservation of Races,'" in Linda Bell and David Blumenfeld (eds), *Overcoming Racism and Sexism*, New York: Rowman & Littlefield, 1995; Paul C. Taylor, "Appiah's Uncompleted Argument: W. E. B. Du Bois and the Reality of Race," *Social Theory and Practice* 26(1) (2000): 103–28.

37 Appiah, *In My Father's House*, p. 31.

38 Appiah, *In My Father's House*, p. 45.

39 For a more detailed discussion of political and cultural theories of race, see Chike Jeffers, "The Cultural Theory of Race: Yet Another Look at Du Bois's 'The Conservation of Races,'" *Ethics* 123(3) (2013): 403–26, 407–22.

40 Tommie Shelby, Sally Haslanger, and Naomi Zack are notable proponents of the political theory of race.

41 W. E. B. Du Bois, *Dusk of Dawn: An Essay Toward an Autobiography of a Race Concept*, New York: The Library of America, 1986, p. 666.

42 Lawrie Balfour, *Democracy's Reconstruction*, Oxford: Oxford University Press, 2011, p. 74.

43 Jeffers, "The Cultural Theory of Race," p. 414.

44 Jeffers, "The Cultural Theory of Race," p. 422.

45 Jeffers, "The Cultural Theory of Race," p. 422.

46 "One cannot think then of democracy in America or in the modern world without reference to the American Negro." W. E. B. Du Bois, *The Gift of Black Folk*, Boston: Stratford Co., 1924, p. 139.

47 Cf. Du Bois, *The Gift of Black Folk*.

48 Jeffers, "Du Bois's 'Whither Now and Why,'" p. 228.

49 Hegel, *Introduction to the Philosophy of History*, p. 90.

50 Du Bois, "Conservation," pp. 817–19.

51 Frank M. Kirkland, "Modernity and Intellectual Life in Black," *Philosophical Forum* 24(1–3) (1993): 136–65, 161.

52 Kirkland, "Modernity and Intellectual Life in Black," pp. 149–61.

53 Cf. Toni Morrison's *The Source of Self-Regard*, New York: Penguin, 2019, pp. 322–5. The preservation of historical memory in adversity and triumph is also a key theme in modern Jewish literature and art. Cf. Jeffers, "Du Bois's 'Whither Now and Why,'" pp. 234–5, 237.

54 Du Bois, "Conservation," p. 815.

55 Kirkland, "Modernity and Intellectual Life in Black," p. 156.

56 Hegel, *Introduction to the Philosophy of History*, p. 67.

57 Hegel, *Introduction to the Philosophy of History*, p. 77.

58 Hegel, *Introduction to the Philosophy of History*, p. 77.

59 Kirkland, "Modernity and Intellectual Life in Black," p. 161.

60 Du Bois, "Conservation," p. 61.

61 Du Bois, "Conservation," p. 58.

62 Du Bois, "Conservation," pp. 816–17.

63 Du Bois, *Dusk of Dawn*, p. 640.

64 W. E. B. Du Bois, "Whither Now and Why," in Herbert Aptheker (ed.), *The Education of Black People: Ten Critiques, 1906–1960*, Amherst: University of Massachusetts Press, 1973, pp. 149–58, p. 150.

65 Du Bois, *Souls*, pp. 204–5.

66 Kirkland, "Modernity and Intellectual Life in Black," p. 158.

67 Cf. Kirkland, "Modernity and Intellectual Life in Black," pp. 155–61.

68 Du Bois, *Souls*, p. 207.

69 Du Bois, *Souls*, pp. 171–2.
70 Cf. Kirkland, "Modernity and Intellectual Life in Black," pp. 145–9.
71 For a canonical account of stereotyping of the black American community, see Hortense J. Spillers, "Mama's Baby, Papa's Maybe: An American Grammar Book," *Diacritics* 17(2) (1987): 64–81.
72 Du Bois, "Conservation," p. 825.
73 Du Bois, "Conservation," p. 822.
74 W. E. B. Du Bois, "The Spirit of Modern Europe," in *W. E. B. Du Bois: The Problem of the Color Line at the Turn of the Twentieth Century*, pp. 139–66, p. 154.
75 Du Bois, "Conservation," p. 821.
76 Christopher Lebron, *The Making of Black Lives Matter: A Brief History of an Idea*, New York: Oxford University Press, 2017, p. 153.
77 Du Bois's commitment to the value of culture for promoting democratic literacy dovetails with his defense of liberal arts and higher education as a basic right of citizenship.
78 W. E. B. Du Bois, "The Song of the Smoke," in *Creative Writings by W. E. B. Du Bois*, Kraus-Thomson Organization, 1985.

Chapter 4 Courting Controversy: Du Bois on Political Rule and Educated "Elites"

1 Ann M. Simmons and Jaweed Kaleen, "Q&A: A founder of Black Lives Matter answers a question on many minds: Where did it go?" *Los Angeles Times*, August 25, 2017, online.
2 Patrisse Cullors, *When They Call You a Terrorist*, New York: St Martin's Press, p. 250.
3 W. E. B. Du Bois, "The Talented Tenth," in Nahum Dimitri Chandler (ed.), *W. E. B. Du Bois: The Problem of the Color Line at the Turn of the Twentieth Century*, New York: Fordham University Press, 2015, pp. 209–42.
4 Cf. Robert Gooding-Williams, *In the Shadow of Du Bois: Afro-Modern Political Thought in America*, Cambridge: Harvard University Press, 2009, pp. 31–7.
5 Booker T. Washington, *Up from Slavery: An Autobiography*,

New York: Floating Boat Press, 2009 [1901], p. 236.

6 Washington, *Up from Slavery*, p. 338.

7 Washington, *Up from Slavery*, p. 336.

8 Joseph S. Cotter, Sr, "Dr Booker T. Washington to the National Negro Business League" (1909), in Joan R. Sherman (ed.), *African-American Poetry of the Nineteenth Century: An Anthology*, Champaign: University of Illinois Press, 1992, p. 334.

9 W. E. B. Du Bois, *The Souls of Black Folk*, New York: Penguin, 1989, p. 49.

10 Manning Marable, *W. E. B. Du Bois: Black Radical Democrat*, Boulder: Paradigm Publishers, 2005, p. 73.

11 Blair L. M. Kelley, *Right to Ride*, Chapel Hill: The University of North Carolina Press, 2010, pp. 6–7.

12 For an opposing view, see Gooding-Williams, *In the Shadow of Du Bois*, p. 37.

13 Du Bois, *Souls*, p. 34.

14 There were numerous anti-black pogroms across the United States from 1910 to 1935, including the East St Louis Riot of 1917, the mob violence of the "Red Summer" of 1919, the Tulsa Riots of 1921, and the Rosewood Massacre of 1923. These violent episodes destroyed prosperous black financial districts and burned down black neighborhoods, resulting in untold loss of life and capital. Cameron McWhirter, *Red Summer: The Summer of 1919 and the Awakening of Black America*, New York: St Martin's Press, 2012, p. 13.

15 Hazel V. Carby, *Race Men*, Cambridge: Harvard University Press, 1998, p. 10.

16 This unfortunate phenomenon parallels Hegel's short commentary on the master–slave dialectic in the *Phenomenology of Spirit* that has come to define Hegel's reception.

17 Du Bois, "The Talented Tenth," p. 209.

18 Du Bois, "The Talented Tenth," pp. 210–12.

19 I will discuss in detail the idea of second slavery in the next chapter. Exclusionary social and institutional conditions persist to expose the African-American community to racial domination after the legal abolition of slavery that "enslaves" black persons in all but name.

20 Du Bois, "The Talented Tenth," pp. 211–13.

21 Du Bois, "The Talented Tenth," p. 213.

22 Du Bois, "The Talented Tenth," p. 219.

23 Jennifer Morton, *Moving up Without Losing Your Way: The Ethical Costs of Upward Mobility*, Princeton: Princeton University Press, 2019, pp. 4–7.

24 See Carby, *Race Men*; Gooding-Williams, *In the Shadow of Du Bois*, pp. 1–19.

25 Gooding-Williams, *In the Shadow of Du Bois*, p. 93.

26 Du Bois, "The Talented Tenth," p. 226.

27 W. E. B. Du Bois, "The Negro College," in *W. E. B. Du Bois: Writings*, New York: The Library of America, 1986, pp. 1010–19.

28 W. E. B. Du Bois, "The Development of a People," in N. D. Chandler (ed.), *The Problem of the Color Line at the Turn of the Twentieth Century: The Essential Early Essays*, New York: Fordham University Press, 2013, p. 257.

29 Du Bois, "Conservation," p. 60.

30 Du Bois, *Dusk of Dawn*, ch. 7.

31 Arash Davari, "On Democratic Leadership and Social Change," in Nick Bromell (ed.), *A Political Companion to W. E. B. Du Bois*, Lexington: University of Kentucky Press, 2018, pp. 241–70, 242.

32 Davari, "On Democratic Leadership and Social Change," p. 243.

33 Davari, "On Democratic Leadership and Social Change," p. 259.

34 Keeanga-Yamahtta Taylor, From #BlackLivesMatter to Black Liberation, Chicago: Haymarket Books, 2016, p. 176.

35 The synthesis of a hybrid model appears to be happening organically. As the BLM movement developed, it released a platform of 40 public policy initiatives: "We recognize that not all of our collective needs and visions can be translated into policy, but we understand that policy change is one of many tactics necessary to move us towards the world we envision." Jaweed Kaleem, "Black Lives Matter has Signed onto a Platform," *Los Angeles Times*, August 1, 2016, online.

36 Olivia Winslow, "Dividing Lines, Visible and Invisible," *Newsweek*, November 17, 2019, online.

37 Marc Kilippino, "Levittown and the Rise of the American Suburb," *PRI*, December 4, 2017, online.

38 Ira Katznelson, *When Affirmative Action was White*, New York: W. W. Norton, 2005, pp. 19–20, 95–6.

39 "The Fair Housing Act," US Department of Justice.

40 Brian J. Charles, "As Fair Housing Act Turns 50, Landmark Law Faces Uncertain Future," *Governing the Future of States and Localities*, April 11, 2018, online. Furthermore, recent census data reveals the homeownership rate for African Americans has fallen to its lowest level since before the civil rights movement.

41 The car mechanic was acquitted by an all-white grand jury. "Ford's mother, Barbara Dunmore Ford, [. . .] that she will believe until her dying day that the grand jury of twenty-three white people did not return a true bill because her son was a black man." Darryl Pinckney, "Yance Ford's 'Strong Island' Is a Form of Justice," *The New Yorker*, September 19, 2017.

42 The ERASE Racism Report, "Civil Rights Rollback: US Government Actions to Reduce Civil Rights in Housing and Public Education," p. 7.

43 "Full Text of President Trump's 2020 State of the Union Speech," *The Wall Street Journal*, February 5, 2020, online.

44 Jaimi Franchi, "Long Island Segregation Drives Educational Inequality 60 Years After Brown v BOE," *Long Island Press*, May 17, 2014, online.

45 Franchi, "Long Island Segregation," online.

46 Du Bois, *Darkwater*, ch. 7; more on this point in chapter 6.

47 Marable, *W. E. B. Du Bois*, p. xii.

48 For further discussion about the contemporary implications of the link between race and trust in forging political solidarity, see T. Shelby, *We Who Are Dark: The Philosophical Foundations of Black Solidarity*, Cambridge: Harvard University Press, 2007, pp. 201–42.

49 Du Bois, "Conservation," p. 58.

50 Margaret Walker, "Amos (Postscript)," *This Is My Century: New and Collected Poems*, Atlanta: University of Georgia Press, 1989.

Chapter 5 A Broken Promise: On Hegel, Second Slavery, and the Ideal of Civic Enfranchisement (1910–1934)

1 W. E. B. Bois, *The Suppression of the African Slave-Trade*, New York: Oxford University Press, 2007, p. 58.

2 During this period, he wrote a history of Africa, African Americans, and blacks around the world: *New Negro* (1915), *The Gift of Black Folk* (1924), *Africa, Its Geography, People and Products* (1930), and *Africa: Its Place in Modern History* (1930). I review his scholarship on Africa in the last chapter.

3 The political significance of Radical Reconstruction remains hotly contested. See Michael Gonchar, "Text to Text: 'Why Reconstruction Matters' and 'Black Reconstruction in America,'" *The New York Times*, December 9, 2015, online.

4 W. E. B. Du Bois, *The Souls of Black Folk*, New York: Penguin, 1989, p. 25.

5 Eric Foner, "The Meaning of Freedom in the Age of Emancipation," *The Journal of American History* 81(2) (1994): 435–60, 441.

6 Kirkland and Balfour analyze the concept of second slavery in some detail. Frank M. Kirkland, "Modernity and Intellectual Life in Black," *Philosophical Forum* 24(1–3) (1993): 136–65, 160; Lawrie Balfour, *Democracy's Reconstruction*, Oxford: Oxford University Press, 2011, ch. 1.

7 As he grew disillusioned with science and reason for fighting racism, he incorporated aesthetic experience as a tool for building a more just society and for fortifying black cultural integrity.

8 Henry Lee Moon, "History of Crisis," *The Crisis* (November 1970): 385.

9 Robert A. Hill, "Marcus Garvey, 'The Negro Moses,'" *Africana Age*, online.

10 Adam Ewing, *The Age of Garvey*, Princeton: Princeton University Press, 2014, p. 1.

11 Shawn Leigh Alexander, *W. E. B. Du Bois: An American Intellectual and Activist*, New York: Rowman & Littlefield, 2015, p. 78.

12 W. E. B. Du Bois, "A Lunatic or a Traitor," in David L. Lewis (ed.), *W. E. B. Du Bois: A Reader*, New York: Henry Holt, 1995, pp. 340–2.

13 W. E. B. Du Bois, *Darkwater: Voices from Within the Veil*, Mineola: Dover, 1999, p. 40; Du Bois, *Autobiography*, p. 188.

14 W. E. B. Du Bois, *Black Reconstruction in America, 1860–1880*, New York: The Free Press, 1992, p. 13.

15 Foner, "The Meaning of Freedom in the Age of Emancipation," p. 444.

16 Of course, enslaved persons had normative authority, except it was *not socially recognized* by the white-controlled polity.

17 David W. Blight, "Quarrel Forgotten or Revolution Remembered? Reunion and Race in the Memory of the Civil War, 1875–1913," in Lyde Cullen Sizer and Jim Cullen (eds), *The Civil War Era: An Anthology of Sources*, Oxford: Blackwell, 2005, pp. 375–97, 378.

18 Du Bois, *Black Reconstruction*, p. 219; Du Bois, *Souls*, p. 24; Balfour, *Democracy's Reconstruction*, p. 17.

19 Cf. Kirkland, "Modernity and Intellectual Life in Black," pp. 136–65.

20 For Du Bois's definition of slavery, see his *Reconstruction*, pp. 9–11.

21 Martha C. Jones, *Birthright Citizens: A History of Race and Rights in Antebellum America*, Cambridge: Cambridge University Press, 2018, p. 5.

22 Jones, *Birthright Citizens*, p. xiii.

23 Michelle Alexander, *The New Jim Crow*, New York: The New Press, 2012, p. 29.

24 Du Bois, *Suppression*, p. 58.

25 Philip Pettit, *Republicanism*, New York: Oxford University Press, 1997, pp. 31–5.

26 Du Bois, *Suppression*, p. 57.

27 Du Bois, *Suppression*, p. 67.

28 For an excellent discussion of the racial injustice of institutions as "a failure of national character," see Christopher Lebron, *The Color of Our Shame*, New York: Oxford University Press, 2008, pp. 18–19.

29 Du Bois, *Reconstruction*, p. 66. Blacks – both free blacks in the North and runaway slaves – joined the Union army in such large numbers that black Americans out-represented whites relative to population size.

30 Alexander Livingston provides an excellent analysis of Du Bois's refrain in *John Brown* that "the cost of liberty is less than the price of repression." The stronger racial domination grows to democratic intervention, the more likely political violence becomes. Livingston's argument is more elegant than

Hegel's blunt claim: "History is a slaughter-bench." Alexander Livingston, "The Cost of Liberty: Sacrifice and Survival in Du Bois's *John Brown*," in Nick Bromell (ed.), *A Political Companion to W. E. B. Du Bois*, Lexington: University Press of Kentucky, 2018, pp. 207–39.

31 Adolph L. Reed Jr, *W. E. B. Du Bois and American Political Thought: Fabianism and the Color Line*, Oxford: Oxford University Press, 1997, p. 11.

32 Reed, ibid., p. 12.

33 Shamoon Zamir, *Dark Voices: W. E. B. Du Bois and American Thought, 1888–1903*, Chicago: University of Chicago Press, 1995, p. 122; Axel R. Schäfer, "W. E. B. Du Bois, German Social Thought, and the Racial Divide in American Progressivism, 1892–1909," *The Journal of American History* 88(3) (2001): 925–49. For a recent discussion of Hegel and race, see Rocío Zambrana, "Hegel, History, and Race," in Naomi Zack (ed.), *The Oxford Handbook of Philosophy of Race*, New York: Oxford University Press, 2017, pp. 251–8; Alison Stone, "Hegel and Colonialism," *Hegel Bulletin* (2017): 1–24; Frank M. Kirkland, "Kant on Race and Transition," in Linda Martín Alcoff, Paul Taylor, and Luvell Anderson (eds), *The Routledge Companion to the Philosophy of Race*, New York: Routledge, 2017, pp. 28–42; Frank M. Kirkland, "Hegel on Race and Development," in Linda Martín Alcoff, Paul Taylor, and Luvell Anderson (eds), *The Routledge Companion to the Philosophy of Race*, pp. 43–60.

34 Zamir, *Dark Voices*, pp. 113–68.

35 Du Bois, *Souls*, p. 5.

36 Du Bois, *Souls*, p. 5.

37 Du Bois, *Souls*, p. 5.

38 Following the Du Bois–Hegel scholars Frank Kirkland and Stephanie Shaw, I favor the methodological shift away from the education of subjective spirit via the master–slave dialectic for conceptualizing race-based forms of social domination. See Dean Moyar, *Hegel's Conscience*, New York: Oxford University Press, 2011, pp. 145–50; Frank M. Kirkland, "Susan Buck-Morss, Hegel, Haiti, and Universal History," *Logos: A Journal of Modern Society & Culture* 11(2–3) (2012), online; Stephanie Shaw, *W. E. B. Du Bois and The Souls of Black Folk*, Chapel Hill: University of North Carolina Press, 2015, pp. 1–10. Robert

Gooding-Williams also explores the Du Bois–Hegel connection without appealing to the master–slave dialectic. However, he focuses on Hegel's philosophy of history and natural spirit, rather than his political philosophy. Robert Gooding-Williams, "Philosophy of History and Social Critique in *The Souls of Black Folk*," *Sur les Sciences Sociales* 26(1) (1987): 99–114.

39 For example, Hegel's political philosophy does not call for the universal, much less democratic, enfranchisement of the rural population. I am indebted to Christopher Yeomans for this point.

40 Du Bois, *Reconstruction*, p. 673. Cf. Balfour's notion of "civic nationalism" in *Democracy's Reconstruction*, pp. 129–36.

41 W. E. B. Du Bois, "Civil Rights Legislation Before and After the Passage of the 14th Amendment," *Lawyer's Guild Review* 6(6) (1946): 640–2; Du Bois, *Reconstruction*, p. 4.

42 G. W. F. Hegel, *Elements of the Philosophy of Right*, New York: Cambridge University Press, 1991, §19.

43 As a family member, she acts on a reason that satisfies her particularity as a desiring subject and has public normative purchase recognizable by the community and by the state through the marriage contract. But the concept is articulated through sensuous particularity – this is *my* family, we play board games on the weekend and drink cherry coke.

44 Hegel, *PhR*, §161, §176.

45 Hegel, *PhR*, §181.

46 Hegel, *PhR*, §§177–8.

47 Hegel, *PhR*, §§182–3.

48 Hegel, *PhR*, §254.

49 Hegel, *PhR*, §230.

50 Hegel, *PhR*, §231. In footnote.

51 Hegel, *PhR*, §257.

52 Du Bois, *Reconstruction*, pp. 219–36.

53 Ludwig Siep, "Hegel's Liberal, Social, and 'Ethical' State," in Dean Moyar (ed.), *The Oxford Handbook of Hegel*, New York: Oxford University Press, 2017, pp. 515–33, p. 523; Charles Taylor, *Hegel*, Cambridge: Cambridge University Press, 1977.

54 Du Bois, *Reconstruction*, p. 13.

55 Du Bois, *Reconstruction*, pp. 29–30.

56 Du Bois, *Reconstruction*, pp. 29, 165–6.

57 Du Bois, *Souls*, p. 11.

58 The following is a narrow selection of scholarship on the topic. Cf. Orlando Patterson's concept of "natal alienation" in *Slavery and Social Death: A Comparative Study*, Cambridge: Harvard University Press, 1982, pp. 5–16. Patterson defines the phenomena: "Not only was the slave denied all claims on, and obligations to, his parents and living blood relations but, by extension, all such claims and obligations on his more remote ancestors and on his descendants. He was truly a genealogical isolate. Formally isolated in his social relations with those who lived, he also was culturally isolated from the social heritage of his ancestors. He had a past, to be sure. But a past is not a heritage. Everything has a history, including sticks and stones. Slaves differed from other human beings in that they were not allowed freely to integrate the experience of their ancestors into their lives, to inform their understanding of social reality with the inherited meanings of their natural forebears, or to anchor the living present in any conscious community of memory. That they reached back for the past, as they reached out for the related living, there can be no doubt. Unlike other persons, doing so meant struggling with and penetrating the iron curtain of the master, his community, his laws, his policemen or patrollers, and his heritage," p. 5. See also Saidiya V. Hartman, *Lose Your Mother: A Journey along the Atlantic Slave Route*, New York: Farrar, Straus, and Giroux, 2008; Sara Clarke Kaplan, "Love and Violence/Maternity and Death: Black Feminism and the Politics of (Un)representability," *Black Women, Gender, and Families* 1(1) (2007): 94–124.

59 Hegel, *PhR*, §159 Add.

60 Balfour, *Democracy's Reconstruction*, pp. 103–4.

61 Du Bois, *Souls*, p. 11; Hegel, *PhR*, §181.

62 Du Bois, *Reconstruction*, p. 9.

63 Du Bois, *Reconstruction*, p. 11.

64 See also Angela Davis, *Women, Race, & Class*, New York: Vintage, 1983, pp. 6–10.

65 Du Bois, *Reconstruction*, p. 11.

66 Du Bois, *Reconstruction*, p. 20.

67 Du Bois, *Reconstruction*, p. 12. Emphasis added.

68 Du Bois, *Reconstruction*, p. 12.

69 Crystal M. Feimster, *Southern Horrors: Women and the Politics of Rape and Lynching*, Cambridge: Harvard University Press, 2009, pp. 169–71.

70 Davis, *Women, Race, & Class*, pp. 7, 14–15, 17.

71 Consider the treatment of immigrant families from Central and South America by ICE. Debbie Nathan, "'They're Taking Everybody,' – Videos Show Texas Troopers Ripping Apart Immigrant Families during Traffic Stops," *The Intercept*, December 10, 2017, online.

72 Du Bois, *Darkwater*, p. 105.

73 Du Bois, *Darkwater*, p. 96.

74 Du Bois, *Darkwater*, p. 96.

75 Toni Morrison, *Beloved*, New York: Knopf, 1987, p. 162.

76 Du Bois, *Souls*, p. 25.

77 Du Bois, *Reconstruction*, pp. 230–5.

78 Du Bois, *Souls*, pp. 119–20; *Reconstruction*, pp. 356–7.

79 My discussion focuses on the wage contract. A full discussion of civil freedom must include the demand for the redistribution of land and resources – the call of reparations for 40 acres and a mule – as well as Du Bois's critique of white-controlled labor unions and his relationship to Marxian ethics later in life, but this is all well beyond the scope of this book.

80 Du Bois, *Reconstruction*, p. 219.

81 Du Bois, *Souls*, pp. 21–5.

82 Du Bois, *Reconstruction*, p. 15.

83 Du Bois, *Reconstruction*, p. 135.

84 Du Bois, *Reconstruction*, p. 7.

85 Du Bois, *Souls*, p. 23; Du Bois, *Reconstruction*, p. 708.

86 Du Bois, *Reconstruction*, p. 670.

87 Du Bois, *Souls*, pp. 20–3.

88 Du Bois, *Souls*, pp. 14, 18.

89 Du Bois, *Reconstruction*, p. 219.

90 Du Bois, *Souls*, p. 21.

91 Du Bois, *Suppression*, pp. 79–82.

92 Indirectly, the Freedmen's Bureau served to enforce the Civil Rights Act of 1866 – the first such act in the country that stipulated rights to be attached to US citizenship.

93 Du Bois, *Reconstruction*, p. 561.

94 Du Bois, *Reconstruction*, pp. 185, 219.

95 Eric Foner, *A Short History of Reconstruction, 1863–1877*, New York: Harper & Row, 1988, p. 134.

96 Du Bois, *Reconstruction*, pp. 78–9, 221–2, 274–5, 601.

97 Du Bois, *Souls*, p. 23.

98 Du Bois, *Souls*, p. 23.

99 Du Bois, *Reconstruction*, p. 223.

100 Du Bois, *Reconstruction*, pp. 29–30.

101 For an alternative view, see Robert Gooding-Williams, *In the Shadow of Du Bois: Afro-Modern Political Thought in America*, Cambridge: Harvard University Press, 2009, p. 4.

102 Du Bois, *Reconstruction*, p. 694.

103 Du Bois, *Reconstruction*, p. 708.

104 Du Bois, *Reconstruction*, p. 635.

105 Ira Katznelson, *Fear Itself: The New Deal and the Origins of Our Time*, New York: Norton, 2013, pp. 227–75.

106 W. E. B. Du Bois, "Du Bois states his reasons for backing President Roosevelt," *People's Voice*, October 21, 1944; Katznelson, *When Affirmative Action was White*, p. 25.

107 For an extended discussion of the racial politics of welfare, see Christopher Lebron, *The Color of Our Shame*, pp. 86–95.

108 *Politico* reports: "The legislation substantially reconstructed the nation's welfare system by giving state governments more autonomy over welfare services while also reducing the federal government's role. [. . .] The act ended welfare as an entitlement program; required recipients to begin working after two years of receiving benefits; placed a lifetime limit of five years on benefits paid by federal funds; [. . .] and required state professional and occupational licenses to be withheld from undocumented immigrants." Andrew Glass, "Clinton Signs 'Welfare to Work' Bill, August 22, 1996," *Politico*, August 22, 2018, online.

109 Bill Chappell, "US Income Inequality Worsens, Widening to a New Gap," *National Public Radio*, September 26, 2019, online.

110 Jennifer Morton, *Moving up Without Losing Your Way: The Ethical Costs of Upward Mobility*, Princeton: Princeton University Press, 2019, pp. 1–2.

111 Information from the reports by the non-profits The State of Working America and Poverty USA.

112 Kayla R. Fontenot, Jessica L. Semega, and Melissa A. Kollar for the US Census Bureau, "Income and Poverty in the United States: 2017" (United States Department of Commerce, 2018), online.

113 A recent study "found that 4.5 percent of families were under half of the poverty line in 1993, but 6.6 percent were in 2004, a nearly 50 percent increase." Dylan Matthews, " 'If the goal was to get rid of poverty, we failed': the legacy of the 1996 welfare reform," *Vox*, June 20, 2016.

114 Lebron, *The Color of our Shame*, p. 95.

115 Unfortunately, due to space constraints, my discussion omits the recent mobilization of fast-food workers and the fight to raise the minimum wage.

116 Alexander, *The New Jim Crow*, p. 180.

117 Alexander, *The New Jim Crow*, pp. 180–1.

118 Ashley Nellis, "The Color of Justice," *The Sentencing Project* 2016.

119 Alexander, *The New Jim Crow*, pp. 31–2.

120 Alexander, *The New Jim Crow*, pp. 218–20.

121 Katherine E. Leung, "Prison Labor as a Lawful Form of Race Discrimination," *Harvard Civil Rights-Civil Liberties Law Review* 53 (2018): 681–708.

122 Philip Pettit, *Just Freedom*, New York: W. W. Norton, 2014, pp. 20–1.

123 Du Bois, *Reconstruction*, p. 694.

124 Nicole Lewis, "What's Really Happening with the National Prison Strike?" *The Marshall Project*, August 24, 2018.

125 Incarcerated Workers Organizing Committee. https://incarcer atedworkers.org/campaigns/prison-strike-2018

126 Steven Greenhouse, "How Walmart Persuades Its Workers Not to Unionize," *The Atlantic*, June 8, 2015.

127 Steven Greenhouse, *The Big Squeeze*, New York: Anchor Books, 2009, p. 139.

128 Greenhouse, "How Walmart Persuades Its Workers Not to Unionize."

129 Shannon Liao, "Amazon Warehouse Workers Skip Bathroom Breaks to Keep Their Jobs, Says Report," *The Verge*, April 16, 2018, online.

130 Ibid.

131 Jon Greenberg, "Bernie Sanders and Walmart Workers," *Politifact*, July 12, 2019, online.
132 Nandita Bose, "Half of Walmart's Workforce are Part-time Workers," *Reuters*, May 25, 2018, online.
133 Michael Sainato, "'We Are Not Robots': Amazon Warehouse Employees Push to Unionize," *The Guardian*, January 1, 2019, online; Michael Sainato, "'I'm Not a Robot': Amazon Workers Condemn Unsafe, Gruelling Conditions at Warehouse," *The Guardian*, February 5, 2020.
134 Du Bois, *Suppression*, p. 196.
135 Du Bois, *Darkwater*, pp. 84–92.
136 E. Tammy Kim, "Black Workers Embody the New Low-wage Economy," *Aljazeera America*, September 12, 2013, online.
137 Ebony Slaughter-Johnson, "Calling Working People of All Colors: A Cue from Du Bois," *People's World*, January 5, 2017.
138 Du Bois, *Reconstruction*, p. 12.
139 Du Bois, *Reconstruction*, p. 12.
140 Du Bois, *Darkwater*, p. 92.

Chapter 6 Du Bois on Sex, Gender, and Public Childcare

1 Chike Jeffers and Robert Gooding-Williams argue that Du Bois's treatment of black sexual norms warrants further study. See their "Introduction to 'The Development of a People,'" *Ethics* 123(3) (2013): 521–4.
2 Michele Elam and Paul C. Taylor, "Du Bois's Erotics," in S. Gillman and A. Weinbaum (eds), *Next to the Color Line: Gender, Sexuality, and W. E. B. Du Bois*, Minneapolis: University of Minnesota Press, 2007, pp. 209–331; Joy James, "Profeminism and Gender Elites: W. E. B. Du Bois, Anna Julia Cooper, and Ida B. Wells-Barnett," in Gillman and Weinbaum (eds), *Next to the Color Line*, pp. 69–95.
3 David L. Lewis (ed.), *W. E. B. Du Bois: A Reader*, New York: Henry Holt, 1995, p. 190.
4 W. E. B. Du Bois, "So the Girl Marries," in *Du Bois*, New York: Library of America, 1986, p. 1005.
5 Tobi Haslett, "The Man Who Led the Harlem Renaissance – and His Hidden Hungers," *The New Yorker*, May 14, 2018;

Mason Stokes, "Father of the Bride," in *Next to the Color Line*, pp. 289–316, 293.

6 Raymond Wolters, *Du Bois and his Rivals*, Columbia: University of Missouri Press, 2002, p. 224.

7 Elam and Taylor, "Du Bois's Erotics," p. 213; James, "Profeminism and Gender Elites," p. 71.

8 According to James, Du Bois was reluctant to acknowledge Wells-Barnett's role in the organization in her "Profeminism and Gender Elites," pp. 82–5; Paula Giddens, "Missing in Action: Ida B. Wells, the NAACP, and the Historical Record," *Meridian* 1(2) (2001): 1–17.

9 Valethia Watkins, "Votes for Women," *Phylon* 53(2) (2016): 3–19; Garth E. Pauley, "W. E. B. Du Bois on Woman Suffrage," *Journal of Black Studies* 30(3) (2000): 384–410.

10 Pauley, "W. E. B. Du Bois on Woman Suffrage," p. 385.

11 Pauley, "W. E. B. Du Bois on Woman Suffrage," p. 386.

12 For further discussion on the historical relationship between suffrage and lynching, see Crystal M. Feimster, *Southern Horrors: Women and the Politics of Rape and Lynching*, Cambridge: Harvard University Press, 2009, chs 3 and 5.

13 Whether his proposed strategy was the reason for the ratification of the nineteenth amendment is a matter of debate among American historians. Linda M. Grasso, "Differently Radical," *American Journalism* 26(1) (2019): 71–98.

14 Watkins, "Votes for Women," p. 8.

15 This section takes inspiration from Balfour's wonderful article: "Representative Women: Slavery and the Gendered Ground of Citizenship," which is the fifth chapter of her *Democracy's Reconstruction*, Oxford: Oxford University Press, 2011.

16 W. E. B. Du Bois, *Darkwater: Voices from Within the Veil*, Mineola: Dover, 1999, p. 100. Cf. Lawrie Balfour, *Democracy's Reconstruction*, pp. 100–7.

17 Du Bois, *Darkwater*, p. 100.

18 To be sure, Du Bois never explicitly confronted the heterosexual assumptions in his writings.

19 Balfour, *Democracy's Reconstruction*, p. 100.

20 Du Bois, *Darkwater*, p. 96.

21 Du Bois, *Darkwater*, p. 95.

22 Du Bois, *Darkwater*, pp. 96, 107.

23 Du Bois, *Darkwater*, p. 96.

24 Curtis J. Evans observes "Du Bois was one of the first social scientists to use the singular 'Negro Church' appellation (1897 seems to be the earliest date)," in "W. E. B. Du Bois: Interpreting Religion and the Problem of the Negro Church," *Journal of the American Academy of Religion* 75(2) (2007): 268-97, 291.

25 W. E. B. Du Bois, *The Souls of Black Folk*, New York: Penguin, 1996, p. 158; Manning Marable, *Race, Reform, and Rebellion: The Second Reconstruction and Beyond in Black America, 1945–2006*, Jackson: University Press of Mississippi, 2007; Aldon D. Morris, *The Origin of the Civil Rights Movement: Black Communities Organizing for Change*, New York: The Free Press, 1984, pp. 4–7; Evelyn Brooks Higginbotham, *Righteous Discontent: The Women's Movement in the Black Baptist Church, 1880–1920*, Cambridge: Harvard University Press, 1994; Albert Raboteau, *Canaan Land: A Religious History of African Americans*, New York: Oxford University Press, 1999; Eddie S. Glaude, Jr, *Exodus! Religion, Race, and Nation in Early Nineteenth-Century Black America*, Chicago and London: The University of Chicago Press, 2000.

26 Du Bois, *Souls*, pp. 5–11. For an excellent defense of the idea of democratic development in Du Bois's thought, one that inspires my account here, see Melvin L. Rogers, "The People, Rhetoric, and Affect: On the Political Force of Du Bois's *The Souls of Black Folk*," *The American Political Science Review* 106(1) (2012): 188–203. Robert Gooding-Williams argues that Du Bois's political theory is a response to Jim Crow in his groundbreaking work, *In the Shadow of Du Bois*.

27 Balfour, *Democracy's Reconstruction*, p. 110.

28 Du Bois, *Souls*, p. 9.

29 Du Bois, *Souls*, p. 158.

30 Higginbotham, *Righteous Discontent*, pp. 53–5; Du Bois, *Black Reconstruction*, pp. 664–7.

31 Higginbotham, *Righteous Discontent*, p. 2. My description of its civic activities is *not* exhaustive.

32 Higginbotham, *Righteous Discontent*, pp. 178–80.

33 Cf. Axel Honneth's claim that a strong democratic public sphere

renders "superfluous" the institutionalization of improved norms. *Freedom's Right*, p. 67.

34 Du Bois, *Black Reconstruction*, p. 638.

35 In other words, rather than assume, as Rawls does in his formulation of the difference principle, that economic inequality is justifiable so long as it benefits the worst off, I contend, with the aid of Du Bois, that the *positive* claims that the worst off make to mitigate their economic vulnerability should inform what, as a result, the best off should be compelled to sacrifice in the interest of justice. This would not yield a strict material equality, but it would provide an alternative normative basis for reasoning about economic justice.

36 Jeffers, "Du Bois's 'Whither Now and Why,'" p. 250.

37 Cf. The Panthers' 10-Point Program's assertions about the "responsibilities of the federal government" to provide public goods. The Black Panthers and the Young Lords eschewed a liberal justification for their demands. With the aid of Du Bois, we can nonetheless construct one. Huey P. Newton, *War Against the Panthers: A Study of Repression in America*, Santa Cruz: Writers and Readers, 1996, pp. 141–6. The historical experience of racial domination helps delineate what the principle of fair equality of opportunity should justify *for all* by focusing on the needs and interests of a particular vulnerable community. But this is a complex issue concerning the nature of the democratic legitimation of public goods that I only flag here and must explore elsewhere in presenting and defending Du Bois's theory of economic justice.

38 Consider that in the US racist dog whistles such as "welfare queen" are used to attack social welfare programs *that also alleviate white poverty*.

39 Du Bois, *On Religion*, p. 41.

40 Du Bois, *Souls*, p. 163; Du Bois, *Dusk of Dawn*, pp. 712–15.

41 Du Bois, *Souls*, p. 155.

42 Du Bois, *Darkwater*, p. 104.

43 Du Bois, *Souls*, p. 158.

44 Higginbotham, *Righteous Discontent*, pp. 95–7, 171–5. See also Mary Church Terrell, "Club Work of Colored Women," *Southern Workman* (1901): 435–38; Linda Gordon, "Black and White Visions of Welfare: Women's Welfare Activism,

1890–1945," *The Journal of American History* 78(2) (1991): 559–90, 584–6.

45 Tucker Carlson, "Mitt Romney Supports the Status Quo," *Fox News*, January 3, 2019, online.

46 Du Bois, *Darkwater*, p. 106.

47 Rasheed Malik, "Black Families Work More, Earn Less, and Face Difficult Child Care Choices," *Center for American Progress*, August 5, 2016, online.

48 Malik, "Black Families Work More, Earn Less, and Face Difficult Child Care Choices," online.

49 Sibyl Schwarzenbach, *On Civic Friendship*, New York: Columbia University Press, 2009, p. 220.

50 "Few say having two full-time working parents is the ideal situation for children in two-parent households," *Pew Research Center*, October 2, 2018.

51 bell hooks, *Feminist Theory: From Margin to Center*, Boston: South End Press, 1984, p. 142.

Chapter 7 Du Bois on Self-Segregation and Self-Respect: A Liberalism Undone? (1934–1951)

1 W. E. B. Du Bois, *Dusk of Dawn: An Essay Toward an Autobiography of a Race Concept*, New York: The Library of America, 1986, p. 697.

2 For early essays from the mid-1930s on the defense of self-segregation, see his "Segregation" (1934), "Separation and Self-Respect" (1934), and "A Negro Nation within the Nation" (1935), in D. L. Lewis (ed.), *W. E. B. Du Bois: A Reader*, New York: Henry Holt, 1995, pp. 557–8, 559–62, 563–70; W. E. B. Du Bois, "Segregation in the North" (1934), "The Board of Directors on Segregation" (1934), and "Counsels of Despair" (1934), in *Du Bois: Writings*, New York: Library of America, 1986, pp. 1239–43, 1252–3, 1254–8.

3 Quoted from Shawn Leigh Alexander, *W. E. B. Du Bois: An American Intellectual and Activist*, New York: Rowman & Littlefield, 2015, p. 85.

4 David Levering Lewis, *W. E. B. Du Bois: The Fight for Equality and the American Century, 1919–1963*, New York: Henry Holt, 2001, pp. 497–8.

5 W. E. B. Du Bois, "Dr. Du Bois Resigns," in Nathan Huggins (ed.), *W. E. B. Du Bois: Writings*, New York: Viking Press, 1986, pp. 1259–60.

6 W. E. B. Du Bois, "Dr. Du Bois Resigns," p. 1260.

7 W. E. B. Du Bois, "Dr. Du Bois Resigns," p. 1262.

8 Manning Marable, *W. E. B. Du Bois: Black Radical Democrat*, Boulder: Paradigm Publishers, 2005, p. xiii.

9 W. E. B. Du Bois, "My Evolving Program for Negro Freedom" (1944), in Lewis (ed.), *W. E. B. Du Bois: A Reader*, pp. 610–18, 614.

10 Du Bois, *Dusk of Dawn*, p. 700.

11 Du Bois, "Dr. Du Bois Resigns," p. 1261.

12 Du Bois, *Dusk of Dawn*, p. 698.

13 His position, in my mind, complements Tommie Shelby's defense of strategic black nationalism in his *We Who Are Dark: The Philosophical Foundations of Black Solidarity*, Cambridge: Harvard University Press, 2007, chs 6 and 7.

14 Du Bois in *The World and Africa* (1947) also stresses the impact of global capitalism and European colonialism on continental Africa and former European colonies around the globe.

15 W. E. B. Du Bois, "A Negro Nation within a Nation," in Lewis (ed.), *W. E. B. Du Bois: A Reader*, p. 570.

16 W. E. B. Du Bois, "The Negro and Communism," in Lewis (ed.), *W. E. B. Du Bois: A Reader*, p. 593.

17 Du Bois, *Dusk of Dawn*, p. 776.

18 Adolph L. Reed Jr, *W. E. B. Du Bois and American Political Thought: Fabianism and the Color Line*, Oxford: Oxford University Press, 1997, pp. 84–9.

19 Du Bois, *Dusk of Dawn*, p. 706.

20 Cf. Reed, *Du Bois and American Political Thought*, p. 87.

21 Du Bois, *Dusk of Dawn*, p. 789.

22 W. E. B. Du Bois, "The Negro and Social Reconstruction," in Herbert Aptheker (ed.), *Against Racism*, Amherst: University of Massachusetts Press, 1985, p. 141. For an opposing view that argues that Du Bois's interest in Marx signaled his "disillusionment with liberalism," see Andrew J. Douglas, *W. E. B. Du Bois and the Critique of the Competitive Society*, Athens: University of Georgia Press, 2019, esp. pp. 23–43.

23 Du Bois, "There Must Come a Vast Social Change in the US," in Lewis (ed.), *W. E. B. Du Bois: A Reader*, p. 621.
24 Du Bois, *Dusk of Dawn*, p. 776.
25 Du Bois, *Dusk of Dawn*, p. 712.
26 Du Bois, "My Evolving Program on Negro Freedom," in Lewis (ed.), *W. E. B. Du Bois: A Reader*, p. 618.
27 Du Bois, *Dusk of Dawn*, p. 707.
28 Du Bois, *Souls*, p. 3.
29 Du Bois, *Souls*, p. 8.
30 Michelle M. Moody-Adams, "Race, Class, and the Social Construction of Self-Respect," *Philosophical Forum* 24(1–3) (1992–3): 251–66, 254.
31 Frank M. Kirkland, "On Du Bois' Notion of Double Consciousness," *Philosophy Compass* 8(2) (2013): 137–48, 138–9; see also Lawrie Balfour, "'A Most Disagreeable Mirror': Race Consciousness as Double Consciousness," *Political Theory* 26(3) (1998): 346–69; Ernest Allen, Jr, "Du Boisian Double Consciousness: The Unsustainable Argument," *The Massachusetts Review* 43(2) (2002): 217–53.
32 Du Bois, *Souls*, p. 8.
33 Du Bois, *Souls*, p. 12.
34 Du Bois, *Souls*, p. 8.
35 Du Bois, *Souls*, p. 8.
36 Du Bois, *Souls*, p. 8.
37 Cf. David S. Owen's "Whiteness in Du Bois's *The Souls of Black Folk*," *Philosophia Africana* 10(2) (2007): 107–26.
38 In recent years, the idea of self-respect figures prominently in debates about racial justice. Tommie Shelby, *Dark Ghettos: Injustice, Dissent, and Reform*, Cambridge: Harvard University Press, 2016; Tommie Shelby, "The Ethics of Uncle Tom's Children," *Critical Inquiry* 38 (2012): 513–32; Melvin L. Rogers, "Rereading Honneth: Exodus Politics and the Paradox of Recognition," *European Journal of Political Theory* 8(2) (2009): 183–206. See also Moody-Adams, "Race, Class, and the Social Construction of Self-Respect"; Laurence M. Thomas, "Rawlsian Self-Respect and the Black Consciousness Movement," *Philosophical Forum* 9 (1978): 303–14 and his "Self-Respect, Fairness, and Living Morally," in Tommy L. Lott and John P. Pittman (eds), *A Companion to African-American*

Philosophy, New York: Blackwell Publishing, 2006, pp. 293–305; Bernard R. Boxill, "Self-Respect and Protest," *Philosophy & Public Affairs* 6(1) (1976): 58–69, and *Blacks and Social Justice*, Lanham: Rowman and Littlefield, 1992, pp. 186–99.

39 Immanuel Kant, *The Metaphysics of Morals*, New York: Cambridge University Press, 1996, p. 29.

40 Immanuel Kant, *Grounding for the Metaphysics of Morals*, Indianapolis: Hackett Publishing Company, 1993, p. 36.

41 Kant, *Grounding*, p. 35.

42 Jacqueline Mariña, "Kant's Robust Theory of Grace," *Con-Textos Kantianos* 6 (2017): 302–20, 304.

43 Immanuel Kant, *Religion and Rational Theology*, New York: Cambridge University Press, 2005, pp. 52–8. "The [moral] law imposes itself on him irresistibly, because of his moral predisposition; and if no other incentive were at work against it, he would also incorporate it into his supreme maxim as sufficient determination of his power of choice, i.e., he would be morally good." Conversely, the universality of moral law compels Kant to reject attributing a "diabolical will" to rational humanity, as if any human being can become so perverse so as to be somehow "beyond" morality.

44 Mariña, "Kant's Robust Theory of Grace," pp. 305–6.

45 Thomas E. Hill, Jr, "Stability, a Sense of Justice, and Self-Respect," in J. Mandle and D. A. Reidy (eds), *A Companion to Rawls*, Chichester: Wiley-Blackwell, 2015, pp. 200–15, 209.

46 Kant, *The Metaphysics of Morals*, pp. 186–7.

47 Cynthia A. Stark, "The Rationality of Valuing Oneself: A Critique of Kant on Self-Respect," *Journal of the History of Philosophy* 35(1) (1997): 65–82, 66–7. Stark's essay focuses on cases of people's "fundamental" ignorance of their own moral value. My concern, however, is not with cases of "genuine" ignorance of the moral law, but with the moral injury to self-respect of sustained racist judgment in a deeply unreasonable world.

48 Stark, "The Rationality of Valuing Oneself," p. 71.

49 This is also the oversight in Hay's defense of the duty to resist oppression in *Kantianism, Liberalism, and Feminism: Resisting Oppression*, New York: Palgrave, 2013.

50 In other words, that public expressions of moral self-regard can

expose one to radical evil and invite violent reprisal confirms that others do not recognize you as a moral equal. The closest that Kant comes to appreciating that self-regard might involve risking one's life is his discussion of the "casuistical question" of whether vaccination against smallpox is morally justifiable. To gain immunity, a person must risk exposing themselves to the disease. Kant, *Metaphysics of Morals*, p. 220.

51 Immanuel Kant, *Critique of Practical Reason*, New York: Cambridge University Press, 1997, p. 27.

52 Of course, no institutional arrangement can eradicate radical evil, which Kant grounds in an innate propensity of human nature. In the *Anthropology* he writes: "In a civil constitution, which is the highest degree of artificial improvement of the human species' good predisposition to the final end of its vocation, animality still manifests itself[.]," p. 232. Yet he concludes: "[Our] volition is generally good, but achievement is difficult because one cannot expect to reach the goal by the free agreement of individuals, but only of a progressive organization of citizens of the earth into and toward the species as a system that is cosmopolitically united," p. 238.

53 Kirkland, "On Du Bois' Notion of Double Consciousness," p. 141; Tommie Shelby invites us to think more carefully about the relevant considerations of forgoing moral self-regard to preserve basic self-respect, i.e., to survive: "There are moments [of] acquiesc[ence] to injustice to avoid serious physical harm, to protect loved ones, to live to fight another day, or to die a more meaningful death at a later time." A new ethics of the oppressed, Shelby hopes, would supplant an ethics of fear, where moral choices are not determined by fear of repercussion. Shelby, "The Ethics of Uncle Tom's Children," p. 517.

54 Du Bois, "Counsels of Despair," p. 1257.

55 Pablo Gilabert helpfully describes such an obligation in Kant's practical philosophy as a "basic positive duty to reasonably contribute to the existence of the basic conditions for other people's exercise of their capacities of autonomous agency" (386) in "Kant and the Claims of the Poor," *Philosophy and Phenomenological Research* 81(2) (2010): 382–418.

56 Barbara Herman, "The Practice of Moral Judgement," *Journal of Philosophy* 82(8) (1985): 414–36, 428.

57 If "internal" resistance is the only viable option for acting in the world, then one's deeds are not identified with the spatiotemporal expression of one's practical agency. The very fact that there is a rift between one's express intentions and what one can ultimately do in the world tracks the moral injury of double consciousness. Herman, "The Practice of Moral Judgement," p. 428.

58 Of course, any moral action invites "risk" inasmuch as it has a spatiotemporal dimension. In a certain sense, "risk" is the ineliminable condition of moral autonomy because we have no guarantee that others will not choose to attack or denigrate us for no reason. However, systematic social injustice of the kind that those subjugated by racial caste experience "pools" or "concentrates" risk in certain vulnerable racial communities in a way that other (white) members of the polity do not experience. And it is precisely the racialization of moral risk that Du Bois's idea of double consciousness helps us understand.

59 In *Anthropology from a Pragmatic Point of View*, Kant distinguishes a legitimate republic from the organized violence of barbaric, despotic, and anarchistic states. These scenarios, however, do not consider that a nominally liberal constitutional regime such as the United States can treat entire sectors of the population as if they were still in the state of nature or part of the fauna of nature, "with no rights that the white man is bound to respect."

60 Kirkland, "On Du Bois' Notion of Double Consciousness," p. 141.

61 John Rawls, *A Theory of Justice*, Cambridge: Harvard University Press, 1999 (rev. edn), p. 386.

62 The more extreme, isolating, and unreasonable the conditions of the color line are, the more unclear (and horrifying) the demands of the moral law can appear to an oppressed individual, as she tries to limit her exposure to evil or avoid becoming its instrument. There are numerous rich illustrations of this dilemma in Africana philosophy and literature. Particularly heartrending are depictions that suggest that respect for the moral law appears to justify destroying one's own – or a loved one's – life. These actions are, at the very least, intelligible from the standpoint of respect for the moral law. Consider

the following illustrations. (1) Frederick Douglass describes a young, half-clothed black woman running from her white captors before leaping off a bridge to her death. She chose death, rather than a lifetime of slavery and sexual brutalization: Frederick Douglass, *My Bondage and My Freedom*, New York: Arno Press, 1968, p. 413. (2) Toni Morrison's *Beloved* culminates with the revelation that Sethe, a runaway slave, takes a handsaw to her toddler's throat once slave-catchers descend on her and her children. She wants to "release" her daughter, Beloved, from life on a Kentucky slave plantation. Sethe explains that she was trying to put her children somewhere "where they would be safe": Toni Morrison, *Beloved*, New York: Vintage, 2007, p. 163.

63 See Crystal M. Feimster, *Southern Horrors: Women and the Politics of Rape and Lynching*, Cambridge: Harvard University Press, 2009, pp. 173–4.

64 Consider the civil disobedience of Rosa Parks. Although she is often described as a weary woman too tired to move, her action was part of a concerted political effort to spark the Montgomery Bus Boycott. Upon her arrest, she was supported by a vocal community that publicly defended her. A. D. Morris, *The Origin of the Civil Rights Movement: Black Communities Organizing for Change*, New York: The Free Press, 1984, pp. 51–3.

65 Robert Gooding-Williams, *In the Shadow of Du Bois: Afro-Modern Political Thought in America*, Cambridge: Harvard University Press, 2009, p. 75.

66 For further discussion of counter-publics in black political thought, see: Evelyn Brooks Higginbotham, *Righteous Discontent: The Women's Movement in the Black Baptist Church, 1880–1920*, Cambridge: Harvard University Press, 1994; Michael C. Dawson, "A Black Counterpublic? Economic Earthquakes, Racial Agenda(s), and Black Politics," *Public Culture* 7(1) (1994): 195–223; Melvin L. Rogers, "Rereading Honneth: Exodus and the Paradox of Recognition," *European Journal of Political Theory* 183(8) (2009): 183–206.

67 Du Bois, "Counsels of Despair," p. 1255.

68 W. E. B. Du Bois, "Does the Negro Need Separate Schools?" *Journal of Negro Education* 4(3) (1935): 328–35, 329.

69 Du Bois, "Separation and Self-Respect," p. 559.

70 Du Bois, "Separation and Self-Respect," p. 560.
71 W. E. B. Du Bois, "Segregation in the North," in *Du Bois: Writings*, New York: Library of America, 1986, pp. 1239–43, 1242.
72 V. P. Franklin, "Educational Philosophy," in Gerald Horne and Mary Young (eds), *W. E. B. Du Bois: An Encyclopedia*, Westport: Greenwood Press, 2001, pp. 68–73, 72–3.
73 Du Bois, "Separation and Self-Respect," pp. 559–60.
74 Du Bois, "Segregation in the North," p. 1244.
75 Derrick A. Bell, Jr, "The Unintended Lessons in Brown v. Board of Education," *New York Law School Review* 49 (2005): 1062.
76 Du Bois, "Segregation in the North," p. 1243.
77 W. E. B. Du Bois, *The Autobiography of W. E. B. Du Bois*, New York: Oxford University Press, 2008; W. E. B. Du Bois, "What is the Meaning of 'All Deliberate Speed'?," in Lewis (ed.), *W. E. B. Du Bois: A Reader*, pp. 419–23. See also Frank M. Kirkland, "The Questionable Legacy of *Brown v. Board of Education*: Du Bois' Iconoclastic Critique," *Logos* 14(2–3) (2015), online.
78 Kirkland, "The Questionable Legacy of *Brown v. Board of Education*," online.
79 M. Goldman, "Frequent Bias Incidents Affect Campus Mental Health, Experts Say," *The Michigan Daily*, October 13, 2017.
80 Goldman, "Frequent Bias Incidents."
81 Du Bois, *Souls*, p. 10.

Conclusion: The Passage into Exile: The Return Home Away from Home (1951–1963)

1 Terry Cowgill, "Veterans Protest Statue to Memorialize 'Communist' W. E. B. Du Bois," *The Berkshire Edge*, June 15, 2018, online.
2 Du Bois first met Crummell at Wilberforce and he profoundly impacted him. The founder of the pan-African movement and a black nationalist, Crummell studied at Cambridge University and had dedicated his life to fighting anti-black racism. He developed a notion of black racial difference that emphasized the ancestral home of continental Africa. He lived for two

decades in Liberia as a missionary and university professor, leading an effort to recolonize Africa by and for black people. Due to financial and political difficulties, he resettled in the United States to direct an episcopal ministry. He continued his political activism, encouraging African Americans to secure positions of leadership in government. With the establishment of the American Negro Academy in 1897, the members of the academy, which included Du Bois, elected the 78-year-old Crummell to be its first president. Du Bois later described his fateful first meeting with Crummell in *Souls*: "Instinctively I bowed before this man, as one bows before the prophets of the world. Some seer he seemed, that came not from the crimson Past or the gray To-come, but from the pulsing Now."

3 W. E. B. Du Bois, *Dusk of Dawn: An Essay Toward an Autobiography of a Race Concept*, New York: The Library of America, 1986, p. 757.

4 Excerpted from Du Bois's letter to Anna Bontemps and quoted from Manning Marable, *W. E. B. Du Bois: Black Radical Democrat*, Boulder: Paradigm Publishers, 1986, p. 190.

5 W. E. B. Du Bois, "I Bury my Wife," in David Levering Lewis (ed.), *W. E. B. Du Bois: A Reader*, New York: Henry Holt, 1995, pp. 142–3, 142.

6 Bettina Aptheker, "Shirley Graham Du Bois's Biographical Writings," *Black Perspectives*, March 11, 2019, online.

7 W. E. B. Du Bois, *The Autobiography of W. E. B. Du Bois*, New York: Oxford University Press, 2008, p. 234.

8 Du Bois, "Russophobia" (1950) and "On Stalin" (1953) in Lewis (ed.), *W. E. B. Du Bois: A Reader*, pp. 769–97.

9 W. E. B. Du Bois, "On Stalin," in Lewis (ed.), *W. E. B. Du Bois: A Reader*, pp. 796–7, 796.

10 Du Bois was under the wrong impression that Soviet Russia had abolished its own color line, even though Jews and Central Asians were disproportionately targeted in Stalin's purges and were denied fair equality of opportunity. In the case of the Soviet apparatchiks, the usually critical Du Bois seemed to acquiesce to the state-sanctioned representation of the Soviet reality and he even celebrated the violent "put down" of wealthy farmers – i.e., the "kulaks" – with the rise of the Soviet state.

11 Manning Marable, "Peace and Black Liberation: The

Contributions of W. E. B. Du Bois," *Science & Society* 47(4) (1983/1984): 385–405; Andrew Lanham, "When W. E. B. Du Bois was Un-American," *Boston Review*, January 13, 2017. http://bostonreview.net/race-politics/andrew-lanham-when-we-b-du-bois-was-un-american

12 W. E. B. Du Bois, *In Battle for Peace: The Story of My 83rd Birthday*, New York: Oxford University Press, 2007, p. 82.

13 Du Bois, *Autobiography*, p. 230.

14 Du Bois, *Autobiography*, p. 255. Du Bois looked without success for a publisher for a new monograph *Russia and America: An Interpretation*; it remains unpublished.

15 Du Bois, *Autobiography*, p. 237.

16 Du Bois, *Autobiography*, p. 237.

17 Scott Christianson, "Du Bois Comes Home from the Grave," *The Berkshire Edge*, May 20, 2014.

18 See, for example, Paul C. Taylor's "What's the Use of Calling Du Bois a Pragmatist?" *Metaphilosophy* 32(1–2) (2004): 99–114, 102.

19 Du Bois had supported the Montgomery Bus Boycott led by King in 1955–6; David Levering Lewis, *W. E. B. Du Bois: The Fight for Equality and the American Century, 1919–1963*, New York: Henry Holt, 2001, p. 557.

20 Du Bois, *Dusk of Dawn*, p. 640.

21 For example, at the 1958 All-African conference in Accra, he asked Graham to deliver a speech on his behalf in which he referred to his audience as his "fellow Africans."

22 Du Bois, *Dusk of Dawn*, p. 639.

23 Interestingly, during this period of Nkrumah's broadened pan-African interest, Ghana's closest ally was Israel. Du Bois himself drew inspiration from Jewish Zionism and looked towards Israel as a model for the founding of a black republic for and by Africans and Afro-descendant peoples. Manning Marable, *African and Caribbean Politics from Kwame Nkrumah to the Grenada Revolution*, London: Verso, 1987, p. 121.

24 He also focused on writing novels and finished *The Black Flame Trilogy*, which included *The Ordeal of Mansart* (1957), *Mansart Builds a School* (1959), and *Worlds of Color* (1961).

25 Henry Louis Gates and Kwame Anthony Appiah, "Introduction

to the First Edition," in *Africana: The Encyclopedia of the African and African American Experience*, 2nd edn, New York: Oxford University Press, 2004, online.

26 Marable, *Du Bois: Black Radical Democrat*, p. 212.

27 Gates and Appiah, "Introduction to the First Edition," online.

28 W. E. B. Du Bois, "A Statement Concerning the Encyclopaedia Africana Project," *EAP History Archive* 1962, online.

29 Du Bois, *Autobiography*, pp. 260, 263.

30 Katrin Flikschuh, "Philosophical Racism," *Aristotelian Society Supplementary* xcii (2018): 91–110, 103.

31 Flikschuh, "Philosophical Racism," p. 103.

32 W. E. B. Du Bois, *Africa, Its Geography, People and Products* and *Africa – Its Place in Modern History*, New York: Oxford University Press, 2007, pp. 42–3.

33 Chike Jeffers, "Appiah's Cosmopolitanism," *Southern Journal of Philosophy* 51(4) (2013): 488–510, 502.

34 My discussion here is indebted to Todd Hedrick's excellent essay, "Race, Difference, and Anthropology in Kant's Cosmopolitanism," *Journal of the History of Philosophy* 46(2) (2008): 245–68.

35 Nkrumah was a prolific writer and theorist in his own right. Cf. his *Consciencism: Philosophy and Ideology for Decolonization*, New York: Monthly Review Press, 1970.

36 W. E. B. Du Bois, *Color and Democracy: Colonies and Peace*, New York: Harcourt, 1945, p. 73.

37 Du Bois, *Color and Democracy*, p. 70.

38 W. E. B. Du Bois, "The African Roots of the War," in Lewis (ed.), *W. E. B. Du Bois: A Reader*, pp. 642–51.

39 Du Bois, *Africa, Its Geography, People and Products* and *Africa – Its Place in Modern History*, p. 45.

40 Du Bois, *Africa, Its Geography, People and Products* and *Africa – Its Place in Modern History*, pp. 42–3.

41 Du Bois, *Color and Democracy*, p. 85.

42 Inés Valdez, *Transnational Cosmopolitanism*, Cambridge: Cambridge University Press, 2019, p. 9.

43 Lewis, *W. E. B. Du Bois: The Fight for Equality*, p. 528.

44 Du Bois, *Autobiography*, p. 258.

45 W. E. B. Du Bois, "The Pan-African Congresses," in Lewis (ed.), *W. E. B. Du Bois: A Reader*, pp. 670–5, 672.

46 W. E. B. Du Bois, *The World and Africa*, New York: Oxford University Press, 2007, pp. 188–9; W. E. B. Du Bois, "Pan-Africanism: A Mission in my Life," in Eugene F. Provenzo, Jr and Edmund Abaka (eds), *W. E. B. Du Bois on Africa*, New York: Routledge, 2016, pp. 237–46.

47 Du Bois, *The World and Africa*, pp. 199–202.

48 Du Bois, *The World and Africa*, p. 189.

49 W. E. B. Du Bois, *The Autobiography of W. E. B. Du Bois: A Soliloquy on Viewing my Life from the Last Decade of its First Century*, New York: Oxford University Press, 2007, p. 259. Emphasis added.

50 Du Bois, *The World and Africa*, p. 208.

51 Chike Jeffers, "Appiah's Cosmopolitanism," pp. 501–8.

52 Du Bois, *Color and Democracy*, pp. 123–6.

53 Lawrie Balfour, "Inheriting Du Bois," *Du Bois Review* 8(2) (2011): 409–16, 413.

54 Cf. Helga Varden, "A Kantian Conception of Global Justice," *Review of International Studies* 37(5) (2011): 2043–57.

55 W. E. B. Du Bois, "Ghana Calls," *Creative Writings*, Millwood: Kraus-Thomson, 1985.

56 Shawn Leigh Alexander, *W. E. B. Du Bois: An American Intellectual and Activist*, New York: Rowman & Littlefield, 2015, p. 132.

57 W. E. B. Du Bois, *In Battle for Peace: The Story of my 83rd Birthday*, New York: Oxford University Press, 2007 [1952], p. 113.

58 Evie Shockley, "du bois in ghana," *Poem-a-Day* by the Academy of American Poets, April 27, 2015, online.

Index